Wisdom and the Renewal of
Catholic Theology

Wisdom and the Renewal of
Catholic Theology

Essays in Honor of Matthew L. Lamb

EDITED BY
THOMAS P. HARMON
AND ROGER W. NUTT

WITH A FOREWORD BY
MICHAEL NOVAK

☙PICKWICK *Publications* · Eugene, Oregon

WISDOM AND THE RENEWAL OF CATHOLIC THEOLOGY
Essays in Honor of Matthew L. Lamb

Copyright © 2016 Wipf and Stock Publishers. All rights reserved. Except for brief quotations in critical publications or reviews, no part of this book may be reproduced in any manner without prior written permission from the publisher. Write: Permissions, Wipf and Stock Publishers, 199 W. 8th Ave., Suite 3, Eugene, OR 97401.

Revised Standard Version of the Bible, copyright 1952 [2nd edition, 1971] by the Division of Christian Education of the National Council of the Churches of Christ in the United States of America. Used by permission. All rights reserved.

The Catholic Edition of the Revised Standard Version of the Bible, copyright 1965, 1966 by the Division of Christian Education of the National Council of the Churches of Christ in the United States of America. Used by permission. All rights reserved.

Pickwick Publications
An Imprint of Wipf and Stock Publishers
199 W. 8th Ave., Suite 3
Eugene, OR 97401

www.wipfandstock.com

PAPERBACK ISBN: 978-1-4982-7841-6
HARDCOVER ISBN: 978-1-4982-7843-0
EBOOK ISBN: 978-1-4982-7842-3

Cataloguing-in-Publication data:

Names: Harmon, Thomas P., editor | Nutt, Roger W., editor | Novak, Michael, foreword.

Title: Wisdom and the renewal of theology : essays in honor of Matthew L. Lamb / edited by Thomas P. Harmon and Roger W. Nutt ; foreword by Michael Novak.

Description: Eugene, OR: Pickwick Publications, 2016 | Includes bibliographical references and index(es).

Identifiers: ISBN 978-1-4982-7841-6 (paperback) | 978-1-4982-7843-0 (hardcover) | ISBN 978-1-4982-7842-3 (ebook)

Subjects: LCSH: Lamb, Matthew L. | Catholic Church—Doctrines.

Classification: BX4827.L35 W55 2016 (print) | BX4827.L35 W55 (ebook)

Manufactured in the U.S.A.   OCTOBER 19, 2016

Contents

Foreword: A Tribute to Father Matthew Lamb | vii
Michael Novak

Acknowledgments | xi

Abbreviations | xii

Contributors | xv

Introduction | 1
Thomas P. Harmon

1. From Cultural Signs to Transcultural Realities: The Contribution of Matthew Lamb for Understanding Lonergan's Metamethod | 11
   Matthew R. McWhorter

2. God's Self-Gift and the Created Supernatural: Matthew Lamb's Lonerganian Account | 37
   John Froula

3. Augustine on Creation: An Exercise in the Dialectical Retrieval of the Ancients | 49
   Matthew Levering

4. Biblical Inspiration in the Theology of St. Thomas Aquinas and Fr. Matthew Lamb | 66
   Matthew J. Ramage

5. Metaphysics and Paul's Use of the Old Testament: The Impact of a Participatory Ontology | 82
   Charles Raith II

6. Monica as Mystagogue: Time and Eternity at Ostia | 104
   Gerald Boersma

7 Psalm 79:8 and St. Augustine's Vision of Education | 126
   Christopher D. Collins

8 The Joy of Christ in Albert the Great's *De corpore domini* | 138
   Sr. Albert Marie Surmanski, OP

9 "Scrutinizing the Signs of the Times": Truth and History in Catholic Social Doctrine | 149
   Thomas P. Harmon

10 Vatican II, St. Thomas Aquinas, and the *Sensus Fidelium* | 175
   David A. Tamisiea

11 Matthew Lamb on Retrieval in Catholic Theology | 205
   Robert J. Barry

Author Index | 223

Subject Index | 226

Foreword

A Tribute to Father Matthew Lamb

As a quite young monk from the Trappist monastery at Conyers, Georgia, the neatly tonsured Father Matt arrived in Rome at the middle point of the Vatican Council in 1964, after the first two sessions, but before the dramatic final two. Like many other excited Catholics in America, Father Matt had been eagerly keeping up-to-date (that is, *aggiornamento'd*) on every morsel of information about the Council, even the juicy tidbits.

One cannot exaggerate how thrilling those days were. Television coverage almost every day. Front-page stories in *The New York Times*, above the fold.

Yes, Father Lamb had been closely following the suspenseful first year at Vatican II, not least the shadowy Vatican intrigue reported by the mysterious "Xavier Rynne" in *The New Yorker*, and gathered up from the *scuttlebutt*—to use a technical theological term of that time—the buzz that hung above the tables in the fragrant coffee shops along the Via della Conciliazione, and inside the restaurants from the "Hilton on the Hill" (where most of the American bishops stayed) to Piazza Navona, famous for stunning scenes starring Marcello Mastroianni and Sophia Loren.

Sadly, nontheological scuttlebutt was at times at the very center of the Council, at least as reporters saw things. In 1964 I was among those reporters. I was working for *Time* that year, and Karen and I had an unlimited expense account so that we could take as many "sources" as we could out to lunch or dinner for interviews and wide-ranging conversations on the state of the church.

If we could have known in those days that the young Father Lamb would become such an important force in the post-Council church, and would found the theology department at Ave Maria University, and if we knew where to find him, we would have taken him to such a restaurant as neither he nor we could ever afford to enter again.

Not long after his days in Rome, Father Matt went on to further and then further studies. It seemed in those days as if further studies never ended. Matt studied one philosophy of history after another, and then the metaphysics they implied, then the different horizons employed, the higher viewpoints, the emergent probabilities. (By the way, that's why Father Matt can always think of another higher viewpoint, horizon, meta-meta . . . and has trouble finishing an explanation.)

Another thing Matt can't finish—he never forgets his friends. Once, he took a train from Germany back to Rome to visit Fred Lawrence and Fred's wife, Sue. Fred had left the seminary, but kept up his studies in Rome under Bernard Lonergan. That's how Fred and Father Matt first met.

Well, one week a few years later, Sue had to stay in the hospital during a scary pregnancy episode, leaving Fred at home with two-year-old Dyer. Like most males, Fred was not quite up to being both mother and father. (How is it most wives seem to do both?) Father Lamb volunteered to help out. He had no idea what he was getting into.

If Fred felt incompetent that week, Father Lamb became completely bewildered. For family chaos the Trappists had not prepared him. A family kitchen was nothing like the world of silence and contemplation. Eventually Father Lamb announced that he must leave. Fred would be better off without him: Be easier to care for one infant, than one infant plus Father Lamb.

When he left Father told Fred and Sue that they could contract with the North American College for a stipend to have a few seminarians come up to help them with their children—that would give them what Newman called a "real apprehension" of the challenges of marriage and children, and why our Lord made it a sacrament of his self-sacrificing love for his body, the church.

Those are days Father Lamb says he truly *verified* his vocation: Celibacy, pure and simple. Some persons *are* meant for celibacy. (And by the way, Fred still agrees that after Father left, his little son settled down, at least as much as boys of two ever do.)

After Germany, Father was called to Marquette, where he fell into heavy-lifting writing and editing—including a memorable festschrift for Father Lonergan. Matt's reputation kept growing. More and more people couldn't follow Father Lamb's arguments—Lonergan does that to people—although they knew Matt was quite deep, and holy, and his writing always sparkled with little diamonds of spiritual wisdom.

Then Father Lamb was invited to Boston College. There he met and inspired a marvelous company. With his old friend Fred Lawrence, and Father Joe Flanagan, SJ, who had also studied under Lonergan, and Father Ernest Fortin, the indomitable Straussian, Father Romanus Cessario, OP, and Mary Ann Glendon of Harvard, he formed a monthly study group centered on Thomas Aquinas's *Summa Theologiae*. Father Lonergan used to complain to Matt that too many had failed to devote time to studying Aquinas.

In the theology department at B.C. Father Lamb faced some notable theological dissent. Some seemed to take Rome as *bête-noire*. In fact, there was a rumor around the Boston area that Father Lamb once petitioned the president of B. C. to put into practice the principles of Affirmative Action, by hiring at least one ethicist in the theology department who agreed with the Magisterium.

Recalling his own days in theological education, when he was expected to study theological classics in Hebrew, Greek, Latin, French, and German—not to mention Italian, for reading *La Civiltà Cattolica* and other Magisterial documents—Father Lamb began to doubt whether American theologians of the future would ever be prepared to pass on the Catholic theological tradition in its fullness. How will they ever be able to grasp the terms of the Greek and Latin Fathers, the millennium and a half of theology after Christ, official church teaching worded in Latin, and even the rest of the Catholic world outside the US?

That is how Father Lamb began to dream of building a place where deeper understanding could be reached. Ave Maria is still moving toward this goal. But even now our graduates are giving a good account of themselves. Most are finding positions rather quickly, while the demand for them keeps growing—thanks to Father Matt's vision, insistence, and perseverance.

In person, too, Father Lamb is a wise counsellor. Doesn't get too excited about difficulties. Urges prayer, patience, and time, time, time. Employs his long experience and the fruits of many inner battles. Knows the mountains and the valleys of the soul in its voyages, its darknesses and lights. Just over ten years ago, he showed immense courage in moving from Boston College to seemingly endless tomato fields in southwest Florida, above which the great Oratory now rises up over large expanses of lawn and campus buildings and hundreds of homes, together reminding one of Tuscany.

The mature, profound, deep, and spiritual papers presented at the conference honoring Father Lamb and their own graduate programs by those sixteen Ave Maria scholars now teaching in other universities and seminaries, and the nine essays in this volume, are a living monument, and a lasting one, to Father Lamb's courage, depth, and wisdom. His maturing students showed also that they learned well the habit of theological friendship.

This is my way of thinking of Father Lamb: *contemplata aliis tradere*. He has passed along to others his own contemplation in the presence of the Love of the Holy Trinity, where all theology begins.

Michael Novak
Ave Maria University

Acknowledgments

THE EDITORS WOULD LIKE to acknowledge the generous assistance they received both in carrying out the conference on which this volume is based and in the preparation of this volume. In particular, the editors would like to thank Michael T. O. Timmis, H. James Towey, Michael Dauphinais, Gregory Vall, Susan Nutt, and Christy Dorer. In addition, the conference and volume could not have come about without support provided by Ave Maria University and the Aquinas Center for Theological Renewal at Ave Maria University.

Thomas P. Harmon would like to thank his wife, Catherine E. Harmon, for her patience and for her editorial advice. He would also like to thank Steven Meyer and Fr. Dempsey Rosales-Acosta, who gave invaluable advice about the faculty development grant application process at the University of St. Thomas and Nicholas McAfee who assisted in the preparation of the indices. Finally, he would like to thank the University of St. Thomas (Houston) for the grant that made it possible for him to organize and attend the conference, "Wisdom and the Renewal of Theology," and Dr. Christopher P. Evans, at that time chairman of the department of theology at UST, for his support. He would also like to thank the excellent editorial staff at Wipf and Stock for their patience and guidance, especially Charlie Collier, Matthew Wimer, and Brian Palmer.

Thomas P. Harmon
Escondido, CA

Roger W. Nutt
Ave Maria, FL

Abbreviations

ABBREVIATIONS FOR BIBLICAL TEXTS follow the *SBL Handbook of Style* (1999). Abbreviations of Augustinian texts follow the *Augustinus-Lexikon* style. For reader convenience, the editors have reproduced those abbreviations of Augustinian texts below along with the other abbreviations used throughout the book.

Not all of the Latin titles below have a standard English translation. Where the editors have thought it prudent, they have chosen to use what they judge to be the most easily recognized English translation in identifying the text, again for the convenience of the reader. Even where the English translation alone is cited, the editors have chosen to use the abbreviation for the Latin title.

beata u.	*De beata uita liber unus* (*On the Happy Life*), St. Augustine
c. acad.	*Contra academicos libri tres* (*Against the Academics*), St. Augustine
CCSL	*Corpus Christianorum Series Latina*
ciu.	*De civitate dei libri uiginti duo* (*The City of God*), St. Augustine
conf.	*Confessionum libri tredecim* (*Confessions*)
De Car.	*Quaestiones disputate de caritate* (*Disputed Questions on Charity*), St. Thomas Aquinas
De Ver.	*Quaestiones disputate de veritate* (*Disputed Questions on Truth*), St. Thomas Aquinas

doctr. chr.	De doctrina christiana libri quattuor (*On Christian Teaching*), St. Augustine
DUI	De unitate intellectus contra Averroistas, St. Thomas Aquinas.
DV	Dei Verbum, the Second Vatican Council's Dogmatic Constitution on Divine Revelation
Gn. Litt.	De Genesi ad litteram libri duodecim, St. Augustine.
GS	Gaudium et Spes, the Second Vatican Counsil's Pastoral Constitution on the Church in the Modern World
In Gal.	Super Epistolam B. Pauli ad Galatas lectura (*Commentary on St. Paul's Epistle to the Galatians*), St. Thomas Aquinas
In Rom.	Super Epistolam B. Pauli ad Romanos lectura (*Commentary on St. Paul's Epistle to the Romans*), St. Thomas Aquinas
LG	Lumen Gentium, the Second Vatican Council's Dogmatic Constitution on the Church
lib. arb.	De libero arbitrio libri tres (*On Free Choice of the Will*), St. Augustine
LSJ	Henry G. Liddell, Robert Scott, and Henry S. Jones, eds., *A Greek-English Lexicon*. Oxford: Clarendon, 1996.
mag.	De magistro liber unus (*On the Teacher*), St. Augustine
ord.	De ordine libri duo (*On Order*), St. Augustine
PL	Patrologiae Cursus Completus Series Latina, edited by Jacques-Paul Migne
Quodl.	Quaestiones Quodlibetales, St. Thomas Aquinas
RSV	Revised Standard Version of the Bible
RSVCE	Revised Standard Version of the Bible, Catholic Edition
RSVCE2	Revised Standard Version of the Bible, 2nd Catholic Edition
S. Eph.	Sancti Thomae de Aquino Super Epistolam B. Pauli ad Ephesios lectura
SCG	Summa contra gentiles, St. Thomas Aquinas

| ST | *Summa theologiae*, St. Thomas Aquinas |
| *uera rel.* | *De uera religion liber unus* (*Of True Religion*), St. Augustine |

Contributors

Robert J. Barry earned his PhD at Boston College in 1996, writing under Rev. Matthew Lamb on the topic of Thomas Aquinas' *De malo*. He teaches Historical and Moral Theology at Providence College, and lives in Providence, RI with his wife Karen and their three daughters.

Gerald Boersma is an Assistant Professor of Theology at St. Bonaventure University. He is the author of The Origins of Augustine's Early Theology of Image: A Study in the Development of Pro-Nicene Theology (New York: Oxford University Press, 2015). In 2015 he was awarded the Patricia H. Imbesi Saint Augustine Fellowship at Villanova University. He received his MA from Ave Maria University and his PhD from the University of Durham. He is a member of the Academy of Catholic Theology.

Christopher D. Collins is Assistant Professor of Theology at the University of Mary in Bismarck, ND, where he and his family also reside. His focus is on moral theology and the early thought of St. Augustine. He received both his MA and PhD from Ave Maria University.

John Froula is an assistant professor at the Saint Paul Seminary School of Divinity in St. Paul, MN, where he teaches classes in Dogmatic and Sacramental Theology. He has degrees from Thomas Aquinas College, the Teresianum, and received his PhD from Ave Maria University, writing his dissertation on the Christology of Aquinas. He has published in the *The Thomist, The Heythrop Journal,* and *Downside Review.*

Thomas P. Harmon is Professor of Theology and Culture at John Paul the Great Catholic University in Escondido, CA. He received his BA in Philosophy from Gonzaga University in Spokane, WA and both his MA and PhD in Theology from Ave Maria University. He is the author of 15 articles, chapters, and reviews. He currently resides in Escondido, CA, with his wife Catherine and their three children. He is a member of the Academy of Catholic Theology.

Matthew Levering is Perry Family Foundation Professor of Theology at Mundelein Seminary. He is the author and editor of numerous books, including *Wisdom and Holiness, Science and Scholarship: Essays in Honor of Matthew L. Lamb*. With Father Lamb, he edited *Vatican II: Renewal within Tradition*, and he and Father Lamb are currently at work on a follow-up volume, to be titled *The Reception of Vatican II at 50: Retrospect and Prospect*. He is the co-editor of *Nova et Vetera* and the chair of the board of the Academy of Catholic Theology. He earned his PhD at Boston College.

Michael Novak is the retired George Frederick Jewett Scholar in Religion, Philosophy, and Public Policy at the American Enterprise Institute. He is author of more than forty-five books and winner of the 1994 Templeton Prize. He is Visiting Distinguished Professor at Ave Maria University and a member of the board of trustees. He resides in Ave Maria, FL.

Matthew R. McWhorter has an MA in philosophy from Georgia State University and a PhD in Theology from Ave Maria University, where he studied under Matthew Lamb. Dr. McWhorter currently teaches philosophy and theology at Holy Spirit College in Atlanta, GA. His research has appeared in academic journals such as *The Modern Schoolman, The Irish Theological Quarterly, New Blackfriars, Angelicum*, and *The Heythrop Journal*.

Matthew J. Ramage is Associate Professor of Theology at Benedictine College and author of the 2013 book *Dark Passages of the Bible: Engaging Scripture with Benedict XVI and Thomas Aquinas*. He earned his MA at Franciscan University of Steubenville and his PhD from Ave Maria University. He is a member of the Academy of Catholic Theology.

Charles Raith II is director of the Paradosis Center for Theology and Scripture and Assistant Professor of Religion and Philosophy at John Brown University in Siloam Springs, AR. He is the author of *Aquinas and Calvin on Romans: God's Justification and Our Participation* (Oxford University Press, 2014), as well as "Calvin's Critique of Merit, and Why Aquinas (Mostly) Agrees" (*Pro Ecclesia*) and "Calvin and Aquinas, Part

II: Condignity and Participation" (*Pro Ecclesia*), along with various other articles. He earned an MDiv from Beeson Divinity School and an MTh from Regent College in Vancouver, Canada. He has the distinct honor of being the first and only Protestant doctoral graduate of Ave Maria University.

Sr. Albert Marie Surmanski, OP is a member of the Dominican Sisters of Mary, Mother of the Eucharist. She earned her BPhil from Ave Maria College in Michigan and her MA and PhD from Ave Maria University in Florida where she is now Instructor in Theology and Research Fellow.

David A. Tamisiea is an Assistant Professor of Theology and director of the undergraduate theology program at Ave Maria University. He is also a PhD candidate in theology at Ave Maria, and is currently working on his dissertation entitled, "The Baptismal Priesthood of the Christian Lay Faithful." Prior to his graduate studies in theology, Mr. Tamisiea was a practicing attorney specializing in civil litigation in the Dallas-Fort Worth area for over ten years. He holds the degrees of BA from the University of Notre Dame, MA in theology from Ave Maria University, and JD from the University of Texas at Austin.

Introduction

Thomas P. Harmon

Gratitude for the wisdom, care, leadership, and counsels of Fr. Matthew L. Lamb in his role as architect of and longtime professor in the Graduate Programs in Theology at Ave Maria University is what prompted the editors to collect this volume of essays in his honor. While it is customary for *Festschriften* to be presented on the occasion of a scholar's retirement or birthday, the present volume was conceived for neither occasion. Instead, the editors conceived the idea for this volume on the occasion of the tenth anniversary of the founding of the Graduate Programs in Theology at Ave Maria University, which Fr. Lamb has done so much to shape.[1] The essays collected here are selected from papers presented at a conference, "Wisdom and the Renewal of Catholic Theology: Celebrating the Graduate Programs in Theology at Ave Maria University," held in February of 2015. We would like to present this volume to Fr. Matthew Lamb in thanks to him as our teacher and the architect of those programs.

For St. Thomas Aquinas, piety extends first of all to God, "for he is supremely excellent, and is for us the first principle of being and government."[2] At the beginning of this introduction, therefore, the editors would like to give thanks and praise to God for his servant and

---

1. Michael Dauphinais and Matthew Levering have already produced an admirable *festschrift* for Fr. Lamb of the traditional variety, *Wisdom and Holiness, Science and Scholarship: Essays in Honor of Matthew L. Lamb*. See that volume for a more traditional account of Fr. Lamb's career and scholarship, as well.

2. *ST* II-II.101.1c.

devoted priest, Fr. Lamb. As St. Augustine—and Fr. Lamb—would, no doubt, remind us, it is God who is the *magister interior*, illuminating the mind as its creator and sustainer. The human, external teacher serves as an adjunct. In the second place, St. Thomas says that we receive "the principles of our being and government" from "our parents and our country, that have given us birth and nourishment. Consequently man is debtor chiefly to his parents and his country, after God."[3] Fr. Lamb has been father to us in three respects. First, he is the architect of the graduate programs in which, for the most part, the contributors to this volume received their theological instruction. Second, he was a professor for all of us. Third, he is a spiritual father to us through his priesthood, having celebrated Mass for us, heard our confessions, baptized our children, and even in a few cases witnessed our wedding vows. Fr. Lamb has therefore exercised fatherly care for our minds, bodies, and spirits academically, liturgically, and interpersonally. There is no adequate repayment to our countries and parents, who gave us life and raised us. Just so, there is no adequate repayment of the debt we owe to Fr. Lamb. We owe so much to his care.

Nevertheless, after offering praise and thanksgiving to God, we want to offer back to him the first fruits of his cultivation. With the exception of Matthew Levering and Robert Barry, who were both students of Fr. Lamb at Boston College, and Amb. Michael Novak, a long-time friend of Fr. Lamb's, the contributors to this volume are all junior faculty members teaching theology in university-level institutions in the United States who received their graduate education at Ave Maria University. With the exception of Gerald Boersma, who received his M.A. at Ave Maria but his doctorate at the University of Durham, those contributors all received doctorates from Ave Maria in theology. This collection of essays therefore represents a taste of what Fr. Lamb was aiming to produce when he moved from Boston College to Ave Maria University in 2004.

When Fr. Lamb departed Boston College in 2004, he gave up a full professorship in one of the most prestigious and well-funded Catholic theological faculties in the world in order to lead the fledgling department of theology at Ave Maria University. He was invited by Matthew Levering and Michael Dauphinais. Michael Dauphinais, now an associate professor and chair of the department of theology at Ave Maria, had read a 1992 article by Fr. Lamb in *America Magazine: The National*

---

3. Ibid.

Catholic Review entitled, "Will there be Catholic Theology in the United States?" That article ends by listing positive signs of renewal in doctoral programs in Catholic theology. But the bulk of Fr. Lamb's article was extremely pessimistic about the prospects for Catholic theology going forward. Fr. Lamb's 1997 *Crisis Magazine* article, "Catholic Theological Society of America: Theologians Unbound," traced the same worrying signs in the United States' premier professional society for theologians.[4] Dauphinais and Levering invited Fr. Lamb to Ave Maria and Fr. Lamb accepted their invitation. All three agreed on the need to address the problems with Catholic graduate theological education in an institutional way through the development of a new graduate program in theology that awarded both the Master's and, especially, the PhD.

What were the main problems Fr. Lamb identified in his two articles, which he aimed to address in designing a new graduate program in theology at Ave Maria? First, Fr. Lamb saw that most doctoral faculty members in Catholic theology departments in the United States had adopted a liberal, Protestant approach to theological education, either consciously or unconsciously. A large number of those faculty members had received doctorates from Protestant programs[5] in what Lamb identified as nondenominational, university-related divinity schools. Those schools understandably had no interest in forming their students in "any Church-related theological tradition"[6]—let alone the Catholic theological tradition. But the educational pedigree of faculty members was only the external symptom of the deficiencies in the training that Catholic doctoral programs were able to provide.

In the actual practice of theology, Fr. Lamb witnessed the pitting of faith against reason and the present against the past due to what he regarded as an uncritical acceptance of Enlightenment antinomies. Those antinomies were leading to the loss of the virtues and skills needed for the science of Catholic theology to flourish. First of all, they fostered a deepening gulf between intellectual training and spiritual formation in

---

4. In 2006, Fr. Lamb helped found the Academy of Catholic Theology. Although the ACT does not mean directly to compete with the CTSA, it is hard to see that there would have been an experienced need for the ACT if the CTSA had been healthy.

5. In 1992, Lamb pointed out that among Catholic theology and religious studies professors 60 percent received their doctorates from Catholic institutions while 40 percent received them from non-Catholic institutions. In 1997, Lamb wrote that more than half of the theological faculties at Boston College and the University of Notre Dame received their doctorates from non-Catholic programs.

6. Lamb, "Theologians Unbound."

the sacramental life of the church. As Fr. Lamb warned, "The intellectual and moral virtues are threatened with extinction without the theological virtues."[7] The study of theology requires the theologian to affirm as true through faith what he cannot so affirm on his own powers. Even on the basis of natural intellectual excellence, however, Fr. Lamb noticed that the intellectual formation in most Catholic theological graduate programs were not laying sufficient emphasis on the serious study of philosophy, "especially the many developments in pre-modern philosophy important in the development of Catholic theological traditions, and to the possible transpositions of these traditions in modern and contemporary philosophical orientations."[8] In order to transpose the ancient, Catholic theological tradition in modern and contemporary contexts, a perennially necessary task that finds expression in the 20th century movement simultaneously toward both *ressourcement* and *aggiornamento*, the modern context has to be known. But the ancient context must also be known. The latter, especially, requires the linguistic skills to be able to read primary texts in their original languages. As Fr. Lamb notes, fulfilment of language requirements in Catholic graduate programs had been reduced to a *pro forma* exercise. Further, none of this rigorous work is possible without the commitment on the part of graduate programs to allow students to engage in serious research without overly burdensome teaching responsibilities. Students must also be free from the necessity of holding down an outside job to support themselves. A focus on leisured research is important not only for students, but even more especially for professors. As Fr. Lamb writes, "If the research is not institutionalized with at least as much care as the teaching, there is a danger that the teaching will be less and less able to meet relevant questions the culture poses to theology."[9] Those who are teaching must continue to learn. With the increasing emphasis on faculty productivity, not only at the level of undergraduate teaching faculty but for those who spend much of their time teaching in graduate programs, the movement away from a research

---

7. Lamb, "Will There Be Catholic Theology," 524. See also Lamb, *Eternity, Time, and the Life of Wisdom*, 58: "As Augustine had indicated how the intellectual and moral excellence advocated by the best of the philosophers could be lived only through his conversion to Jesus Christ, so Aquinas indicates how the intellectual and moral virtues are integrated within the absolutely supernatural communion with the Triune God operative in the theological virtues of faith, hope, and charity."

8. Lamb, "Will There Be Catholic Theology," 531.

9. Ibid., 532.

focus that Fr. Lamb noticed in 1992 has only accelerated in recent years. It is understandable but still regrettable.

The work of transposition in theology is not merely a matter of the reacquisition of language skills, however. Transposition does not only take skill, but also highly demanding and difficult theoretical activity. In the first place, we post-moderns face a peculiar challenge to the work of transposition in the form of an intellectual potion that combines historicism with the myth of historical progress, which we have all imbibed to some degree. Fr. Lamb remarks, "Historicism claims that historicity leaves us only with incommensurable series of conventions, and so without culture transcending norms."[10] If historicism is the case, then all interpretation of texts becomes an act of will or an imposition through power rather than a work of wisdom.[11] Returning to theology as a work of wisdom requires a thoroughgoing critique of historicism, to which Fr. Lamb has contributed theoretically in his many works on eternity and time[12] and in practice through his scholarship on pre-modern figures. But combatting historicism is only the beginning. As Fr. Lamb observes, "transposition is not a translation or transliteration from one set of texts to another. Rather, it involves judgment and thus knowledge of the realities referred to in the texts one is studying. Reaching up to the mind of an Augustine or an Aquinas means reaching up to the realities they knew."[13] Cultivation of a particular technique or method is never enough. Before transposition can be accomplished, each theologian must first grasp the realities to which the texts of the great thinkers of the past referred.

For Fr. Lamb, therefore, the challenges to Catholic theology stem from an abandonment of the wisdom approach to theology that "attunes the mind to the whole of reality, to the whole pattern in which all the

---

10. Lamb, "Temporality and History," 839.

11. See Lamb, *Eternity, Time, and the Life of Wisdom*, 22–23, where he talks about this phenomenon in light of Spinoza's foundation of the historical-critical method. See also ibid., 57: "From late medieval nominalism and voluntarism, moderns are used to reading the creative and redemptive action of God as an expression of his power and will, rather than as an expression of his wisdom."

12. Some highlights, by no means exhaustive, include his book, *Eternity, Time, and the Life of Wisdom*; "Historicity and Eternity"; "Eternity and Time in St. Thomas Aquinas's Commentary on the Gospel of John"; "Nature is Normative for Culture"; "Temporality and History"; "Eternity Creates and Redeems Time"; "Augustine and Aquinas on Eschatology"; "The Question of Truth in Revealed Religion."

13. Lamb, "Lonergan's Transpositions," 6.

parts can be understood as reaching their full purpose and nature,"[14] which itself is only fully grasped in the knowledge of the Missions of the Son and Holy Spirit in bringing fallen creatures into communion with the Triune God. The higher does not negate the lower, as Fr. Lamb never tires of reminding his students; rather, it is the intelligible that creates the sensible. The sapiential approach to theology therefore requires as its precondition both an intellectual conversion that is attuned to the difference between both the sensible and the intelligible[15] and the created and the uncreated, but also a metaphysics adequate to that conversion. Fr. Lamb identifies the wisdom approach as belonging to the patrimony of the Fathers of the Church and the best of the schoolmen, especially St. Augustine and St. Thomas Aquinas. He traces its abandonment to the late medieval nominalists and voluntarists who inaugurated the shift from wisdom to power that finds its home in the main project of modernity all the way through the Enlightenment and up to our own post-modern era. In the task of theological renewal, the theologian can find no better guides than the great patristic and medieval theologians like St. Augustine and St. Thomas Aquinas. But this task requires a thoroughgoing critique of historicism, an understanding of the historical differences in our own modes of expression vis-à-vis theirs, the linguistic skills to read their texts well, the humility and docility to approach their texts with the willingness to learn, the rigorous cultivation of the virtues of theological science and wisdom that will allow the mind to grasp not only the meaning of their texts, but the realities to which their texts point, and the cultivation of the theological virtues, without which the task of the theologian is fruitless, since theology is a subalternated science to the science of God and the blessed, which comes to us in the form of articles that must be believed through the virtue of faith, desired as possible through the virtue of hope, and ardently cleaved to through the enlivening virtue of charity. As Fr. Lamb himself puts it, "Fidelity to the Church demands more—not less—commitment to deepening and broadening one's intelligence to appreciate the unity of theological and philosophical wisdom."[16] This is the goal toward which Fr. Lamb directed his energies in the formation of the graduate programs from which the contributors to this volume have benefited.

---

14. Lamb, *Eternity, Time, and the Life of Wisdom*, 57.
15. This is what Augustine accomplishes in book 7 of his *Confessions*.
16. Lamb, "Letter of Welcome."

As Fr. Lamb conceived it, the graduate programs he founded and to some degree gave birth to address the problem of historicism through a core seminar sequence in the history of western philosophy and theology on what he calls the "dialectic of the ancients and the moderns." Fr. Lamb's insight, which also bears the influence of his former Boston College colleagues and friends, Bernard Lonergan, SJ and Ernest Fortin, AA, is that in order to appropriate the Catholic theological tradition, the contemporary theologian must grapple with the nature of modernity and what effects modern thought has had on Catholic theology. That involves a pushing back to the origins of modernity in the intellectual and political projects of the late Middle Ages and early modern period. In Lamb's articulation, the nominalism and voluntarism of the late Middle Ages effect an eclipse of judgment that leads to a movement away from wisdom and toward the will to power. Early modern political philosophy then reduces the goals of human living from theoretical excellence and moral virtue to technical prowess in service of the *libido dominandi* and disordered appetite.[17] But these various mutations are performed without adequately refuting what came before. The eclipse of judgment and the reduction of politics to technique amount to a narrowing of reason and lead to the production of long-term bias and cycles of moral, political, and intellectual decline that result in the destruction of reason through historicism. What is needed, then, is a new dialectic comparing the main stream of historicist and proto-historicist thought found in modernity with ancient and medieval nonhistoricist thought. In light of this dialectic, the stream of reflection from pre-modern sources comes to light once again as a live option, having been dismissed either hastily or maliciously by its early modern opponents. Only in this way will the Catholic theologian be able to appropriate the Catholic tradition adequately and also be able to escape the various deformations common to our age that prevent a wisdom approach to theology, which alone can do justice to the mysteries of the faith. Fr. Lamb therefore instituted the ancients and moderns seminars in a two-year cycle that read through the great books in philosophy and theology in the Western tradition. Through this cycle,

---

17. To see how Fr. Lamb himself performs the dialectic of the ancient and modern, see the first chapter of his book, *Eternity, Time, and the Life of Wisdom*, "The Resurrection and Christian Identity as *Conversatio Dei*," comparing the *Confessions* of, on the one hand, St. Augustine and St. Teresa of Avila and, on the other, of Jean-Jacques Rousseau.

students have had the opportunity to engage in this much-needed dialectical purgation of bias.

As begins to become clear from Fr. Lamb's emphasis on the dialectic of the ancient and modern, Fr. Lamb is also keenly attentive to the theologico-political implications of theology, both in general and for us today. One of the unique features of the programs he designed was that he wanted to show how the question of faith and reason is reflected in the political orders in which we live. Catholics and Catholic theologians are not simply free-floating citizens of creation, but concrete men and women who live in concrete political orders that have a real, shaping influence on their own concerns and judgments. His approach here is grounded thoroughly in the methods of St. Augustine's *City of God*.[18] Ancient philosophers had, of course, noticed the profound ways in which the most authoritative opinions of the day as found embodied in political constitutions held sway in the judgments of the multitude. Augustine noticed how one's education under political law affected not only the citizen, but also the Christian's own understanding of the faith. In order to disentangle the earthly city and the city of God and to reveal the transpolitical way of life lived by Christians, a dialectical engagement between the two cities was necessary: hence, the *City of God*. Likewise in his own teaching and in his writing,[19] Fr. Lamb has sought to provide his own students with the opportunity to engage in a similar dialectic that reveals both the unchanging nature of the relationship between the two cities and the particular modifications it undergoes in liberal democratic regimes. Without that crucial dialectic, Catholic theologians will be decisively shaped by the opinions of the earthly city rather than the city of God.

Fr. Lamb's theoretical articulation of the challenges for Catholic theology and his proposal for a retrieval of the sapiential approach to theology find their written articulation in many, many works of his own scholarship; but they also find institutional articulation in the Patrick F. Taylor Graduate Programs in Theology at Ave Maria University. Because of the work of Fr. Lamb at Ave Maria, we think there is much more cause for hope now than there was at its initial publication that there can be a positive answer to Fr. Lamb's question, "Will there be Catholic theology

---

18. One of Fr. Lamb's regularly taught doctoral courses is a seminar that carefully reads and reflects on St. Augustine's *City of God*.

19. See, for example, his excellent edited volume, *Catholicism and America: Challenges and Prospects*.

in the United States?" We hope this volume provides empirical evidence that there will be. All of the contributors have, with his help, attempted to reach up to the mind of Matthew Lamb. We hope that these humble offerings provide some evidence that, with his help, we have managed to grasp something of the divine realities to which he has worked devotedly and with fatherly care to point out to us. As Fr. Lamb frequently remarks with a glint in his eye, it could take centuries to renew Catholic theology, so there's not a moment to lose. And as Fr. Lamb himself said in another context, "The mission is as rock solid old and as refreshingly new as the gift and achievements of the mind itself enlightened by faith. We are not alone. The vast communion of saints and scholars beckons us into the Infinite Holiness, Intelligence, and Love who is blessed for ever and ever. Amen."[20]

BIBLIOGRAPHY

Aquinas, Thomas. *Summa Theologiae*. Translated by the English Dominican Friars. New York: Benzinger Bros., 1947.

Dauphinais, Michael, and Matthew Levering, eds. *Wisdom and Holiness, Science and Scholarship: Essays in Honor of Matthew L. Lamb*. Naples: Sapientia, 2007.

Lamb, Matthew L. "Augustine and Aquinas on Eschatology." In *Aquinas the Augustinian*, edited by Michael Dauphinais and Matthew Levering, 167–89. Washington, DC: Catholic University of America Press, 2007.

———. "Catholic Theological Society of America: Theologians Unbound." *Crisis Magazine* (December 1, 1997). http://www.crisismagazine.com/1997/catholic-theological-society-of-america-theologians-unbound (accessed March 25, 2016).

———. *Catholicism in America: Challenges and Prospects*. Edited by Matthew L. Lamb. Ave Maria, FL: Sapientia, 2012.

———. "Challenges for Catholic Graduate Theological Education." In *Theological Education in the Catholic Tradition*, edited by Patrick W. Carey and Earl C. Muller, 108–30. New York: Crossroad, 1997.

———. "Eternity and Time in St. Thomas Aquinas's Commentary on the Gospel of John." In *Reading John with St. Thomas Aquinas: Theological Exegesis & Speculative Theology*, edited by Michael Dauphinais and Matthew Levering, 127–39. Washington, DC: Catholic University of America Press, 2005.

———. "Eternity Creates and Redeems Time: The Theology of History in St. Augustine." In *Divine Creation in Ancient, Medieval, and Early Modern Thought: Essays Presented to the Rev. Robert Crouse*, edited by M. Treschow, et al., 117–40. Leiden: Brill, 2007.

———. *Eternity, Time, and the Life of Wisdom*. Naples, FL: Sapientia, 2007.

———. "Historicity and Eternity: The Transpositions of Bernard Lonergan." *Lonergan Workshop* (1994) 179–227.

20. Lamb, "Challenges," 130.

———. "Letter of Welcome to Ave Maria University's M.A. and PH.D. Programs in Theology." http://www.avemaria.edu/Portals/0/PDFs/Graduate%20Catalog.pdf.

———. "Lonergan's Transpositions of Augustine and Aquinas." In *The Importance of Insight: Essays in Honor of Michael Vertin*, edited by John J. Liptay and David Liptay, 3–21. Toronto: University of Toronto Press, 2007.

———. "Nature is Normative for Culture." *Nova et Vetera* 3 (2005) 153–62.

———. "The Question of Truth in Revealed Religion." In *Jerusalem, Athens, and Rome: Essays in Honor of Fr. James Schall, SJ*, edited by Marc D. Guerra, 70–79. South Bend: St. Augustine's, 2013.

———. "Temporality and History: Reflections from St. Augustine and Bernard Lonergan." *Nova et Vetera* 4 (2006) 815–50.

———. "Will There Be Catholic Theology in the United States?" *America: The National Catholic Review* (May 26, 1990) 523–34.

1

From Cultural Signs to Transcultural Realities

The Contribution of Matthew Lamb for Understanding Lonergan's Metamethod

Matthew R. McWhorter

INTRODUCTION

BERNARD LONERGAN IS OFTEN categorized as a "transcendental Thomist." In what respect is Lonergan's work "transcendental"? Lonergan's student Matthew Lamb argues that close attention to Lonergan's work will observe that his method in theology does not comprise an attempt to integrate Catholic thought with the transcendental idealism of Kant. Rather, Lamb maintains that Lonergan's method is better characterized as a "metamethod" which orients a Catholic theologian beyond various historical contexts toward transhistorical or transcultural realities. When considered in light of Lamb's interpretation, Lonergan's metamethod may be understood as directing Catholic theologians to supplement their study of cultural signs with a focus upon the primary task of theology, namely, the discernment of the signified realities. For

Lonergan, such leads the theologian to the attainment of a state of authenticity which is fostered by ongoing conversions (intellectual, moral, and religious). This threefold conversion is, for Lonergan, the foundation of all authentic theological praxis.

LAMB AND LONERGAN

After corresponding from the Trappist monastery where he was located outside of Conyers, Georgia, Matthew Lamb met Bernard Lonergan in Rome at the Gregorian University in September 1964.[1] Lonergan directed Lamb's STL thesis there the following year.[2] Their scholarly relationship and friendship continued thereafter. Lonergan wrote to Lamb after returning to Canada, discussing how his faith in God supported him through his struggle with cancer in late 1965.[3] Each theologian held the work of the other in high regard. Lamb would later describe Lonergan as a "Catholic intellectual genius."[4] Lonergan, referring to Lamb's doctoral dissertation written in 1974 under the direction of Johann Baptist Metz at the University of Münster, writes, "The effort of drawing on his learning and of entering into his thought is highly rewarding."[5]

Due to Lamb's personal relationship with Lonergan, Lamb's writings offer students and contemporary scholars of Catholic theology a significant resource for understanding Lonergan's teachings. The present study aims to serve as an expository analysis of Lamb's treatment of Lonergan's methodology. Special emphasis will be given to the benefit of interpreting Lonergan's method in light of Lamb's realism. Lonergan's method must be understood in this respect in order to interpret his critiques of conceptualism and classicism.[6]

Lamb observes that Lonergan's writings are typically divided into two eras.[7] The earlier era involves Lonergan's Thomistic studies such as *Grace and Freedom* and *Verbum*, as well as Lonergan's primary work

---

1. See: Lamb, "Historicity and Eternity," 179–80; Lamb, "Lonergan's Transpositions," 3.

2. See: Lamb, "Analogy for the Divine Self-Gift," 115n. This article is an abridgment of Lamb's STL thesis.

3. See Mathews, "Biographical Perspective," 151.

4. Lamb, "Historicity and Eternity," 179.

5. Lonergan, "Forward," xii.

6. Lamb refers to Lonergan's "critique of classicism" in "Response to Principe," 102.

7. Lamb, "Lonergan's Transpositions," 6.

Insight.[8] The later era is exemplified by Lonergan's *Method in Theology*.[9] Lamb describes Lonergan's early work as a response to transcendental idealism and Lonergan's later work as a response to dialectical materialism.[10]

In a similar way, Lamb's writings may also be chronologically distinguished according to a thematic development which occurs during the 1990s: while Lamb's early writings emphasize theological praxis in relation to socio-economic and political criticism,[11] his later writings consider the relation of history to eternity as well as the need for Western society to reacquire wisdom, a virtue eclipsed by the modern cultural emphasis upon the virtue of science.[12] Lamb's earlier works evince an interest in the Frankfurt School of critical theory, as likely influenced by the similar work of his doctoral dissertation director, Johann Baptist Metz.[13] The thematic shift in Lamb's work correlates with a concern he raises in the early 1990s that the doctoral research of Catholic theologians in the previous decade was disproportionately focused upon "contemporary figures and questions," with the increasing risk that Catholic doctrinal and theological traditions will be left solely to historians.[14] Lamb's contention that historical research comprises only one phase of Catholic theological method (discussed below) should be interpreted in light of this concern.

---

8. To these may be added *Collection, Understanding and Being*, and *Philosophical and Theological Papers 1958–1964*.

9. To this era may be added *A Second Collection, A Third Collection*, and *Philosophical and Theological Papers 1965–1980*.

10. See the discussion in: Lamb, "Orthopraxis," 71–73.

11. See, for example: Lamb, "Response to Lonergan"; "Production Process"; "Orthopraxis"; "Praxis and . . . Empirical Method" (which is "Orthopraxis" with slight revisions, such as a new introduction, deletions, and an edited conclusion); "Methodology" (where 315–41 is a revision of Lamb, *History, Method, and Theology*, 4–41); *Solidarity with Victims* (where chapter 5 is a revision of the earlier "Orthopraxis" article); "Christianity within the Political Dialectics"; "Dialectics of Theory and Praxis"; "Social and Political Dimensions"; and chapter 7 of *Eternity, Time, and the Life of Wisdom*.

12. See, for example, Lamb, "Historicity and Eternity"; "Divine Transcendence"; chapter 3 of *Eternity, Time, and the Life of Wisdom*; "Temporality and History"; "Millennial Challenges"; "Lonergan . . . Gregorian Years."

13. See, for example, Lamb, *Solidarity with Victims*, 28–60. For reference to Metz as Lamb's dissertation director, see Lamb, *History, Method, and Theology*, xxv.

14. See Lamb, "Response to Principe," 98–9. See also Lamb, "Will There Be Catholic Theology"; "Challenge"; "Catholic Theological Society of America."

LONERGAN AND TRANSCENDENTAL THOMISM

Lonergan is frequently categorized as exemplary of a twentieth century school of theology and philosophy dubbed "transcendental Thomism." This movement, according to Joseph Donceel, has the Beligian thinker Joseph Maréchal as its progenitor.[15] Maréchal, Donceel states, was in turn influenced by Maurice Blondel, Pierre Rousselot, and Pierre Scheuer.[16] Many advocates of transcendental Thomism characterize Lonergan's work as an expression of their school of thought. Lamb, for example, cites Gerald McCool in this respect.[17] One might also consider the studies of Otto Muck,[18] or the popular work of Richard McBrien.[19] At the other extreme, critics of transcendental Thomism also interpret Lonergan's work as an example of Maréchal's school of thought. See, for example, the studies of Frederick Wilhelmsen,[20] E. L. Mascall,[21] John Knasas,[22] Ronald McCamy,[23] and Romanus Cessario.[24] Yet a third set of interpreters of Lonergan question the legitimacy of categorizing Lonergan's work under the heading "transcendental Thomism."[25] Donceel argues

---

15. See Donceel, "Transcendental Thomism." See also his general discussion in "Symposium." For a critique of Donceel as a representative of Transcendental Thomism, see Cullen, "Transcendental Thomism."

16. Donceel, "Transcendental Thomism," 68. See also Maréchal, "Cahier V"; and Matteo, "Marechal's Dialogue."

17. Lamb, "Divine Transcendence," 76. Lamb cites McCool, *Unity to Pluralism*, 34–35; and *Neo-Thomists*, 160.

18. See: Muck, *Transcendental Method*, 255–84. Also see Muck, "Logical Structure," 349 and 353. Lamb maintains that Muck has misinterpreted Lonergan's method. See: Lamb, "Wilhelm Dilthey's Critique," 321n1.

19. See McBrien, *Catholicism*, 148.

20. See Wilhelmsen, "Priority of Judgment," 475.

21. See Mascall, *Openness of Being*, 48, 84.

22. See Knasas, "Transcendental Thomism and *De Veritate*," 230–32; Knasas, "Intellectual Dynamism," 15–16; Knasas, *Being and Some . . . Thomists*, 22n27. For a critique of transcendental Thomism that does not consider Lonergan, see Knasas, "Transcendental Thomism . . . Texts." For a defense of Lonergan vis-à-vis Knasas, see Wilkins, "Dialectic." For Knasas's response, see Knasas, "Why for Lonergan."

23. See McCamy, *Out of a Kantian Chrysalis*, 30nn5–6, 156. McCamy argues that Lonergan has been influenced by Maréchal with respect to particular doctrines. See McCamy, *Kantian Chrysalis*, 166n19.

24. For Cessario, see the discussion at Lamb, "Contemplata Tradere," 319. Lamb cites Cessario, *Short History*, 87–88.

25. See, for example, the discussion at Lamb, "Contemplata Tradere," 319–20n 30, citing Henle, *American Thomistic Revival*, 348. Also see Kerr, *Twentieth-Century*

that while Maréchal did influence Henri de Lubac and Karl Rahner directly, Maréchal's influence upon Lonergan was indirect and Lonergan "disagrees with Maréchal in fundamental doctrines."[26] Lamb supports Donceel's hesitation to categorize Lonergan as a follower of Maréchal.[27] At the same time, Donceel does discuss Lonergan alongside other transcendental Thomists.[28] Why? To ask whether Lonergan is a transcendental Thomist is to ask two questions. First, in what respect is Lonergan a transcendental thinker? Second, to what extent is Lonergan a Thomist? It is the first question that the present discussion addresses.

AN INTRODUCTION TO LONERGAN'S METAMETHOD

Donceel indicates that a transcendental Thomist will use a transcendental method which is implicit in Aquinas and explicit in Kant.[29] Lonergan does refer to his theological method as a "transcendental method."[30] But if by "transcendental" one signifies Kantian critical idealism, Lamb explicitly rejects such an interpretation of Lonergan. Lamb indicates that there are "profound differences between Lonergan's transcendental method and German *Transzendentalphilosophie* . . ."[31] Elsewhere, he argues, "Lonergan does not try to claim that some idea or concept is present in all or many cultures. As Giovanni Sala has clearly established, it is simply flat out wrong to view Lonergan's understanding of the 'transcendental' and the 'a priori' as anything but a profound critique of the Kantian orientation."[32] In yet another selection, Lamb maintains that Sala compellingly establishes that, "Lonergan adopted Aquinas's cognitional theory in order to provide a thorough criticism of Kantian philosophy."[33]

Catholic Theologians, 111–12 and 111n19, where Kerr appeals to Tracy who questions this characterization of Lonergan. See Tracy, *Achievement*, 28–29.

  26. Donceel, "Transcendental Thomism," 72–73.
  27. Lamb, "Dilthey's Critique," 321n1.
  28. See Donceel, *Searching Mind*, 127.
  29. Donceel, "Transcendental Thomism," 71.
  30. See, for example, Lonergan, *Method*, 13, section subheading.
  31. Lamb, "Methodology," 378n28.
  32. Lamb, "Notion of the Transcultural," 59. With respect to the reference to Sala, Lamb refers his reader to Sala, *Das Apriori*. Also see the helpful contrasts in Sala, "Concept of the Transcendental."
  33. Lamb, "*Contemplata Tradere*," 319. As well as again citing Sala's *Das Apriori*, here Lamb also refers his reader to Sala, *Lonergan and Kant*; and Sala, "What Use is Kant . . . ?"

Lamb concedes that the category of "transcendental Thomism" is indeed applicable to the work of those thinkers who were genuinely influenced by Maréchal.[34] But Lamb does not agree with characterizing Lonergan's work in this regard. He observes that Lonergan writes that he did not study Maréchal's work directly.[35] Lamb states that when Lonergan first heard of Maréchal's work, Lonergan understood it only in connection with Augustine's concern with *veritas* and Aquinas's concern with *esse*.[36] In order to distinguish Lonergan from Maréchal, Lamb points to a comparative study by Michael Vertin who outlines many differences between the two thinkers.[37]

How does Lonergan himself describe his method as "transcendental"? When considering Muck's *The Transcendental Method* and the evaluation of Lonergan's work found therein, Lonergan writes,

> I conceive method concretely. I conceive it, not in terms of principles and rules, but as a normative pattern of operations with cumulative and progressive results. I distinguish the methods appropriate to particular fields and, on the other hand, their common core and ground, which I name transcendental method. Here, the word, transcendental, is employed in a sense analogous to Scholastic usage, for it is opposed to the categorial (or predicamental). But my actual procedure also is transcendental in the Kantian sense, inasmuch as it brings to light the conditions of the possibility of knowing an object in so far as that knowledge is *a priori*.[38]

In a passage which serves to comment on this text of Lonergan, Lamb maintains that Lonergan employs the word "transcendental" primarily in a Scholastic sense, "where the transcendental is distinguished from the categorical as something not bound to one of Aristotle's predicaments."[39] An interpretation of Lonergan which gives primacy to Kant as a herme-

---

34. Lamb, "*Contemplata Tradere*," 319–20. See also Lamb, "Lonergan's Transpositions," 7.

35. Lamb, "*Contemplata Tradere*," 320n31, citing Lonergan, "*Insight* Revisited," in *Second Collection*, 265. Also see the similar discussion in Lonergan, *Understanding and Being*, 349–50.

36. Lamb, "Divine Transcendence," 77.

37. See Lamb, "Lonergan's Transpositions," 7 and 19n18, citing: Vertin, "Maréchal, Lonergan," 411–22.

38. Lonergan, *Method*, 13n4. Lamb cites this passage in Lamb, "Methodology," 378n28.

39. Lamb, "*Contemplata Tradere*," 320.

neutical key is liable to be led astray by the modern connotations of the word "transcendental." As such, Lamb observes that in Lonergan's later thought (beginning in 1974 after the publication of *Method in Theology*), Lonergan begins to speak of his method in different terms as a "generalized empirical method."[40] Further, Lamb observes that elsewhere in *Method in Theology*, Lonergan describes his method not only as "transcendental" but also as "transcultural." There, Lonergan writes, "the transcendental method . . . is, in a sense, transcultural. Clearly it is not transcultural inasmuch as it is explicitly formulated. But it is transcultural in the realities to which the formulation refers, for these realities are not the product of culture . . ."[41] Lonergan's reference to transcultural "realities" here is of key importance; this topic will be explored at greater length below.

Also helpful for distinguishing Lonergan from Kant is to understand Lonergan's method by Lamb's descriptive term "metamethodology."[42] Lamb explains his rationale for employing this phrase. He writes, "In discussions within the German context, I have found it helpful not to refer to Lonergan's method as transcendental but as meta-method. The differences between Lonergan's method and *Transzendentalphilosophie* (Kant or Husserl) are rather basic. Perhaps of equal significance are the differences between meta-method and the transcendental Thomist trend initiated by Maréchal . . . Also instructive are the misunderstandings which arise when Lonergan is grouped into this trend . . ."[43] When discussing Lonergan's "transcendental method of methods or metamethodology," Lamb observes that, "it entails a completely new understanding of method. It is not a set of objectivistic rules or axioms to be followed blindly by the adepts of the method, but an appropriation of the creative and critical structures of human subjectivity, in every aspect of theory or praxis."[44]

Lamb's reference to "appropriation" in this passage is important for grasping his understanding of Lonergan's method. Self-appropriation, Lamb explains, is central to Lonergan's metamethodology: "The key to metamethod lies in its invitation to a self-appropriation of the praxis of human understanding and performance in all spheres of human activity

---

40. Lamb, "Orthopraxis," 73; Lamb, "Praxis and . . . Empirical Method," 62; Lamb, *Solidarity with Victims*, 129.

41. Lonergan, *Method*, 282, as quoted in Lamb, "Transcultural," 61.

42. Lamb, "Methodology," 284.

43. Lamb, "Dilthey's Critique," 321n1.

44. Lamb, "Methodology," 366.

whatever they might be."⁴⁵ Lamb elaborates further a few lines later in the same essay: "The key, once again, is self-appropriation which involves not only what factually is (e.g., all the manifold concrete situations resulting from equally diverse social, political, philosophical, scientific, aesthetic, etc. traditions); but also uncovers within these factual situations certain dynamically related and recurrent operations of human historical subjectivity capable of grounding a critical evaluation of those situations."⁴⁶ A metamethodology must be transcendental because any method of a particular science is categorical and thus cannot be universalized as grounding all other methodologies.⁴⁷ In this respect, Lamb maintains elsewhere that Lonergan's "*generalized* empirical method" is "applicable not only to theology but whole series of basic issues in the sciences and scholarly disciplines."⁴⁸ Since it is "transcendental," Lonergan's metamethod relates to all of the various methods of the sciences. Lamb writes, "Lonergan's transcendental method or metamethodology has effectively cut through the Gordian knot of objectivism; it provides a compelling account of why the natural sciences are successful by calling attention to the related and recurrent operations capable of yielding cumulative and progressive results, not only in the physical sciences, but in all spheres of human performance."⁴⁹ Such a metamethodology is not abstract from the particular methods of the different sciences in the sense of being an ideal. In the same essay, Lamb explains, "Lonergan has come up with such a novel version of transcendental method that the present writer has found it advisable to refer to it with the less philosophically loaded expression of metamethod . . . In the measure that Lonergan was able to radically correct the Kantian program of transcendental method, to that extent he would also avoid any charge of obscurantism in seeking to relate his transcendental method with the many methods operative in natural and human sciences."⁵⁰

The non-Kantian reading of Lonergan which Lamb promotes is implicit in another way as well, namely, with respect to Lonergan's affirmation of the continued value and validity of metaphysics as a philosophical

---

45. Ibid., 354.
46. Ibid., 355.
47. See the discussion at ibid., 363.
48. Lamb, "Orthopraxis," 86; Lamb, *Solidarity with Victims*, 142.
49. Lamb, "Methodology," 284. See also the reference to "scientistic objectivism" at ibid., 354.
50. Ibid., 354.

discipline. According to Lamb, the functional specialization of theological foundations in sacred theology "needs metaphysics since there is no one-to-one correlation between conscious acts and natural realities and revealed realities."[51] Lamb maintains that, for Lonergan, foundations or fundamental theology should utilize metaphysics for the sake of articulating "general theological categories" which would be employed in all the other theological specializations.[52] As an example, Lamb maintains that the specialization of systematics should employ a "critical metaphysics."[53] Elsewhere, Lamb provides a general admonition regarding the continued importance of metaphysics for theology: "without metaphysics there is a danger that theology will succumb to the voluntarism, fideism, and fundamentalism that fails to appreciate how the absolutely supernatural revelation of Christ Jesus redeems and perfects nature."[54]

THE FOUNDATION OF LONERGAN'S METAMETHOD: COMMON COGNITIVE OPERATIONS

As discussed above, Lamb contends that Lonergan's metamethodology is not presented as an ideal theory apart from actual human cognitive performances in the various sciences, but rather it recognizes those common cognitive operations which are employed in the various specialized methods of the sciences.[55] What is "the normative pattern of operations" which comprises Lonergan's meta-method? In an oft-quoted passage found in the introduction to *Insight*, Lonergan states, "Thoroughly understand what it is to understand, and not only will you understand the broad lines of all there is to be understood but also you will possess a fixed base, an invariant pattern, opening upon all further developments

---

51. Lamb, "Lonergan's Transpositions," 10–11.

52. Ibid., 11 and 20n34, quoting Lonergan, *Method*, 287. There Lonergan states that by "metaphysics" he means an "integral heuristic structure" and refers his reader to *Insight*, 390–96.

53. Lamb, "Divine Transcendence," 84. For the meaning of "critical metaphysics" for Lamb, see the note just above leading to *Insight*, 390–96.

54. Lamb, "Nature is Normative," 161.

55. See also Lamb, "Methodology," 286.

of understanding."⁵⁶ Lonergan's purpose in his work *Insight* is to call attention to such invariant cognitive structures.⁵⁷

Lonergan affirms that there are common cognitive operations found at "different levels of consciousness," namely, the empirical, intellectual, critical, and responsible levels.⁵⁸ Such operations, Lamb indicates, comprise human "experiencing, understanding, judging, deciding, acting . . ."⁵⁹ The act of insight is associated particularly with the intellectual level.⁶⁰ Lonergan differentiates the third and fourth levels as involving "judgments of fact" and "judgments of value."⁶¹ There are also hints of a fifth level. For example, describing "the praxis of self-appropriation," Lamb states that such "elicits an awareness of the subject's own . . . drives toward attentiveness, intelligence, critical rationality, responsibility, and love."⁶² Lamb's reference to "love" as a fifth common cognitive operation here touches upon the exegetical question of whether for Lonergan a fifth level of consciousness exists which involves being in love with God⁶³ (there is a scholarly question whether, for Lonergan, there is also a sixth level of consciousness—although what might comprise the associated cognitive operation at this level is unclear in Lonergan's text).⁶⁴

Lamb treats the first three levels of cognitive operations (experience, understanding, and judgment) in his STL thesis.⁶⁵ There, he writes

---

56. Lonergan, *Insight*, 22. For a helpful short introduction to Lonergan on insight, see Crowe, "Stare at a Triangle."

57. See Crowe's discussion concerning Lonergan's later qualifications regarding the acquisition of "insight into insight" in Crowe, "For a Phenomenology," 71–83.

58. Lonergan, *Method*, 9. See also Lonergan, *Insight*, 592.

59. Lamb, "Methodology," 307.

60. Lamb refers to the four levels as "attention, insight, reasonableness, responsibility," in ibid., 311.

61. Lonergan, "Philosophy and the Religious Phenomenon," 134.

62. Lamb, "Methodology," 359.

63. The question of a fifth level of consciousness derives from a comment made by Lonergan at the end of a lecture in 1972. See Lonergan, "Lecture 2: The Functionality Speciality 'Systematics,'" in *Philosophical and Theological Papers 1965–1980*, 193. The lecture also appears in Lonergan, *Philosophy of God*, 21–44. See also Vertin, "Lonergan on Consciousness."

64. The question of a sixth level of consciousness involves a passage found in a posthumously published essay from 1977–1978. See Lonergan, "Philosophy and the Religious Phenomenon," 134. For dating information, see Crowe, "Lonergan's 'Philosophy and the Religious Phenomenon,'" 122. See also Byrne, "Consciousness."

65. See: Lamb, "Analogy," 122–24. Also see the discussion in Kanaris, *Bernard Lonergan's Philosophy*, 35–36. See also the study of these three levels in Smith, "Is There a Thomist Alternative," 631–33.

that each level of consciousness is oriented toward an ontological element of a concrete entity as its proper correlate: empirical consciousness is oriented to potency, intelligent consciousness to form, and critical consciousness to act or existence.[66] Lamb describes the transition from one level of consciousness to the next again in a later essay: "As the questions for understanding arise out of the data of empirical consciousness and go beyond (transcend) them by asking their meaning; as questions for reflection arise out of hypothetical formulations of meaning and go beyond (transcend) them by asking if they are true or false; as deliberation arises out of knowledge and goes beyond it (transcends) by responsible decisions and action; so one can question the quest(ion)ing drive of human knowing and doing itself without retreating into obscurantism..."[67] Part of the normativity of such cognitive operations, Lamb maintains elsewhere, is for the human knower to remain open to new experiences, new understandings, new judgments, new responsible decisions. Observing that Lonergan's work uncovers "the related and recurrent operations of the subject-as-subject," Lamb argues that, "these operations constitute the open structures of freedom; they ground both the worlds of science and of day-to-day living."[68] At all levels of consciousness, a subject's openness is found preeminently in his or her act of questioning. Lamb writes, "The normativity of intelligence is precisely this ongoing openness to all further questions... The openness is precisely an openness to questions all of which seek and demand correct answers... The norm is not in the answer but in the desiring question."[69]

Despite this reference to the *normativeness* of such cognitive operations, one should not confuse normativity in this discussion with what is non-natural. In a later essay, Lamb states that the normative cognitive operations under consideration are those which are proper to human nature *as such*. There he writes,

> The human mind as most divine in us, and the image of God in us, has a nature. There are patterns or natural ordered orientations of human understanding and judging and loving, which we do not make up ourselves or acquire from a culture or tradition... We either act according to the natural order or pattern within our rational nature, or we fail to live as genuinely

---

66. Lamb, "Analogy," 123.
67. Lamb, "Methodology," 308.
68. Ibid., 307.
69. Lamb, "Historicity and Eternity," 213–14.

as human beings ought to live. As rational, human nature has a transcultural core. The human mind and soul transcend while being immanent in cultures . . . Wisdom attends to these transcultural patterns and ordered orientations.[70]

In addition to construing Lonergan's account of such normative cognitive operations as a description of the transcultural nature of the human mind, Lamb maintains in a different early essay that this pattern of operations is not only normative but *factual*. He states, "Lonergan's transcendental method strives for coherence but frankly admits its radical incompleteness. The operations of conscious intentionality are indeed both factual ("is") and normative ("ought"). Yet this fusion of the factual and the normative is not the indicative ("always already") possession of *Geist* within the world of theory but is the imperative ("not yet") beckoning of concrete human strivings toward attentiveness, intelligence, reasonableness and responsible love."[71] Lamb's reference to attentiveness, intelligence, reasonableness, and responsibility in this passage is an allusion to what he names elsewhere as Lonergan's four "transcendental imperatives."[72] In his writings, Lamb frequently alludes to these imperatives or transcendental precepts[73]—as well as to the opposite modes of behavior.[74]

The transcendental imperatives, according to Lonergan, are "permanent" and their "sustained observance" is what engenders genuine human progress.[75] Such imperatives, Lamb states, are "the transformative values" upon which "Lonergan's dialectical analysis takes a critically grounded stand . . ."[76] He explains that, "from that stand within intellectual or noetic orthopraxis," such imperatives, for Lonergan, provide criteria in accordance with which other traditions and cultures may be evaluated.[77] In this way, Lamb asserts that "historical religions" can be

70. Lamb, "Nature is Normative," 158.

71. Lamb, "Orthopraxis," 72; Lamb, "Praxis and . . . Empirical Method," 60–61; Lamb, *Solidarity with Victims*, 127–28.

72. See the discussion in Lamb, "Social and Political Dimensions," 264.

73. See, for example, Lamb, "Transcultural," 60, 69; Lamb, "Production Process," 290.

74. See, for example, Lamb, "Transcultural," 68; Lamb, "Production Process," 292; Lamb, "Methodology," 307, 360, 370.

75. Lonergan, *Method*, 53.

76. Lamb, "Orthopraxis," 82; Lamb, "Praxis and . . . Empirical Method," 72; Lamb, *Solidarity with Victims*, 138.

77. Lamb, "Orthopraxis," 82; Lamb, "Praxis and . . . Empirical Method," 72; Lamb, *Solidarity with Victims*, 138.

subjected to evaluation: "Insofar as historical religions have tended to oppose the unfolding of human attention, intelligence, reasonableness, and responsibility they have been guilty of alienating religious expressions from an authentic experience of the God-question."[78]

What does Lamb mean by "authentic experience" in this statement? Authenticity, Lonergan teaches, is associated with the attainment of self-transcendence.[79] Such comprises a state which a subject can choose and will,[80] yet one which can also be lost.[81] To the extent that traditions, cultures, and historical religions are transformed in accordance with the transcendental imperatives, to that extent such precepts can be understood as "transcultural." On this point, Lamb writes, "Neither reflection on theology nor reflection on method are ends in themselves. They are meant to promote a creative and critical collaboration with all humans in the tasks of transforming ourselves and our world into more attentive, intelligent, reasonable, and responsibly loving life."[82]

Although these precepts are called "transcendental imperatives," Lamb argues that they should not be understood as simply a set of *a priori* rules or regulative ideas in the Kantian sense. He writes, "If one has misread Lonergan's notion of transcendental method as just a variation on Kantian or Neo-Kantian themes, then one can imagine that Lonergan is developing a set of rules, or regulative ideas, which ought to be helpful (if one is sympathetic) or harmful (if one is not) in restructuring how theology and/or religious studies departments go about doing whatever they do."[83] In contrast to understanding these precepts as deontological rules, such "imperatives" should be understood instead as expressions of a subject's "unrestricted desire for meaning and value," a desire which a subject can pursue or ignore.[84]

In a later essay, Lamb indicates that historical cultures and Lonergan's transcultural imperatives are not mutually exclusive, but rather the latter are co-present and embedded in the former. He writes,

---

78. Lamb, "Methodology," 312.
79. See Lonergan, *Method*, 104.
80. Ibid., 51.
81. Ibid., 110.
82. Lamb, "Orthopraxis," 87; Lamb, "Praxis and . . . Empirical Method," 77; Lamb, *Solidarity with Victims*, 143.
83. Lamb, "Transcultural," 65.
84. Lamb, "Methodology," 302.

> Within any culture there is present, insofar as any culture is constituted by human minds and human actions, both a transcendental and an immanent dimension. Any genuine culture is both transcultural and incultural. It is transcultural insofar as it fosters the beauty of the aesthetic, the truth of intelligence, the goodness of morality, the holiness of the religious. These transcultural dimensions are not merely "ideals" or "ideas" reserved in some eternal thought: They are transcultural orientations that are always inculturated in particular achievements of beautiful art, achievements of genial intelligence, achievements of moral goodness, achievements of religious holiness.[85]

Further, according to Lamb, it is because the Gospel contains this transcultural component that it may be efficaciously proclaimed to all cultures in history: "The transcultural dimension of the Gospel is in no way antithetical to, but really makes possible, the inculturation of the Gospel in myriad cultures. Because the Gospel is absolutely supernatural and totally the free gift of an all-loving Triune God, the Gospel must be proclaimed and inculturated among all nations and cultures."[86]

THE FOUNDATION OF ACADEMIC THEOLOGY: ONGOING THREEFOLD CONVERSION

Lonergan's metamethodological imperatives seek to inculcate human agents in the common human cognitive operations discussed above, facilitating what Lamb refers to as "noetic praxis."[87] Participation in this praxis, for Lamb, is what comprises the special task of academic theology: "Theology is a reflective noetic praxis which mediates the transformative values and narratives of religion to cultures and societies."[88] It is by abiding in such a normative cognitive orthopraxis that establishes, for Lamb, the foundation of contemporary academic theology. He writes, "To critically mediate the Christian message from the present into the future means that the very foundations of theology cannot be located in the past—whether in scriptural, patristic, conciliar, or other ecclesial traditions—and then mediated theoretically into the present. Rather the foundations are in the praxis of the present as actually oriented toward

---

85. Lamb, *Eternity, Time, and the Life of Wisdom*, 110.
86. Ibid., 111.
87. Lamb, "Transcultural," 65.
88. Lamb, *Solidarity with Victims*, 14, citing Lonergan, *Method*, xi–xii.

the eschatological kingdom of God."[89] Such praxis, Lamb indicates later in the same essay, involves a particular kind of criticism: "It is important to understand the conception of critique that is the basis of metamethod. As providing the framework for creative collaboration, metamethod sees the critical justification of the entire theological enterprise as an ongoing process. It cannot be theoretically deduced—unless one adopts a classicist conception of critique."[90] At the basis of a theologian's critical praxis is a process of ongoing intellectual, moral, and religious conversion. In the same essay, Lamb writes, "Lonergan sees intellectual, moral, and religious conversion as the very foundation of theology."[91] In a later essay, Lamb relates each conversion to the acquisition of certain kinds of virtues: "The three conversions are articulated in terms of the religious conversion to Jesus Christ (theological virtues), the intellectual conversion appropriating the detailed experiences of intellectual and rational consciousness (intellectual virtues), and the moral conversion appropriating the exigencies of our rational self-consciousness (moral virtues)."[92]

Since academic theology is understood from a Lonerganian perspective as a critical noetic praxis, one should give special attention to Lonergan's doctrine of intellectual conversion in order to grasp his construal of the theological task. On this topic, Lamb maintains, "Noetic praxis as intellectual conversion can no longer be taken for granted. It must be thematized explicitly in an anthropocentric turn to the questioning human subject whereby we appropriate our own cognitive desires and expectations with their related and recurrent operations."[93] Lamb sees previous thinkers in the Christian tradition as having undergone the same threefold conversion he mentions here. Lamb explicitly refers to Augustine in this respect: "to know the reality of the divine friendship Augustine narrates, one must, like him, undergo a process of intellectual, moral, and religious conversion."[94] Similarly, Lamb maintains that what is needed to understand Aquinas's theology and cognitional theory

---

89. Lamb, "Methodology," 342.

90. Ibid., 380n41.

91. Ibid., 369, citing Lonergan, *Method*, 130–32, 235–44, and 267–93.

92. Lamb, "Lonergan . . . Gregorian Years," §3. The section number is cited here rather than the page number since the article cited has not yet been published in *Gregorianum*.

93. Lamb, *Solidarity with Victims*, 15, citing his own *History, Method, and Theology*, 357–529.

94. Lamb, "Temporality and History," 829.

is not simply a critical historical reconstruction but rather a theologian participating in the same ongoing process of conversion (intellectual, moral, and religious).[95]

Lamb also indicates that undergoing the threefold conversion process is the hermeneutical key needed to understand Lonergan as an interpreter of Aquinas: according to Lamb, Lonergan underwent this necessary intellectual conversion in his attempt "to reach up to the mind of Aquinas . . ."[96] Lamb explains, "This conversion had to be made explicit, otherwise the achievements of theology from Augustine to Aquinas would continue to be misunderstood, as in decadent scholasticism and nominalism. In order to retrieve Aquinas' cognitional theory from the deformations into which it had fallen at the hands of too many so-called Thomists, Lonergan wrote *Verbum* . . ."[97] Without such conversion, Lamb warns that "theology as such ceases."[98] He indicates that the Thomist response to Descartes in the seventeenth century failed because it lacked such an intellectual conversion:

> When Descartes's *cogito ergo sum* was enunciated most could not distinguish thinking from knowing, and eternity was increasingly defined as the simple and total negation of time. Thomists opposed Cartesian thinking with the dependence of the mind on sensations, perceptions, and images. So realism came to imply an empiricism unable to deal with the systematic tasks of metaphysics and theology . . . Universals could not be concrete but only nominal, as metaphysics and theology was farmed out to grammarians and logicians. The stage was set for Spinoza's claim that any transcendence of nature was a contradiction of nature.[99]

In contrast to an empiricist's emphasis upon the bodily senses as the sole criterion of truth, Lamb argues that for Aquinas the bodily senses can yield only metaphors for the divine, not proper analogies.[100]

Given its importance for the task of theology, one must ask: What is intellectual conversion for Lonergan?[101] Although Lamb relates intel-

---

95. Lamb, "Divine Transcendence," 78.
96. Ibid.
97. Ibid., 101n13.
98. See Lamb, "Response to Principe," 101.
99. Lamb, "Historicity and Eternity," 221.
100. Ibid., 212, citing Aquinas, *ST* I, 13, 6 and 16.
101. See Barden, "On Intellectual Conversion."

lectual conversion to the theological virtue of faith, Lonergan's account of intellectual conversion cannot be identified strictly with a graced act of assent to Catholic teachings (that is, as conversion from non-belief in teachings about Christ to belief). Rather, Lamb explains that, for Lonergan, intellectual conversion "is the discovery and appropriation of the related and recurrent operations of human intelligence in act."[102] Intellectual conversion entails a "shift toward interiority" and "rational self-appropriation."[103] Describing the phrase "rational self-appropriation," Lamb states that such language "is a transposition of the ancient call to a self-knowledge of the soul."[104]

As an example of intellectual conversion, Lamb sends his reader to books five through nine of Augustine's *Confessions*.[105] The three conversions are interrelated and connected to Lonergan's transcendental imperatives. For example, referring to "religious conversion," Lamb states that it "is intrinsically related to intellectual and moral conversions. Intelligence, goodness, and holiness are integral with each other, not in terms of some classical ideal but in the ongoing practice of striving for ever fuller attentiveness, intelligence, reasonableness, responsibility, love."[106]

THREE PHASES IN THEOLOGICAL METHOD: CRITICAL HISTORY, KNOWLEDGE OF REALITIES, RESTATEMENT

Lonergan's metamethod as applied to the task of Catholic academic theology should be understood in connection with the theological movements of *ressourcement* and *aggiornamento* popular in the twentieth century.[107] The former, according to Lamb, involves a historical task which proceeds by "identifying authors or historical agents, situating their actions and/or works in time and place, studying their historical contexts and sources..."[108] Theological research at this phase involves the same procedures

---

102. Lamb, "Historicity and Eternity," 182. See also Gregson, "Desire to Know."
103. Lamb, "Historicity and Eternity," 185.
104. Ibid., 187.
105. Lamb, "Temporality and History," 823.
106. Lamb, "Social and Political," 277–78. See also Carmody, "Desire for Transcendence."
107. Lamb, "Divine Transcendence," 76. See also the discussion at Lamb, "Historicity and Eternity," 184–85.
108. Lamb, "Response to Principe," 100. See also Lamb, "Historicity and Eternity," 193–94; Lamb, "Temporality and History," 842.

which occur in historical science.[109] Lamb explains in a later essay that, "the first phase is constituted by the light of reason researching the data, interpreting them, charting their history, and discerning the underlying differences in their histories."[110] Such historical considerations comprise a "retrieval" or a "return to the sources" (*ressourcement*). On this point, Lamb refers his reader to a statement of Lonergan at the end of *Verbum*, where Lonergan asserts that his study had been a work of retrieval in an effort to establish "the *vetera* . . ."[111] This is an allusion to Leo XIII's phrase *vetera novis augere et perficere*, "to build up and perfect the old with the new."[112] Lamb maintains that the first phase of Lonergan's theological method should be understood as an application of this Leonine decree.[113]

Lamb observes that some thinkers unfortunately stop at this first historical phase in their work and proceed no further.[114] He contends that, "for critical historians to begin to become real theologians, and not just comparative textologists, they are going to have to develop personally and communally against the drift of many Enlightenment presuppositions still biasing modern and postmodern cultures."[115] As such, a "critical historian's main objective" in proper theological work requires a transition to a second, methodological phase.[116] Lamb explains, "While a critical historian might not need to know faith, the spiritual life, or the mystery of the Trinity to do textual criticism, establish sources, compare one set of texts with another set of texts (after all, anyone who can read can begin to do that!), it is something else if he or she is going to engage in a history of faith, prayer, or theology as an *intellectus fidei*."[117] What

---

109. Lamb, "Historicity and Eternity," 190. See also Lamb, "Temporality and History," 840; Lamb, *Eternity, Time, and the Life of Wisdom*, 8.

110. Lamb, "Lonergan . . . Gregorian Years," §3.

111. Lamb, "Lonergan's Transpositions," 5 and 18n7, which quotes not *Verbum* but observes a similar statement in *Insight*. See: Lonergan, *Insight*, 769. For the passage in *Verbum*, see Lonergan, *Verbum*, 222 and 226.

112. See: Lonergan, *Verbum*, 222 and 226. See also Leo XIII, *Aeterni Patris*, 24.

113. See Lamb, "*Contemplata Tradere*," 318–19, quoting Lonergan, "Scope of Renewal," in *Philosophical and Theological Papers 1965–1980*, 298. See also Lamb, "Lonergan's Transpositions," 4.

114. See: Lamb, "Response to Principe," 103n10.

115. Lamb, "Temporality and History," 845.

116. Lamb, "Historicity and Eternity," 194. See also: Lamb, "Temporality and History," 842.

117. Lamb, "Response to Principe," 100. See also: Lamb, "Historicity and Eternity," 194; Lamb, "Temporality and History," 842–43.

Lamb is describing in this passage is the need for Catholic thinkers to transition from the propaedeutic task of history to the proper task of theology. In contrast to critical history, Lamb maintains, "the task of a genuine theology is to realize how theology's subject is nothing less than the reality of the mysterious God."[118]

It is here that Lamb's realism merits special attention as a key for interpreting Lonergan's metamethod. For Lamb, the second phase of theology will transition from the study of historical *signa* to knowing the transhistorical *res* signified.[119] Lamb's emphasis here is on knowing realities, not signs. Such requires not attention to the data of sense but rather to "the data of consciousness..."[120] At the second phase of the theological task, Lamb maintains that a theologian "should move on to understand the objects, processes, events, and realities referred to in those critically established sources."[121] Elsewhere, Lamb similarly refers to the goal of "theologically understanding *the realities* referred to in all of our sacred texts and theological traditions."[122] He states in the same selection: "We can know the realities an Augustine or a Hildegard or an Aquinas knew, just as we can know the realities of our own experiencing, understanding, judging, deciding, loving. These realities are never without mediations, and while the cultural mediations differ profoundly, those mediations are just that, they mediate."[123] The interpretation of cultural *signa* is thus only an initial concern of theology; the proper task of theology entails attentiveness to the transcultural *res*. Lamb explains, "One of the basic and central points that Lonergan makes is that genuine transpositions rest on knowing the realities referred to in the texts one is studying. Thus, transposition is not a translation or transliteration from one set of texts to another. Rather, it involves judgment and thus knowledge of the realities referred to in the texts one is studying. Reaching up to the mind of an Augustine or an Aquinas means reaching up to the realities they knew."[124]

118. Lamb, "Divine Transcendence," 85.

119. See Lamb, "Divine Transcendence," 84, citing Lonergan, *Method*, 189. See also Lamb, "Response to Principe," 99–100.

120. Lamb, "Historicity and Eternity," 190. See also Lamb, "Temporality and History," 840.

121. Lamb, "Response to Principe," 100.

122. See: Lamb, "Transcultural," 69; emphasis is Lamb's.

123. Ibid.

124. Lamb, "Lonergan's Transpositions," 6. Later at p.13, he reiterates this same point: "[T]he analysis of the ancient texts requires attention to the realities those texts affirm."

Here one may ask: What are the realities with which theology is properly concerned? In this respect, Lamb refers to both "natural realities and revealed realities."[125] Regarding natural realities, Lamb considers Lonergan's example of "the one intelligible reality, man, humanity" which "unfolds by means of matter into a material multiplicity of men . . ."[126] In the same passage, Lamb affirms that, "humankind is one intelligible reality."[127] The discussion here intersects with Lonergan's doctrine of "concrete universality."[128] A concrete universal is a universal *in re*: The "concrete" in this sense is not what is material or sensual but simply what is *real*. Lamb elsewhere refers to human cognitive operations as realities.[129]

Regarding revealed realities, Lamb refers to "the mysteries of faith, the sacred realities themselves,"[130] as well as to "the most real reality there is, God."[131] Such "divine realities," he states elsewhere, "are transcendentally immanent in human history."[132] Knowing such realities requires cultivating a sense of careful discernment at the level of judgment. In this respect, Lamb's realism is a critical realism not only with respect to the first phase of theology (which involves a critical approach to historiography), but also with respect to the theologian's relation to sacred realties and to God. He writes, "Our knowledge and love of God requires at the very minimum all the efforts at critical realism and objectivity which any sane person would require in any interpersonal relationship."[133]

Upon knowing theological realities, a theologian should then transition to a third methodological phase which involves the transposition of the cultural signs under consideration in light of the realities experienced and known firsthand. If the first phrase of critical history concerns a recovery of the *vetera* and the second phase concerns a theologian's orientation to the signified realities, such a renewed expression of that

---

125. Ibid., 10–11.

126. Lamb, "Transcultural," 55, where Lamb quotes an early study of Lonergan, then unpublished. See Lonergan, "Essay," 34.

127. Lamb, "Transcultural," 55.

128. Ibid., 49.

129. Lamb, "Divine Transcendence," 92. See also Lamb, "Response to Principe," 103.

130. Lamb, "Divine Transcendence," 81.

131. Ibid., 82.

132. Lamb, "Response to Principe," 101.

133. Lamb, "Historicity and Eternity," 210.

experience is required as a third phase in light of the Leonine call, *novis augere et perficere*. A transposition, Lonergan explains, involves "a restatement of an earlier position in a new and broader context."[134] Here then there is a shift from *ressourcement* to *aggiornamento*.

In a later writing, Lamb compares the first phase of critical history and the third phase of restatement to the *via inventionis* and the *via doctrinae* which Augustine describes in *De doctrina Christiana* (books I–III and book IV, respectively).[135] Each phase, Lamb states, has particular cognitive operations found at each level of consciousness (experiencing, understanding, judging, and deciding).[136] During the phase of restatement, a theologian must discern how he or she can best communicate recovered theological knowledge in his or her present context. On this point, Lamb elaborates, "The task of recovering wisdom traditions of the past is not a task of archaism, a mere restoration of some past epoch. Quite the contrary, a genuine dialectic requires that the recovery of past and repressed wisdom traditions be transposed into very different contexts in order, for example, to counteract the baneful effects of their loss."[137] A transposition or restatement does not aim so much at novelty as at the goal of facilitating theological communication. Lamb indicates that a theologian may find some amount of success by focusing upon the interrelationship between God, the mysteries of faith, and internal cognitive operations. Speaking about how for Lonergan academic sacred theology remains a "subaltern science" in the Scholastic sense, Lamb writes, "the theoretical mediation has to be transposed into an explanatory interiority to convey some fruitful if limited understanding of revealed mysteries..."[138]

The validity of a restatement is found to the extent that what is substantive for the past thinker is preserved.[139] Lamb also maintains that the success of a transposition depends upon the second phase of the theological task (namely, the theologian genuinely knowing the signified

---

134. See Lamb, "Lonergan's Transpositions," 5 and 18n10, quoting Lonergan, "Horizons and Transpositions," in *Philosophical and Theological Papers 1965–1980*, 410.

135. See Lamb, "Lonergan ... Gregorian Years," §3.

136. See ibid.

137. Lamb, "Temporality and History," 818.

138. See Lamb, "Lonergan ... Gregorian Years," §3.

139. See Lamb, "Lonergan's Transpositions," 8 and 19n26, citing Lonergan, *Method*, 352. For Lonergan, preservation of the "substance" of a seminal theological work comprises part of the fourth factor of continuity in systematics. See the overall discussion in ibid., 351–53.

realities). He writes, "The validity of these transpositions depends upon more than a marshalling of the relevant texts . . . Anyone who wants to know the truth of these texts must move to a knowledge of what the texts signify."[140] As Lamb concisely observes elsewhere, "one cannot transpose what one does not know."[141]

A further criterion for assessing the validity of a theological restatement concerns whether it exemplifies the kind of cognitive praxis cultivated by Lonergan's more general transcendental method (described above). Lamb notes that, for Lonergan, it is a theologian's manifestation of authenticity, attained by cultivating a noetic praxis regulated by the transcendental imperatives, which warrants the genuineness of his or her theological transposition.[142] Lamb states that, "in *Method in Theology* [Lonergan] wrote of achieving authenticity in self-transcendence, and how the religious effort toward authenticity is an apostolate constituted by prayer, penance, and a religious love of all shown in good deeds."[143]

Once an authentic restatement has been communicated, a theologian need not conclude that his or her task is then complete. Rather, Lamb emphasizes that Lonergan's theological method involves an ongoing self-corrective process.[144] This process entails a recurrent return to the theological realities under consideration as well as an attempt to unveil what may be hidden in previous theological contexts. On this point, Lamb writes, "Transposition is rendering explicit, in a fuller context, what was latent but operative in another context."[145]

SUMMARY

Due to Lamb's personal relationship with Lonergan and lifelong study of his work, Lamb is an invaluable guide to Lonergan's thought. Lamb's work aims to differentiate Lonergan's doctrine from transcendental Thomism by describing Lonergan's teachings not in terms of a rapprochement with Kant but rather in terms of a metamethod which outlines cognitive

---

140. Lamb, "Historicity and Eternity," 188.

141. Lamb, "Lonergan's Transpositions," 4.

142. Lamb, "Historicity and Eternity," 186, citing Lonergan, "Horizons and Transpositions," then unpublished. See: Lonergan, *Philosophical and Theological Papers 1965–1980*, 410.

143. Lamb, "Historicity and Eternity," citing Lonergan, *Method*, 104 and 119.

144. Lamb, "Lonergan's Transpositions," 4.

145. Lamb, "Historicity and Eternity," 186.

operations common to all sciences. The particular methodological foundation of academic theology as a special science is to be found in a theologian's participation in an ongoing conversion process. This process is operative throughout a theologian's work: it ensures that a theologian will not stop with historical reconstructions alone, but he or she will attend also (and primarily) to the signified transcultural realities. It is in this way that theology will remain living and thriving.

BIBLIOGRAPHY

Barden, Garrett. "On Intellectual Conversion." *Journal of Macrodynamic Analysis* 3 (2003) 117–41.

Byrne, Patrick H. "Consciousness: Levels, Sublations, and the Subject as Subject." *Method: Journal of Lonergan Studies* 13 (1995) 131–50.

Carmody, Denise Lardner. "The Desire for Transcendence: Religious Conversion." In *The Desires of the Human Heart: An Introduction to the Theology of Bernard Lonergan*, edited by Vernon Gregson, 57–73. New York: Paulist, 1988.

Cessario, Romanus. *A Short History of Thomism*. Washington DC: Catholic University of America, 2005.

Crowe, Frederick. "For a Phenomenology of Rational Consciousness." *Method: Journal of Lonergan Studies* 18 (2000) 67–90.

———. "Lonergan's 'Philosophy and the Religious Phenomenon'." *Method: Journal of Lonergan Studies* 12 (1994) 121–24.

———. "'Stare at a Triangle . . .' A Note on How to Get an Insight and How Not To." *Method: Journal of Lonergan Studies* 19 (2001) 173–80.

Cullen, Christopher M. "Transcendental Thomism: Realism Rejected." In *The Failure of Modernism: The Cartesian Legacy and Contemporary Pluralism*, edited by Brendan Sweetman, 72–86. Mishawaka, IN: American Maritain Association, 1999.

Donceel, Joseph. *The Searching Mind: An Introduction to a Philosophy of God*. Notre Dame, IN: University of Notre Dame, 1979.

———. "A Symposium: Thomistic Scholars." *Listening* 9 (1974) 157–63.

———. "Transcendental Thomism." *The Monist* 58 (1974) 67–85.

Gregson, Vernon. "The Desire to Know: Intellectual Conversion." In *The Desires of the Human Heart: An Introduction to the Theology of Bernard Lonergan*, edited by Vernon Gregson, 16–35. New York: Paulist, 1988.

Henle, Robert J. *The American Thomistic Revival*. St. Louis: St. Louis University Press, 1999.

Kanaris, Jim. *Bernard Lonergan's Philosophy of Religion: From Philosophy of God to Philosophy of Religious Studies*. Albany, NY: State University of New York Press, 2002.

Kerr, Fergus. *Twentieth-Century Catholic Theologians*. Malden, MA: Blackwell, 2007.

Knasas, John. *Being and Some Twentieth Century Thomists*. New York: Fordham University Press, 2003.

———. "Intellectual Dynamism in Transcendental Thomism: A Metaphysical Assessment." *American Catholic Philosophical Quarterly* 69 (1995) 15–28.

———. "Transcendental Thomism and *De Veritate* I, 9." In *Thomistic Papers VI*, edited by John Knasas, 229–50. Houston, TX: Center for Thomistic Studies, 1994.

———. "Transcendental Thomism and the Thomistic Texts." *Thomist* 54 (1990) 81–95.

———. "Why for Lonergan Knowing Cannot Consist in 'Taking a Look.'" *American Catholic Philosophical Quarterly* 78, no. 1 (2004) 131–50.

Lamb, Matthew. "An Analogy for the Divine Self-Gift." *Lonergan Workshop* 14 (1998) 115–54.

———. "Catholic Theological Society of America: Theologians Unbound." *Crisis Magazine* (December 1, 1997) 36–37.

———. "The Challenge of Graduate Theological Education." In *Theological Education in the Catholic Tradition: Contemporary Challenges*, edited by Patrick W. Carey and Earl C. Müller, 108–30. New York: Crossroads, 1997.

———. "Christianity within the Political Dialectics of Community and Empire." *Method: Journal of Lonergan Studies* 1 (1983) 1–30.

———. "*Contemplata Tradere*: Embodied Interiority in Cessario, Pinckaers, and Lonergan." In *Ressourcement Thomism: Sacred Doctrine, the Sacraments, and the Moral Life: Essays in Honor of Romanus Cessario, O.P.*, edited by Reinhard Hütter and Matthew Levering, 312–29. Washington DC: Catholic University of America Press, 2010.

———. "The Dialectics of Theory and Praxis within Paradigm Analysis." In *Paradigm Change in Theology: A Symposium for the Future*, edited by Hans Küng and David Tracy, 63–109. New York: Crossroad, 1989. Originally published in *Lonergan Workshop* 5 (1985) 71–114.

———. "Divine Transcendence and Eternity: The Early Lonergan's Recovery of Thomas Aquinas as a Response to Father McCool's Question." In *Continuity and Plurality in Catholic Theology: Essays in Honor of Gerald A. McCool, S. J.*, edited by Anthony J. Cernera, 75–106. Fairfield, CT: Sacred Heart University Press, 1998.

———. *Eternity, Time, and the Life of Wisdom*. Naples, FL: Sapientia, 2007.

———. "Fr. Bernard J. F. Lonergan S.J., The Early Gregorian Years." *Gregorianum*. forthcoming.

———. "Historicity and Eternity: Bernard Lonergan's Transpositions and Differentiations." *Lonergan Workshop* 10 (1994) 179–227.

———. *History, Method, and Theology: A Dialectical Comparison of Wilhelm Dilthey's Critique of Historical Reason and Bernard Lonergan's Meta-Methodology*. Missoula, MT: Scholars, 1978.

———. "Lonergan's Transpositions of Augustine and Aquinas: Exploratory Suggestions." In *The Importance of Insight: Essays in Honour of Michael Vertin*, edited by John J. Liptay and David Liptay, 3–21. Toronto: University of Toronto Press, 2007.

———. "Methodology, Metascience, and Political Theology." *Lonergan Workshop* 2 (1981) 281–403.

———. "The Millennial Challenges Facing Catholic Intellectual Life." *Nova et Vetera* (English Edition) 11 (2013) 969–91.

———. "Nature is Normative for Culture." *Nova et Vetera* (English Edition) 3 (2005) 153–162.

———. "The Notion of the Transcultural in Bernard Lonergan's Theology." *Method: A Journal of Lonergan Studies* 8 (1990) 48–73.

———. "Orthopraxis and Theological Method in Bernard Lonergan." *Catholic Theological Society of America Proceedings* 35 (1980) 66–87.

———. "Praxis and Generalized Empirical Method." In *Creativity and Method: Essays in Honor of Bernard Lonergan*, edited by Matthew Lamb, 53–77. Milwaukee: Marquette University Press, 1981.

———. "The Production Process and Exponential Growth: A Study in Socio-Economics and Theology." *Lonergan Workshop* 1 (1978) 257–307.

———. "A Response to Bernard Lonergan." *Catholic Theological Society of America Proceedings* 32 (1977) 22–30.

———. "Response to Walter Principe." *Catholic Theological Society of America Proceedings* 46 (1991) 98–107.

———. "The Social and Political Dimensions of Lonergan's Theology." In *The Desires of the Human Heart: An Introduction to the Theology of Bernard Lonergan*, edited by Vernon Gregson, 255–84. New York: Paulist, 1988.

———. *Solidarity with Victims: Toward a Theology of Social Transformation*. New York: Crossroad, 1982.

———. "Temporality and History: Reflections from St. Augustine and Bernard Lonergan." *Nova et Vetera* (English Edition) 4 (2006) 815–50.

———. "Wilhelm Dilthey's Critique of Historical Reason and Bernard Lonergan's Meta-Methodology." In *Language Truth and Meaning: Papers from the International Lonergan Congress 1970*, edited by Philip McShane, 115–66 and 321–32. Notre Dame, IN: University of Notre Dame Press, 1972.

———. "Will There Be Catholic Theology in the United States?" *America: The National Catholic Review* (May 26, 1990) 523–34.

Leo XIII. *The Restoration of Christian Philosophy: Aeterni Patris*. Boston, MA: Pauline, n.d.

Lonergan, Bernard. *Collection: Papers by Bernard J. F. Lonergan*. Toronto: University of Toronto Press, 1993.

———. "Essay in Fundamental Sociology." In *Lonergan's Early Economic Research: Texts and Commentary*, by Michael Schulte, 15–43. Toronto: University of Toronto Press, 2010.

———. "Foreword." In *History, Method, and Theology: A Dialectical Comparison of Wilhelm Dilthey's Critique of Historical Reason and Bernard Lonergan's Meta-Methodology*, by Matthew Lamb, ix–xii. Missoula, MT: Scholars, 1978.

———. *Grace and Freedom: Operative Grace in the Thought of St. Thomas Aquinas*. Toronto: University of Toronto Press, 2000.

———. *Insight: A Study of Human Understanding*. Toronto: University of Toronto Press, 2008.

———. *Method in Theology*. Toronto: University of Toronto Press, 2003.

———. *Philosophical and Theological Papers 1958–1964*. Toronto: University of Toronto Press, 1996.

———. *Philosophical and Theological Papers 1965–1980*. Toronto: University of Toronto Press, 2004.

———. "Philosophy and the Religious Phenomenon." *Method: Journal of Lonergan Studies* 12, no. 2 (1994) 125–46.

———. *Philosophy of God and Theology: The Relationship between Philosophy of God and the Functional Specialty, Systematics*. Philadelphia: Westminster, 1974.

———. *A Second Collection*. Toronto: University of Toronto Press, 1996.

———. *A Third Collection*. New York: Paulist, 1985.

———. *Understanding and Being: The Halifax Lectures on Insight*. Toronto: University of Toronto Press, 1995.

———. *Verbum: Word and Idea in Aquinas*. Toronto: University of Toronto Press, 2005.

Maréchal, Joseph. "Cahier V." In *Le Point de Départ de la Métaphysique*, in *A Maréchal Reader*, 65–231. Edited and translated by Joseph Donceel. NewYork: Herder and Herder, 1970.

Mascall, Eric L. *The Openness of Being: Natural Theology Today*. Philadelphia: Westminster, 1971.

Mathews, William A. "A Biographical Perspective on Conversion and the Functional Specialties in Lonergan." *Method: Journal of Lonergan Studies* 16 (1998) 133–60.

Matteo, Anthony M. "Marechal's Dialogue with Kant: The Roots of Transcendental Thomism and the Search for Ultimate Reality and Meaning." *Ultimate Reality and Meaning* 22 (1999) 264–75.

McBrien, Richard P. *Catholicism: New Study Edition*. New York: HarperCollins, 1994.

McCamy, Ronald. *Out of a Kantian Chrysalis? A Maritainian Critique of Fr. Maréchal*. New York: Lang, 1998.

McCool, Gerald A. *From Unity to Pluralism: The Internal Evolution of Thomism*. New York: Fordham University Press, 1989.

———. *The Neo-Thomists*. Milwaukee: Marquette University Press, 1994.

Muck, Otto. "The Logical Structure of Transcendental Method." *International Philosophical Quarterly* 9 (1969) 342–62.

———. *The Transcendental Method*. New York: Herder and Herder, 1968.

Sala, Giovanni. "The Concept of the Transcendental in Kant and Lonergan." In *Going Beyond Essentialism: Bernard J.F. Lonergan, An Atypical Neo-Scholastic*, edited by Cloe Taddei-Ferretti, 147–73. Naples, Italy: Istituto Italiano per Gli Studi Filosofici, 2011.

———. *Das Apriori in der menschlichen Erkenntnis*. Meisenheim, Germany: Hain, 1971.

———. *Lonergan and Kant: Five Essays on Human Knowledge*. Toronto: University of Toronto Press, 1994.

———. "What Use is Kant for Theology?" In *Wisdom and Holiness, Science and Scholarship: Essays in Honor of Matthew L. Lamb*, edited by Michael Dauphinais and Matthew Levering, 293–314. Naples, FL: Sapientia, 2007.

Smith, Marc. "Is There a Thomist Alternative to Lonergan's Cognitional Structure?" *Thomist* 43 (1979) 626–36.

Tracy, David. *The Achievement of Bernard Lonergan*. New York: Herder and Herder, 1970.

Vertin, Michael. "Lonergan on Consciousness: Is There a Fifth Level?" *Method: Journal of Lonergan Studies* 12 (1994) 1–36.

———. "Maréchal, Lonergan, and the Phenomenology of Knowing." In *Creativity and Method: Essays in Honor of Bernard Lonergan*, edited by Matthew L. Lamb, 411–22. Milwaukee: Marquette University Press, 1981.

Wilhelmsen, Frederick D. "The Priority of Judgment over Question: Reflections on Transcendental Thomism." *International Philosophical Quarterly* 14 (1974) 475–93.

Wilkins, Jeremy. "A Dialectic of 'Thomist' Realisms: John Knasas and Bernard Lonergan." *American Catholic Philosophical Quarterly* 78 (2004) 107–30.

2

God's Self-Gift and the Created Supernatural

Matthew Lamb's Lonerganian Account

John Froula

"THE PRESENT ARTICLE IS no more than a footnote to a broader and richer theology of God's self-gift."[1] So wrote Matthew Lamb in his article, *An Analogy for the Divine Self-Gift,* a shortened version of his STL thesis written under Bernard Lonergan at the Gregorian University.[2] What is offered here and now is no more than a footnote to the footnote, a toe note. I would like to point out the breadth and richness of Fr. Lamb's understanding of the created supernatural, which focuses on Lonergan's explanation of Christ's act of existence or *esse*. In that explanation we see how God gives himself immediately, without buffers, and how the recipient of the gift thereby participates in the Trinitarian relations. Fr. Lamb's understanding of God's self-gift, and the created supernatural as the necessary consequent term of God's self-gift, serves as a foundation for much of theology, sapientially bringing together many of the different themes and emphases of the graduate theology program at Ave Maria University.

---

1. Lamb, *Analogy,* 145.
2. For further explanation of how the article came to be, see ibid., n1.

And so follows a brief account, with a little further explanation, of some of the wisdom that Fr. Lamb received from Lonergan in his own theological formation.

Our starting point in trying to understand the created supernatural in general will be God's communication of self in the hypostatic union, and the character of the created supernatural element of the incarnation in that communication. The insight into God's incarnational self-communication then offers us further insight into the other distinct ways God gives himself, their corresponding created supernatural realties, and their participation in the Trinitarian relations.

The existence of the created supernatural, which would include not only the act of being assumed in the human nature of Christ, but also the light of glory, habitual or sanctifying grace, and the habit of charity, is something revealed and not known naturally.[3] To understand what is revealed it is helpful to have as an analogy something that is naturally known by us. Maurice de la Taille, in a laudable but ultimately unsatisfactory attempt, makes the composition found in created things an analogy for the divine self-gift, that is, the composition of act and potency, and the composition of *esse* and essence.[4] In the hypostatic union, then, according to de la Taille, the act or *esse*, which is divinity, gives actuation to the potency of human nature.[5] The created actuation of the human nature given by God is then what constitutes the hypostatic union.

De la Taille's explanation is critiqued by Fr. Lamb on many levels.[6] Even if the analogy were accurate, it seems de la Taille is laboring under a too complicated philosophy. It is not accurate to introduce actuation as a third principle distinct from act and potency. It is not true, for instance, that the soul has act, the body potency, and the body exists by actuation that is distinct from the act of the whole. Rather, it is the composite being in its unity that has act and potency as principles.[7]

---

3. For a scriptural understanding of the revealed nature of the life of grace, see 1 Cor 2:7–13.

4. See de la Taille, *Created Actuation*, 30.

5. Ibid., 38.

6. The occasion for the critique of Lamb was not simple disagreement, but the contention of de Letter that Lonergan and de la Taille were basically on the same page concerning God's self-gift, a contention Lamb shows to be false. Lamb saw Lonergan misinterpreted, and corrected the misinterpretation, not for the last time. See de Letter, *God's Self-Gift*, 402–22; also see de Letter, *Created Actuation by Uncreated Act*, 60–92.

7. This would be true not only of things whose matter and form depend on the

On the level of the analogy, act is not self-limiting, but limited by potency. God is never limited by his self-gift the way created act is always limited by potency. This is a fundamental analogical disconnect between composed finite realities and the union of giver and receiver in God's self-communication. Also, the principles of finite reality, potency, form, and *esse*, are precisely principles of a supposit, and not subsisting things or substances in composition. If a single created thing with multiple principles is used to understand how God gives himself to creation, it would not be surprising if a kind of pantheism resulted.[8] Nor would it be surprising if in an effort to avoid pantheism the principles of composition are thought of as more separate than they really are.

Instead of using composed, created, natural reality as an analogy for God's self-gift, Lonergan uses what we can know about God with natural knowledge. We, by human reason, can arrive at God's simplicity, and so are able to know, still by reason, that God's being is his understanding and his will. It is by one act that God knows himself necessarily and all contingent created reality.[9] It is by one act that God loves himself and all that he loves into being. It is by one act that God is present to himself necessarily and to all contingent created temporal things. So to draw out analogically this unity of act with a diversity of terms, both necessary and contingent, to the created supernatural realities, it is by one act of being that God is God necessarily and that God is man contingently in the incarnation. The one divine *esse* is therefore the constituent cause

---

existence of the composite; it would even be true of the human whose soul does not depend on the existence of the composite, and so survives death. It is still the soul or form of the composite person. See Aquinas, *DUI* 1.38.

8. "Judaeo-Christianity would never countenance a presentation of God's self-gift to men in terms of an informing action on God's part." Lamb, *Analogy*, 134.

9. "God's *esse*, *intelligere*, and *velle* are absolutely identical; his act of knowing and willing what is necessary is the same act by which he knows and wills what is contingent. In the Incarnation this means that the same divine infinite esse by which the Word is God is also the unique constitutive cause of his being man contingently." Ibid., 117–18.

"As to an analogy with what we know in a natural way, we have not sought understanding from a finite composite being to say that, just as a finite being is composed of essence and existence, so the incarnate Word is in some similar fashion composed of a human essence and a the divine act of existence. Our analogy, rather, has been derived from the fact that what is contingently true of God must necessarily be resolved into that infinite act as its cause, and some contingent being as a consequent term." Lonergan, *Constitution of Christ*, 153.

of hypostatic union.[10] The union of the hypostatic union stems from the unity of the divine person who now exists through human nature.[11] Christ has one act of existence by which he is, simply-speaking; by which he *is*, God and man.[12]

That is not to say that there is nothing created about the hypostatic union. The act of assumed humanity is the necessary, consequent, created, *ad extra* term of the assumption.[13] Assumed human nature is that by which Christ is human and is distinct from the divine nature with its own reality and intelligibility.[14] But Christ subsists by the divine *esse*.[15]

10. "[T]he constitutive reason or cause of the hypostatic union does not tell us why the Son is a person, or why he is God, or why he is man, but why it is the same one who is God and who is man [. . .] it is through the constitutive reason or cause of the hypostatic union that the same one who is also God is also man." Ibid., 135.

11. In *ST* III.6, St. Thomas Aquinas does speak of mediation in the hypostatic union in the sense that the principles of the human nature, mind, soul, body have a certain order and functionality in human nature, but there is no mediation between the human nature assumed and the Word who assumes it to himself. Christ's body is the body of the Word; one need not merely affirm that Christ's body is the body of the soul of the Word. The union does not mediate the natures.

12. "It may be worthwhile mentioning in conclusion that it is only within the conceptual framework of a mixed relation that one can understand Aquinas's teaching on the number of *esses* in Christ. For Aquinas Christ is one being, *ens*, by the *esse personale* of the Logos, but he is one *ens* by the *esse personale* only because the created relational *esse*, i.e., the real relational effect in the humanity, comes to be and is united to the Logos in such a way that the Logos subsists in it." Weinandy, *Does God Change*, 98.

13. St. Thomas does hold in *ST* III.2, 7 that the union of the divine nature and the human nature is something created because the human nature has a relation to the divine *in re*, and the divine nature has a relation to the human nature *secundum rationem*. In doing so he is considering the union in terms of the things united. Yet because union is several in one, union can also be considered as that in which the several are united. That is how St Thomas considerers union in *ST* III.2, 9, and that is how Lonergan conceives Christ's union when explaining that it has one constitutive cause.

14. "Fr. Lonergan explicitly rejects the notion that the humanity strictly exists. God *is* 'per esse divinum,' he *is* God by the divine esse, and he *is* man by the divine esse. But he is God by the divine essence or nature, and he is man by the human nature. Thus the divine esse does not make the humanity real, for essence as a principle of being has a reality proper to itself. If it did not, the assumption of human nature by the Word would be the assumption of nothing—which does not square too well with Constantinople III." Lamb, *Analogy*, 118.

15. "As for the hypostatic union, we shall defend a single esse in Christ, in such a way as to maintain that the divine esse is the sole constitutive cause of the union itself, that the humanity of Christ lacks its own proper and proportionate esse, and yet that the same humanity is actuated by a created esse not proper to it—not, indeed, in order that it might exist, but rather that it be actually assumed." Lonergan, *Constitution of Christ*, 72n25.

GOD'S SELF-GIFT AND THE CREATED SUPERNATURAL

The act of assuming on God's part is the same act or divine *esse* whereby the Word is God, and the act that gives unity—that is existence—to the hypostatic union.[16]

So it is that the obediential potency of human nature to be assumed is brought into act by the unity of the Word assuming human nature to himself.[17] This created act is the *esse secundarium* as explained by St. Thomas in the *De unione Verbi incarnati*.[18] Therefore, there is not some third thing that is union, some actuation, which stands between the human nature of Christ and his divinity. The divine hypostatic gift requires an adequate created term to be received, the act of Christ's humanity assumed.[19] The gift of God's self, bringing humanity into communion with himself, is a personal gift, and cannot be explained by an actuation, but by a personal presence or union with another. The reality of the relation is the reality of the terms. And so God's gift of self in the incarnation, and in

---

16. Analogously, God's act of creation is not dependent on the thing created, but vice versa: God's act of creation is constituted by the divine power. That is not to say that God can create an object separate from himself without the object really being there with its own intelligibility. The real relation is in the object as created. But the object is the term of the divine power, not the creative act itself. God always determines, never is determined. He knows and loves creation into being with the knowledge and love that is his own being, his own power, and his own freedom.

17. Fr. Lamb agrees with de la Taille that the created supernatural surpasses all connaturality, and so is an act of an obediential, not natural, potency. See Lamb, *Analogy*, 132.

18. "Therefore just as Christ is one simply because of the unity of the supposit, and two in a certain respect, because of the two natures, thus he has one *esse* simply because of the one eternal *esse* of the eternal supposit. But there is also another *esse* of this supposit, not inasmuch it is eternal, but inasmuch as it is made man in time. Which it is, even if it is not accidental *esse*—since man is not predicated accidentally of the Son of God, as was said above—it is nevertheless not the principle *esse*, but subordinate. But if in Christ there were two supposits, then each supposit would have its own principle *esse*. And thus in Christ there would be twofold *esse* simply speaking." Aquinas, *De unione* 4; author's translation.

19. St. Thomas does speak of the Word as the terminus of the assumption because the union took place in the person in *ST* III.3.1. That does not deny that the human nature of Christ receives act as a term when it is assumed, the act of being assumed. The Word is not assumed, but assumes human nature and so gives himself to it.

the created supernatural in general, is always immediate.[20] It is a direct personal gift.[21]

Both to apply the above explanation of God's self-gift and the created supernatural, and to clarify it, we will now move on to the other created supernatural realities. It would be helpful here to provide some explanation of what the supernatural is, and to offer some explanation as to why Lonergan might consider there to be four created supernatural realities. Abbot Anscar Vonier, in his work on the human soul, defines the supernatural as follows: "[T]he state of the created and finite spiritual being into which it is raised by a direct act of God, separate from the act that created the spirit, following upon that first act and making the spirit inherently capable of seeing God face to face."[22] Vonier goes on to say "that it implies contradiction that God should ever create a spirit to which the supernatural would be a necessary psychological complement, as such a being would be another God."[23] In other words, only God by nature enjoys himself beatifically. No finite nature can entail a necessary union with the infinite. That nature would be infinite, or God. Face to face vision with God is a supernatural gift.

20. Michael Stebbins explains that Lonergan considered the divine concourse with creation to be direct. See Stebbins, *The Divine Initiative*, 223. St. Thomas Aquinas speaks to this also when he explains how God works in every worker. Not only is God the final end and the first efficient cause, but he is the one present upholding forms and powers. "And since the form of a thing is within the thing, and all the more, as it approaches nearer to the First and Universal Cause; and because in all things God himself is properly the cause of universal being which is innermost in all things; it follows that in all things God works intimately." *ST* I.105.5.

21. The immediacy of God's self-gift in no way detracts from an understanding of secondary causality so central to Catholic theology, but rather illuminates the nature of secondary causality when God is the non-competitive primary cause. The sacraments, for instance, are not God's way of keeping us at arm's length while he uses something besides himself as a source of grace. The sacraments are not sticks God uses to poke us. Rather, the sacraments are the means of contact with God, means willed by God and suited to us. See *ST* III.62.6. The humanity of Christ is not some kind of transition zone between God and sinful humanity, but the way through which God himself acts for sinful humanity's salvation. God's instruments make God immediate to us by their adequation to us, not by providing God something he does not already possess in full perfection. Veneration of an image of Christ is in fact a veneration of Christ, not a veneration of something that venerates Christ. Mary's mediation does not add to Christ's but participates in the one mediation, and so on. Catholic theology presents a direct and immediate divine concourse with its proper adequated secondary means that God wills.

22. Vonier, *The Human Soul*, 283.

23. Ibid., 284.

Under the rubric of this account of the supernatural we will look at another instance of the created supernatural: the light of glory in heaven. The light of glory is not itself the beatific vision. The light of glory, like the created act of Christ's humanity assumed, is an adequate *ad extra* and necessary term for receiving God's self-gift. In the case of the incarnation the divine self-gift resulted in personal union in which created human nature does not have a proportionate act of existence. Human nature is personally assumed. With the light of glory, the self-gift of God is for God to be united to a human person who does have a proportionate act of existence such that the created light is accidental, God being united without any intermediary in the extreme intimacy of the divine concourse, such that the essence of God is known without the mediation of concepts.[24]

Sanctifying grace, another created supernatural reality, is the created *ad extra* term that elevates the person in an adequate way to be dwelt in by the Trinity. Sanctifying grace is not the divine indwelling, it does not call down the divine indwelling, but rather God dwelling in the person activates his obediential potency to be a temple of God by possessing a qualitative habit,[25] making the person a child of God and participate in the divine nature.[26] Sanctifying grace is the foundation for direct contact with God by the theological virtues.[27] Charity, for its part, is the necessary consequent term of union with God. It is the one theological virtue that

---

24. See Aquinas, *ST* I.12.

25. See Aquinas, *ST* I-II.110.2.

26. Fr. Lamb shows that in St. Thomas's early *Scriptum* (I dist. 14, q. 2, art. 1 qla. 2) there can be found a mutual priority thesis in which habitual grace causes the mission of the Holy Spirit by way of a dispositive quasi-material cause, and the mission causes habitual grace in other respects. This contrasts with the *Summa* in which grace does not dispose one to receive the Holy Spirit, but rather to have him in the sense of use and enjoyment as explained in *ST* I.43.3. And in *ST* III.7.13 St. Thomas says plainly that grace is caused in man from the divine presence, as light in the air form the presence of the sun. See Lamb, *Analogy*, 152–53.

27. "God is in man, not only as in inanimate things, but because he is more fully known and loved by him, since even by nature we spontaneously love, desire, and seek after the good. Moreover, God by grace resides in the just soul as in a temple, in a most intimate and peculiar manner. From this proceeds that union of affection by which the soul adheres most closely to God, more so than the friend is united to his most loving friend, and enjoys God in all fullness and sweetness. Now this wonderful union, which is properly called 'indwelling,' differing only in degree of state from that with which God beatifies the saints in heaven, although it is most certainly produced by the presence of the whole Blessed Trinity—nevertheless is attributed in a peculiar manner to the Holy Ghost." Leo XIII, *Divinum illud munus* 1.

guarantees the beatific vision, so long as it is present, and is the response that is the measure of union with God.[28]

There are not any more created absolutely supernatural realities in the strict sense because nothing else of its very nature implies face to face vision. Nothing else is meritorious *per se*. There are other gifts from God that go into the supernatural life, and so are supernatural virtually. Faith and hope do not attain the end of beatific life unless they are informed by charity, which is the bond of union. Infused moral virtues do not exist without charity. It is the connaturality of charity between the human and God that gives the gifts of the Holy Spirit their formality. With respect to why habitual grace implies face to face vision, its consequent outcome is glory, and it is by impediment and degree, not a qualitative deficiency, that grace does not enable vision.[29] The light of glory is directly related to face to face vision. St. Thomas primary uses soteriological arguments for why Christ saw the face of God in his human nature, yet one can see by a careful reading that face to face vision is proper to Christ in his human nature because of the nearness of the two natures as they exist in one divine person.[30]

---

28. "Now as to the connection of these mysteries among themselves and with our ultimate end: (1) since this end consists in the beatific vision in which the divine essence itself enters in a created intellect, and (2) since we are elevated to this end through justification, in which an uncreated Gift is given to us, and finally (3) since the hypostatic union is the cause and source both of our justification and of our attainment of this end though perseverance in justice, one can discover this remarkable similarity in these three instances, namely, that in them not only is God's infinite perfection united to creatures, but also this very union involves the existence of a created appropriate contingent term. In the hypostatic union there is present besides the infinite act of existence of the Word a secondary substantial act of existence as a term received in Christ's human essence, just as in the justification of a sinner besides the uncreated gift of the Holy Spirit there is also present as a term sanctifying grace received in the soul as an accident, and in the beatific vision, in addition to the divine essence, which in a way fills the function of an intelligible species, there is just such a term in the light of glory." Lonergan, *Constitution of Christ*, 153–54.

29. See St. Thomas's doctrine of prevenient and subsequent grace in *ST* I-II.111.3.

30. "For the nearer a recipient is to an inflowing [*influenti*] cause, the more does it partake in its influence." *ST* III.7.1. "To Christ, inasmuch as He is the Natural Son of God, is due an eternal inheritance, which is the uncreated beatitude through the uncreated act of knowledge and love of God, i.e., the same whereby the Father knows and loves Himself. Now the soul is not capable of this act, on account of the difference of natures. Hence it behooved [*oportebat*] it to attain to God by a created act of fruition which could not be without grace." *ST* III.7.1, ad 2.

GOD'S SELF-GIFT AND THE CREATED SUPERNATURAL 45

According to Lonergan, each of the four created supernatural realities, Christ's *esse secundarium*, the light of glory, habitual grace, and charity, participates in a different Trinitarian relation, Paternity, Filiation, Active Spiration and Passive Spiration, respectively.[31] The created supernatural realities in relation to God are *ad extra*, or outside of God, and so are created by God and not by any one person to the exclusion of the others. But nothing prevents the created supernatural realities from having different created likenesses to different Trinitarian relations as ways of participating in the divine nature. Moreover, it makes sense that the divinely revealed created supernatural realities participate specially in the divinely revealed relations in God, and that the created consequent supernatural conditions of God's self-gift participate in the uncreated self-gift of the Trinitarian relations.

Here are just a few words about each of these four relations and their connection to the created supernatural realities, merely to point out how rich this theology is, and how worthy of consideration and development.

The created secondary *esse* of Christ is a participation in the relation of Paternity. Fr. Lamb writes: "As a created participation in the very relation of Paternity, the secondary *esse* in the Incarnation grounds a real relation to the Word alone."[32] We could also draw an analogy between the act of being assumed and Paternity in that Paternity in the Trinity is a foundational relation in the life of the Trinity, and the assumed humanity of Christ is foundational in the life of grace.

The light of glory participates in Filiation, the relation of the Son or Word to the Father. It relates us to the Father as adoptive sons to the highest degree. It unites us by way of intellectual contact, and so is like Filiation, the generation by way of intellect.

Sanctifying grace is a participation in Active Spiration, grounding a special relation to the Holy Spirit, and participating in the sending action of Father and Son.[33] In the Father's and the Son's one sending of the Holy

---

31. "First, there are four real divine relations, really identical with the divine substance, and therefore there are four very special modes that ground the external imitation of the divine substance. Next, there are four absolutely supernatural realities which are never found uninformed, namely, the secondary act of existence [*esse*] of the incarnation, sanctifying grace, the habit of charity, and the light of glory." Lonergan, *Triune God*, 471–73.

32. Lamb, *Analogy*, 144–45.

33. Fr. Lamb's theology of the missions of the Son and Holy Spirit, closely linked to a discussion of the priority of the interpersonal, is largely based on Lonergan's extremely well developed and understudied Trinitarian works. While an integral part of

Spirit, the Trinity dwells in us, and grace is the created act corresponding to that dwelling.[34] Sanctifying grace is the fruitful source of the spiritual life as the Father and Son as one principle are the fruitful source of the Holy Spirit.

Charity participates in passive spiration, grounding the special relation to the Father and the Son, and so by love we are caught up in a participation of the Holy Spirit's relation to the most intimate union of Father and Son as one principle. The church becomes bonded as one in charity as the Father and Son are one in nature by the bond of the Holy Spirit. Charity poured out in our hearts makes us like the Holy Spirit poured out. The Holy Spirit's mission divinizes us so we can respond to God's infinite love.

Fr. Lamb's understanding of the created supernatural as a consequent term of God's immediate and personal gift of himself is a unifying point for many of the features and prevalent themes of the graduate theology program at Ave Maria University that he was so instrumental in developing. It is tempting here to reproduce large parts of the *curricula vitae* of the professors there and show how one part or another of their work touches on Fr. Lamb's earlier insight, wittingly or no. That would be cumbersome. Instead, by way of presentation of some general themes, one can see how Fr. Lamb's thought provides a key for seeing the sapiential wholeness of theology, and provides a door for entry into further elaboration. The vine has many branches.

In the theology program at Ave Maria University there is the prominence of the notion of self-gift. God's self-gift is the basis for the entire order of grace. There is the absolute primacy of God's initiative in the life of grace, and in the created causal order in general as well. There is the irreducible distinction, yet inseparability, between the natural and the supernatural, and the complete gratuity of the supernatural, grounded in the distinction between nature and personal relations of the Trinity. There is a recognition of how important analogy is to Theology. There is an understanding of Christ that is both Ephesian and Chalcedonian,

---

An Analogy for the Divine Self-Gift (145–53), it deserves its own fuller treatment not provided here.

34. "Hence, the divine love actively constituting the missions common to the three Persons who communicate to men the infinite good which is themselves. The divine love passively constituting the mission is the "dilectio notionalis" in which the Father and Son love men and thereby send them the Spirit who is this love. Thus, in sending the Spirit, the entire Trinity comes and dwells in us." Lamb, *Analogy*, 147.

that is, one does not have to abandon the strong sense of Christ's unity in order to affirm equally strongly that Christ has two natures.[35] This Christology recognizes the beatific vision in the human nature of Christ. The supernatural character of the act of his assumed humanity makes the beatific vision connatural to it.

Also, I would propose that a proper understanding of the theology of beauty depends on a proper understanding of the created supernatural as that which is principally beautiful in the created order. For Balthasar, the Neoplatonic mindset is a destroyer of the notion of beauty because it does not recognize the proper communicative form through which glory radiates, but sees mediations as obstacles to God.[36] In view of this critique we can see that by putting up any *tertia quid* buffer between the creator and the creature, true unitive concourse between creator and creature by which the infinite discloses itself in finite expression, is denied. A notion of beauty informed by faith demands the immediacy of divine concourse.

Lastly, perhaps a bit more tenuously, the word and deed of God's special interaction in salvation history are inseparable. Unlike other words and actions which are mediations in the created order, and so distinct by distinct modes of mediation, the divine word and deed exemplified in Christ, are both instances of the unmediated revelatory divine self-gift.

In closing, here is a good summation from Jeremy Wilkins. He writes: "In the theological understanding of St. Augustine, St. Thomas Aquinas, and Fr. Lonergan, the Trinity is an eternal order of giving and receiving, of divine self-communication. The order of grace is a created communication of that same order. Divine intersubjectivity consists in an ordered, contemplative love of the divine Good and all things in that Good, and human intersubjectivity is fulfilled in the created communication of that same ordered, contemplative love. In the deepest and most important sense, this is indeed the one and only reality 'communicated for its own sake.'"[37]

---

35. If created composition is the analogue that is being used, and if it is too literally taken that the Son is to his humanity as created being is to created essence, then Monophysitism results. If the Son to his humanity is seen too like form's relation to matter, then Apollinarianism results. If the union of Christ is seen as mediated by some third thing, then Nestorianism results.

36. See Balthasar, *The Glory of the Lord*, 426–27. Balthasar's discussion about the beatific vision and Christ's role in it should be read in light of the insistence on the immediacy of the divine concourse as explained by Fr. Lamb and in light of *ST* III.9.2.

37. Wilkins, *Method, Order, and Analogy*, 592.

BIBLIOGRAPHY

Aquinas, Thomas. *De unitate intellectus contra Averroistas.* http://www.corpusthomisticum.org/oca.html (accessed March 28, 2016).

———. *Summa Theologiae.* Translated by Fathers of the English Dominican Province. 5 vols. New York: Benziger Bros., 1947.

———. *De unione Verbi incarnati.* Translated by Roger Nutt. Lueven: Peeters, 2015.

Balthasar, Hans Urs, von. *The Glory of the Lord, A Theological Aesthetics, I: Seeing the Form.* Translated by Erasmo Leiva-Merikakis. San Francisco: Ignatius, 2009.

de la Taille, Maurice. *The Hypostatic Union and Created Actuation by Uncreated Act.* Translated by Cyril Vollert. West Baden Springs, IN: West Baden College, 1952.

De Letter, P. "The Theology of God's Self-gift." *Theological Studies* 24 (1963) 402–22.

———. "Created Actuation by Uncreated Act: Difficulties and Answers." *Theological Studies* 18 (1957) 60–92.

Lamb, Matthew L. "An Analogy for the Divine Self-Gift." *Lonergan Workshop* 14 (1998) 115–53.

Leo XIII. *Divinum illud munus.* http://w2.vatican.va/content/leo-xiii/en/encyclicals/documents/hf_l-xiii_enc_09051897_divinum-illud-munus.html (accessed March 28, 2016).

Lonergan, Bernard. *The Ontological and Psychological Constitution of Christ.* Translated by Micheal G. Shields. Toronto: University of Toronto Press, 2002.

———. *The Triune God: Systematics.* Translated by Michael G. Shields. Toronto: University of Toronto Press, 1988.

Stebbins, Michael J. *The Divine Initiative: Grace, World-Order, and Human Freedom in the Early Writings of Bernard Lonergan.* Toronto: University of Toronto Press, 1995.

Vonier, Anscar. *The Human Soul and Its Relations with Other Spirits.* London: Herder, 1925.

Weinandy, Thomas G. *Does God Change: The Word's Becoming in the Incarnation.* Still River, MA: St. Bede's, 1985.

Wilkins, Jeremy D. "Method, Order, and Analogy in Trinitarian Theology: Karl Rahner's Critique of the "Psychological Approach.'" *Thomist* 74 (2010) 563–92.

3

Augustine on Creation

An Exercise in the Dialectical Retrieval of the Ancients

Matthew Levering

THE CURRENT PROFUSION OF popular science books that promote atheism calls to mind a remark of Matthew Lamb's: "Could it be that modernity provides the best communication networks in world history, but has nothing substantive to communicate?"[1] In his writings, Lamb frequently explores the relationship of the "ancients" and the "moderns." Can the moderns learn something from the ancients, and vice versa?[2]

---

1. Lamb, *Eternity, Time, and the Life of Wisdom*, 126.

2. This is why I have advocated a *Ressourcement* Thomism, that is to say, a fully contemporary theology that learns gladly from (and imitates) the patristic, liturgical/typological, and historical-critical engagement that marks the *nouvelle théologie*, while integrating these insights within a constructive retrieval of central aspects of Aquinas's theology (and without fearing to appropriate, as well, the insights of the Baroque scholastic and neo-scholastic periods). Aquinas helps the modern Catholic systematician move up and down the ladder of tradition, so as to appreciate tradition's plurality and unity. After all, Aquinas's questions and many of his conclusions arise from the Latin and Greek Fathers, and the theology of the last seven centuries (especially among Catholics, but also in the great Protestant and Orthodox scholasticisms) can neither be understood nor appreciated without recognizing its debts to Aquinas.

In his *Eternity, Time, and the Life of Wisdom*, Lamb reflects on this question in dialogue with Jürgen Habermas. Arguing that each time period needs the insights that have been achieved in earlier time periods, Lamb suggests that "[t]he roots of dogmatism and nihilism in modernity, as in other epochs, is the fallacy of misplaced normativeness. It is the process of making the products of intelligence and reason as normative rather than the questioning praxis of intelligence and reason."[3] When insights are measured in light of the questions that arise from them, both their truth and their limitation can be seen. When a time period does not perceive the limitations of its own insights, these insights are mistakenly thought to be exhaustive accounts of reality. We imagine that we have reached (or at least nearly reached) the end of human questioning, as though we have conclusively captured what there is to know, or as though even the reality of our own minds (let alone God) can be measured by our finite concepts. As Lamb observes, "We create something that is intelligent and marvelously rational, then we project onto it the powers of our own creative intelligence and reason. Religious, who recognize intelligence and reason as divine in origin, call this idolatry; secularists term it reification."[4]

Among Lamb's central concerns, therefore, is that we not "hand over the natural sciences to empiricist and instrumentalist philosophies."[5] Indebted to Bernard Lonergan, Lamb demonstrates a keen appreciation of modern scientific insights. He finds that "empirical sciences in the modern age are examples *par excellence* of research communities engaged in raising ever further relevant questions and correcting previous errors."[6] However, modern natural science goes astray when it conceives of its results in an empiricist and positivist mode, which illegitimately narrows the scope of reality. Lamb warns that in the Cartesian worldview, "The pivotal role of judgment was collapsed into a curious type of Platonic du-

---

Aquinas returns those who study his theology not only to the Fathers, but also to the Scriptures. This insight inspired the young Matthew Lamb, in his translation of and profound introduction to Aquinas's *Commentary on Ephesians*. I like to cite the fact that in the *secunda pars* of his *Summa theologiae* alone, Aquinas quotes more than half the chapters of the entire Old Testament and quotes from all the Old Testament books with the exceptions of the very short books of Obadiah, Haggai, and Zephaniah.

3. Lamb, *Eternity, Time, and the Life of Wisdom*, 132.
4. Ibid.
5. Ibid., 137.
6. Ibid., 138.

alism, now recast in terms of body versus mind, sensations versus ideas. Since no human ideas (even the *ego cogito*) could survive Descartes's universal doubt, the empiricists simply transferred *necessity* and *certainty* to sensations or perceptions."[7] The result was to cut off whole domains of human questioning, in a manner that made "reason into a monistic absolute, as if reason could be completely expressed, as if all questions would be fully answered."[8] Lamb's target here is rationalistic monism, which has no room for inquiry into realities (including the mind itself, and even more importantly including the infinite God) that cannot be empirically measured.

As Lamb makes clear, the solution is not simply to return to the ancients as though the moderns have attained no insights. This would falsely presume that all truth that can be acquired has been gained in the past. Instead, the solution is found in "a dialectic of enlightenment that differentiates the genuine exercise of reason from the abuse of reason to subject nature and persons as instruments to another."[9] This dialectical discernment (which also applies to religious practice) welcomes all genuine questioning, ancient and modern. It presumes that such questioning has produced coherent answers, even if these answers must inevitably be incomplete, given the inexhaustible character of reality. It also includes *theological* reasoning in faith. Challenging the Nietzschean presumption that truth in general and religious truth in particular are rightly apprehended in terms of power and violence, Lamb observes that "[a]mong the many tasks of a dialectic of enlightenment, or a second enlightenment, is the recognition that religious faiths and practices do not by definition lack intelligence and reason."[10] Since dialectical discernment enables us to eschew both the myth of "necessary unilinear progress" and the rejection of past communities of inquiry, we moderns can recognize that our science and scholarship still needs to take account of earlier "achievements in wisdom, in moral goodness, and in common sense."[11] Specifically, Lamb calls for a retrieval of certain "normative achievements" of Augustine and Aquinas.[12]

---

7. Ibid., 140.
8. Ibid., 141.
9. Ibid., 144.
10. Ibid., 146.
11. Ibid., 147.
12. Ibid., 148.

Clearly, Augustine's theology of creation lacks a modern understanding of evolutionary biology, or of the Big Bang and the formation of the cosmos. In this regard, the modern achievements of natural science are outstanding and normative for ongoing research and study. Yet, Augustine's theology of creation includes elements that anticipate and go beyond modern science in significant ways. In the spirit of Lamb's dialectical engagement with the ancients and the moderns, this essay retrieves Augustine's *The Literal Meaning of Genesis* in dialectical engagement with some contemporary popular scientists. Let me first introduce the perspective of these contemporary scientists regarding the origins of the cosmos, and then turn to Augustine's theology of creation in his *The Literal Meaning of Genesis*.

DOES QUANTUM GRAVITY SUFFICE TO ACCOUNT FOR THE ORIGIN OF THE UNIVERSE?

In *A Universe from Nothing: Why There Is Something Rather than Nothing*, the physicist Lawrence Krauss argues that "all signs suggest a universe that could and plausibly did arise from a deeper nothing—involving the absence of space itself."[13] In modern physics, Krauss suggests, "the very distinction between something and nothing has begun to disappear."[14] He explains that "quantum gravity not only appears to allow universes to be created from nothing—meaning, in this case, I emphasize, the absence of space and time—it may require them. 'Nothing'—in this case no space, no time, no anything!—*is* unstable."[15] Krauss also argues that there may be "a multiverse, either in the form of a landscape of universes existing in a host of extra dimensions, or in the form of a possibly infinitely replicating set of universes in a three-dimensional space as in the case of

---

13. Krauss, *A Universe from Nothing*, 183. On the cover of this book, the prominent novelist Ian McEwan enthuses, "We have been living through a revolution in cosmology as wondrous as that initiated by Copernicus. Here is the essential, engrossing, and brilliant guide." After earning his doctorate in physics from MIT, Krauss taught at Yale and Case Western before becoming Foundation Professor and Director of the Origins Project at Arizona State University. For Krauss, believers in God must posit a nothingness in which "something" already is: "if one requires that the notion of true nothingness requires not even the *potential* for existence, then surely God cannot work his wonders, because if he does cause existence from nonexistence, there must have been the potential for existence" (ibid., 174).

14. Ibid., 182–83.

15. Ibid., 170.

eternal inflation."[16] Such a multiverse, he thinks, would do away with the need for identifying a "prescribed 'cause' for our universe," since it would relativize "the question of what determined the laws of nature that allowed our universe to form and evolve."[17] Krauss denies that there is an all-powerful creative "external agency existing separate from space, time, and indeed from physical reality itself."[18]

Krauss's views are commonplace in contemporary popular science. Thus, in their *Origins*—a book written as a companion to a NOVA television special on PBS—Neil deGrasse Tyson and Donald Goldsmith begin chapter one with the claim, "In the beginning, there was physics."[19] And in their *The Grand Design*, Stephen Hawking and Leonard Mlodinow remark at the outset of their first chapter, titled "The Mystery of Being," that "philosophy is dead."[20] On the basis of quantum physics, Hawking and Mlodinow posit that "a great many universes were created out of nothing. Their creation does not require the intervention of some supernatural being or god. Rather, these multiple universes arise naturally from physical law."[21] This "physical law" is the original "nothing." Toward the end of the book, Hawking and Mlodinow identify the law of gravity as the key: "Because there is a law like gravity, the universe can and will create itself from nothing . . . Spontaneous creation is the reason there is something rather than nothing, why the universe exists, why we exist. It is not necessary to invoke God to light the blue touch paper and set the universe going."[22]

16. Ibid., 176.
17. Ibid.
18. Ibid., 171.
19. Tyson and Goldsmith, *Origins*, 33.
20. Hawking and Mlodinow, *The Grand Design*, 5.
21. Ibid., 8–9.

22. Ibid., 180. Earlier they observe that quantum theory's explanation of the space-time continuum "removes the age-old objection to the universe having a beginning, but also means that the beginning of the universe was governed by the laws of science and doesn't need to be set in motion by some god." Ibid., 135. Their work has value, obviously, when they stick with their expertise, physics. In this regard they helpfully summarize the insights of the twentieth century into the first moments of the universe: "In the early universe—when the universe was small enough to be governed by both general relativity and quantum theory—there were effectively four dimensions of space and none of time. That means that when we speak of the 'beginning' of the universe, we are skirting the subtle issue that as we look backward toward the very early universe, time as we know it does not exist! We must accept that our usual ideas of space and time do not apply to the very early universe." Ibid., 134. Quantum theory

In sum, these influential scientists envision a finite universe emerging from a finite entity (obviously not "nothing"), the law of gravity. Does Augustine, a bishop and theologian trained in rhetoric and philosophy, merit a place at the table in this discussion?

AUGUSTINE'S THEOLOGY OF CREATION

Although contemporary scientists generally overlook it, the emergence of all finite things from an original, non-spatio-temporal finite reality is not a new idea. Gregory of Nyssa and Augustine had already conceived of something broadly similar. Paul Blowers states that "Augustine generally agrees with Gregory of Nyssa (and with Philo's second version of simultaneous creation) that the whole Hexaemeral narrative represents the simultaneous moment when God created the orderly sequence according to which the sensible world would emerge in space and time."[23] Like Gregory, Augustine proposes a theory of *rationes seminales* by which all things are included in an original creation.[24] Augustine conceives of an original formless creation of "heaven and earth," which he calls "the very beginning of creation in its inchoate state," prior in origin (though not in time) to its reception of form.[25] Although all things are in a certain way present in this original creation, however, the original creation cannot be the source of its own *existence*. For giving and sustaining the being of things, a transcendent Creator is needed. To set the stage for my discussion of Augustine on the creation of "heaven and earth," therefore, I begin with a brief portrait of Augustine's view, in *The Literal Meaning of Genesis*, of the transcendent, triune Creator.

---

holds that "[g]iven the state of a system at some time, the laws of nature determine the *probabilities* of various futures and pasts rather than determining the future and past with certainty." Ibid., 72. Earlier Hawking and Mlodinow defined a "law of nature" as "a rule that is based upon an observed regularity and provides predictions that go beyond the immediate situations upon which it is based." Ibid., 27.

23. Blowers, *Drama*, 155. For background in Philo, see ibid., 54–61. Blowers discusses Gregory of Nyssa and Augustine on ibid., 146–59.

24. For Gregory, "The Creator is a grand Sower whose founding (καταβολή) of the world is an instantaneous 'throwing down' of the seeds of created things that funds the orderly and sequential production (κατασκευή)." Blowers, *Drama*, 146. See also Hart, *The Experience of God*, 26.

25. 1.6.12. See also 1.14.28; 1.15.29-30; 5.5.16.

The Transcendent Triune Creator

Augustine interprets Proverbs 8:23 as a reference to the eternal Word of God. Recall that Proverbs 8 is a description of personified Wisdom, depicted as the first creature, present in the creation of all other things. Augustine's version of Proverbs 8:23 reads, "Before the ages He [God] established me" (RSV: "Ages ago I was set up, at the first, before the beginning of the earth"). Augustine attributes these words to the Son of God. Indeed, according to John 1, it was through the divine Son that the "ages" were created: "all things were made through him, and without him was not anything made that was made" (Jn 1:3).[26] No mere creature, not even the angels, "is before the ages." For Augustine, the angels' creation marks the beginning of the "ages."[27] On this basis, Augustine concludes that in Proverbs 8:23 the divine Son is speaking, since he is the Wisdom that the author of Proverbs dimly perceived. Here Augustine appeals again to Psalm 104:24, "In wisdom you have made them all."[28]

Likewise, Augustine interprets Genesis 1:3, where God creates by saying, "Let there be," to be another sign of the Father's creating all things in the Word.[29] In Augustine's view, the Son's presence is already signaled in Genesis 1:1, "In the beginning God created the heavens and the earth." This is so because the Son *is* the "beginning," since God the Father creates all things in the Son. As John 1:2 teaches, "He was in the beginning with God." Proceeding further along these lines, Augustine reasons that Genesis 1:3—"And God said, 'Let there be light'"—indicates the perfecting in the Word of the formless spiritual and material creation ("the heavens and the earth") that God created "in the beginning."[30] In this way, creation receives form by imitating the divine Image or Exemplar. Here Augustine moves easily from the pattern of creation to the pattern of redemption. He states that the incarnate Son has redeemed us from a "formless" life: "For when it [the rational creature] is turned away from

---

26. All citations from the Bible in this chapter are from the RSVCE.

27. *Gn. Litt.* 5.19.38.

28. Ibid.

29. See ibid., 1.4.9. This statement comes at the outset of the six days, and therefore, as we will see below, Augustine associates it with God's giving form to the formless matter that God has created in Gen 1:1.

30. For the roots in the Christian *Hexaemeron* tradition of Augustine's view that Gen 1:1 describes the creation of formless spiritual and corporeal matter, see Torchia, *Creatio ex nihilo*, 38. See also Swift, "Six Days of Creation," 317–28.

changeless Wisdom, its life is full of folly and wretchedness," whereas true "formation consists in turning to the changeless light of Wisdom, the Word of God."[31]

As we would expect, the Holy Spirit likewise plays a central role in Augustine's discussion of the Creator. Genesis 1:2 states that "the Spirit of God was moving over the face of the waters." This verse, Augustine remarks, completes the sacred author's expression of the Trinitarian nature of God. Augustine suggests that the Spirit's presence indicates that God creates with supreme benevolence; we should understand that "it is not out of any need but out of His goodness that His love is directed towards His works."[32] The Spirit's presence shows that creatures participate in God's goodness, which is appropriated to the Spirit. This point is amplified for Augustine by the fourth verse of Genesis 1. When God speaks his Word in Genesis 1:3, "Let there be light," the Spirit's presence is indicated by the very next verse, "And God saw that the light was good." Augustine observes that the creature is thus "established, according to its capacity, in the good will and benevolence of God."[33] This interpretation depends upon the connection of the Holy Spirit with "the Divine Goodness and Love."[34] In the Holy Spirit, God loves us into existence and lovingly sustains our existence; and he creates us "by His coeternal Word, that is, by the interior and eternal forms of unchangeable Wisdom."[35]

"Heaven and Earth" and the Day of Creation

Does the triune God create all things at once? In considering this question, Augustine finds Genesis 2 to be especially helpful. In his version, Genesis 2:4–6 reads, "This is the book of the creation of heaven and earth when day was made. God made heaven and earth and every green thing of the field before it appeared above the earth, and all the grass of the field before it sprang forth. For God had not rained upon the earth, and there was not a man to till the earth. But a spring rose out of the earth and watered all the face of the earth." For Augustine, the most significant verse

31. Ibid., 1.5.10.
32. Ibid., 1.5.11.
33. Ibid., 1.5.11.
34. Ibid., 1.7.13.
35. Ibid., 1.10.20. On the Trinitarian dimension of Augustine's theology of creation, see Williams, "Creation," 254.

here is the fourth: "This is the book of the creation of heaven and earth when day was made" (RSV: "These are the generations of the heavens and the earth when they were created. In the day that the Lord God made the earth and the heavens").

The first question that Augustine asks of Genesis 2:4 is whether "heaven and earth" are here the same as the heaven and earth mentioned in Genesis 1:1. He argues the answer must be no, since Genesis 1:1 "seems to mean that God made something apart from any day, before He made day," whereas Genesis 2:4 suggests that day has already been made when "heaven and earth" are created.[36] According to Augustine, Genesis 1-2 thereby distinguishes God's creative act before "the creation of day" from God's creative work "when day was made" (Gen 2:4).[37] Since "heaven and earth" are created both before *and* after the creation of "day," the author of Genesis must intend for us to perceive that he has in mind two different senses of "heaven and earth." Puzzling over these two distinct creations of "heaven and earth," Augustine proposes that Genesis 1:1, "In the beginning God created the heavens and the earth," is about the creation of "matter unformed and formable, both spiritual and corporeal" as "the substratum of what was to be made."[38] The second creation of "heaven and earth" in Genesis 2:4 is the creation of all things, in the sense of the bestowal of form.[39] But why would Genesis 1-2 proceed in this fashion? Augustine considers that the answer is at least partly that Genesis 1-2 aims to help us distinguish the original creation of all things from the historical unfolding of things—while at the same time insisting that "God created everything at one time."[40]

What about the meaning of "day" in Genesis 1:5 and 2:4? In Genesis 1-2, there is an evident mystery in the term "day," not only because Genesis 2:4 indicates that "day" is made before the heavens and the earth, but also because Genesis 1:5 and Genesis 1:11-12 tell us that "day" and vegetation appear before the sun is created.[41] It is exegetically fitting, therefore, to distinguish the "day transcending our knowledge and experience" from the "days marked by the course of the sun after the proper

---

36. *Gn. Litt.*, 5.1.1.
37. Ibid.
38. Ibid., 5.5.13.
39. See Ibid., 5.3.5; 5.5.16.
40. Ibid., 5.3.6.
41. Ibid., 5.2.4.

lapse of time for each kind."[42] According to Augustine, the seven "days" of Genesis 1:5–2:3 depict the transcendent "day": they are the *one* "day" of creation "seven times repeated," a repetition that "took place without lapse of time" and that manifests "an order based not on intervals of time but on causal connections."[43] Augustine argues that in fact this "day" refers to the creation of the *angels* and to their knowledge of "the whole array of creatures arranged in hierarchical order."[44] The view that everything was created on one "day" fits with Sirach 18:1, which in Augustine's version reads, "He made all things together" (RSV: "He who lives for ever created the whole universe").[45]

Augustine goes on to explain that just as the various parts of the tree exist in the tree's seed "primordially, not in the dimensions of bodily mass but as a force and causal power," so also the whole universe is present in the original creation.[46] He observes in this vein, "In the seed, then, there was invisibly present all that would develop in time into a tree. And in this same way we must picture the world, when God made all things together, as having had all things together which were made in it and with it when day was made."[47] The original creation is like soil containing seeds, and thus containing invisibly and in potency all the things that have come to be through the unfolding of natural causes under the guidance of divine providence.[48] Augustine therefore denies that Genesis 2:9, "out of the

42. Ibid., 5.4.10.
43. Ibid., 5.3.6; 5.4.11.
44. Ibid., 5.5.15.
45. Ibid., 5.17.35.
46. Ibid, 5.23.44.
47. Ibid., 5.23.45. McGrath comments, "The image of a seed provided Augustine with a suitable analogy on which he could draw to support his more-general thesis about the role of potential existing entities within the earth before their appearance in mature form when the conditions were right . . . Yet Augustine was emphatic that these *rationes seminales* are not 'seeds' in the normal sense of the term. The notion of the seed is heuristic, providing an inexact, though helpful, means of visualization for the theologically difficult notion of a hidden force within nature through which latent things are enacted." McGrath, *Fine-Tuned Universe*, 102. As McGrath emphasizes, the *rationes seminales* should not "be understood as distinct physical entities that were embedded within the original creation, as seeds lie in the ground. Rather, Augustine seems to have conceived of them as dormant 'virtual' entities, enabling the natural world to emerge in its own way and in its own time." Ibid., 103. See also Torchia, *Creatio ex nihilo*, 36; McMullin, "Introduction," 8–16.
48. Williams helpfully emphasizes that for Augustine things are not "created simply with immanent capacities for growth," as though "their subsequent history does

ground the Lord God made to grow every tree that is pleasant to the sight and good for food," *adds* something to the original creation. God's original creation is already "very good" (Gen 1:31) and "finished" (Gen 2:1–2). God's original creation needs no addition and receives none.

Since Augustine considers that the six "days" depict the created order as known by the angels, he also associates the angels with the "light" or "day" of Genesis 1:3–5. Their knowledge of the created order begins with the "firmament" or sky (Genesis 1:6–8); then the sea and earth (Genesis 1:9–10), with all plants and trees "in the earth potentially."[49] Next come the sun, moon, and stars (Genesis 1:14–8) and the waters, along with the sea-creatures and birds of the air (Genesis 1:20–21) which are present "potentially in the numbers which would come forth under appropriate influences in the course of time."[50] Last come the animals, of which the human being is the highest (Genesis 1:24–30), again "created potentially, for time would bring them into view in the ages to come."[51]

But how is God the Creator of the things that are produced through natural causes? Augustine recognizes that "there are some who think that only the world was made by God and that everything else is made by the world according to His ordination and command, but that God Himself makes nothing."[52] Against this view, Augustine underscores the significance of God's providential governance. He cites Jesus' statements that "My Father is working still" and "the Father who dwells in me does his works" (Jn 5:17; 14:10), as well as Paul's remark that "God gives it a body as he has chosen, and to each kind of seed its own body."[53] In short, God now creates in a different way: "He now creates from what already exists, whereas in the beginning creatures were made by Him when none

---

no more than unfold what has been there from the beginning in terms of natural processes. The *rationes* do indeed contain the potential in things for natural development, but they also specify the ways in which things in the world may be acted upon by God." Williams, "Creation," 252.

49. *Gn. Litt.* 5.5.14.

50. Ibid.

51. Ibid. As Augustine emphasizes, "In the earth from the beginning, in what I might call the roots of time, God created what was to be in times to come." Ibid., 5.4.11. In this regard Williams states that, "for Augustine, the *temporal* character of the created world is axiomatic: it is a world in motion, a set of processes in which potential is realized." Williams, "Creation," 252.

52. *Gn. Litt.*, 5.20.40.

53. 1 Cor 15:38

of them existed at all."⁵⁴ All things are contained in the *rationes seminales* of the original creation, and God's providential governance draws them out at the appropriate time.

As we would expect, therefore, Augustine interprets the two creation accounts—the creation of humans in Genesis 1:27 and the creation of Adam in Genesis 2:7—to mean that man was made in potency in the original creation and later came to be in the course of history. Specifically, Augustine argues that like "the grass of the field before it sprang forth," humans were included by God in the original creation, "in some hidden form" and "in the hidden recesses of nature."⁵⁵ The creative act portrayed in Genesis 2:7 pertains not to the original creation that Genesis 1:27 describes, but rather to God's ongoing work over the course of history. As Augustine puts it, "The original creation, therefore, of the two [humans] was different from their later creation. First they were created in potency through the word of God and inserted seminally into the world when He created all things together."⁵⁶ In the original creation, neither an adult human, nor an infant, nor even the semen was present in a visible or empirically detectable manner. Humans existed in the original creation, but only "[i]nvisibly, potentially, in their causes, as things that will be in the future are made."⁵⁷

When Augustine summarizes his position on the creation of man and woman, he states that "God by His almighty power made what would appear in the future; and when He who is before the ages created the beginning of the ages, in what we might call the germ or root of time, He created man to be formed later in due time."⁵⁸ Augustine stresses that he does not mean that a person born in the year 354 AD has actually existed since the original creation. Rather, "when God created all things simultaneously, He created man in the sense that He made the man who was to be, that is, the causal principle of man to be created, not the actuality of man already created."⁵⁹

---

54. *Gn. Litt.* 5.4.11.

55. Ibid., 6.1.1.

56. Ibid., 6.5.8.

57. Ibid., 6.6.10. Even so, Augustine accepts that Gen 2:7 accurately describes the way by which the first man and woman, as flesh-and-blood individuals, came to be in the history of the world.

58. Ibid., 6.8.13.

59. Ibid., 6.9.16.

CONCLUDING REMARKS

For Augustine, something that now exists can be said to exist in three ways: in the Word, where all things that God creates are known eternally; in the original creation or "the elements of the universe, where all things destined to be were made simultaneously"; and in its own time, when it comes to be in actuality.[60] In his *A Fine-Tuned Universe*, the theologian and scientist Alister McGrath praises Augustine's understanding of creation as "classic, both in the sense of establishing a norm and offering a resource for future generations."[61] McGrath thinks that Augustine's approach offered three enduring insights: the created order (including time) had a beginning; the created order included "embedded causalities which emerge or evolve at a later time"; and God providentially directs the emergence or unfolding of these "embedded causalities."[62] These insights enable Augustine to describe creation in a manner that broadly accords with contemporary scientific theories of evolution and the Big Bang, so long as God's providential governance retains a place.[63]

Whereas McGrath appreciates Augustine's *The Literal Meaning of Genesis* largely in relation to evolutionary biology and theories of emergent complexity, I have surveyed Augustine's theology of the transcendent triune Creator and of the creation of "heaven and earth" with an eye to modern scientific views of the emergence of the universe. I have done so in the spirit of Matthew Lamb's suggestion that while "[m]odern science has vastly extended human knowledge of the empirical and particular," there now needs to be a retrieval of past achievements in the "cognitive and philosophical mediation of the whole."[64]

Recall the arguments from Krauss and Hawking/Mlodinow with which I began. For Krauss, "all signs suggest a universe that could and

---

60. Ibid., 6.10.17.

61. McGrath, *A Fine-Tuned Universe*, 97.

62. Ibid., 107. McGrath adds a fourth enduring insight, which can be integrated into the second and third: "The image of a dormant seed is an appropriate but not exact analogy for these embedded causalities." Ibid.

63. Blowers notes that the *rationes seminales* "are not simply a kind of creaturely DNA"; instead, although "they are potencies or creational 'codes' of a sort," they do not "merely realize natural processes based on immanent capacities for growth," because they are under divine providential governance. See Blowers, *Drama*, 157. Blowers cites early works linking Augustine's theory to evolution: Woods, *Augustine and Evolution*; McKeough, *Meaning of* Rationes Seminales; Zahm, *Evolution and Dogma*.

64. Lamb, *Eternity, Time, and the Life of Wisdom*, 15.

plausibly did arise from a deeper nothing—involving the absence of space itself."[65] For Hawking and Mlodinow, "Because there is a law like gravity, the universe can and will create itself from nothing . . . Spontaneous creation is the reason there is something rather than nothing, why the universe exists, why we exist. It is not necessary to invoke God to light to blue touch paper and set the universe going."[66] With respect to such views, Augustine helps especially in two ways. First, he makes clear that no one supposes that the transcendent Creator God merely "set the universe going" as an *external* instigator. Rather, God, who is one and three (a mystery of unity and communion, of supreme wisdom and love), creates the universe from nothing by the gift of finite existence, a gift that establishes and sustains the very core of every finite thing. As infinite eternal presence, God is present to all time and space in bestowing the gift of existence. Thus God's gift of existence does much more than "set the universe going." Second, Augustine helps us to see that the "deeper nothing" of which Krauss speaks, or the quantum law of gravity as described by Hawking and Mlodinow, is *not* nothing. Indeed, Augustine's original "formless" creation is in certain respects much like Krauss's original "deeper nothing." Formless creation, like the quantum law of gravity, does not exist in a spatio-temporal way. The same can be said for the *rationes seminales* of all things in the original creation.

Augustine also can remind us that real creation *from nothing*, unlike the emergence of all things from an original law (or from an original formless state, or from *rationes seminales*), involves the radical gift of being and the sustaining of all things in being. In short, Augustine not only offers something broadly similar to the hypothetical scenario described by Krauss and Hawking/Mlodinow, but he also makes clear that their hypothetical scenario does not in fact *answer to the problem* identified by the doctrine of creation. Focused solely upon empirical realities, Krauss and Hawking/Mlodinow have not actually understood the real problem, which has to do with being itself. As Augustine is aware, only the transcendent God can give existence, as opposed to merely producing emergent realities or to propagating new things.

Yet, even if Augustine's understanding of creation offers fruitful (though inexact) parallels to contemporary scientific insights, does Augustine's approach to Genesis 1–2 work exegetically? After all, Augustine's

---

65. Krauss, *A Universe from Nothing*, 183.

66. Hawking and Mlodinow, *The Grand Design*, 180.

text of Genesis 2:4, "This is the book of the creation of heaven and earth when day was made," is not accepted today in contemporary critical versions of the text of Genesis. Augustine also thinks that Genesis 1–2 *intends* to teach us something both through the contrasting references to the creation of "heaven and earth" that we find in Genesis 1:1 and Genesis 2:4, and through the contrast between the creation of "day" in Genesis 1:5, the seven "days" of Genesis 1:1–2:3, and the "day" of creation in Genesis 2:4. In Augustine's exegesis, each occurrence of "heaven and earth" and "day" receives extensive speculative interpretation. By contrast, contemporary historical-critical interpretation obviously takes a quite different approach, one grounded in a much richer knowledge of the ancient near-Eastern context. Augustine affirms that if the intended meaning of a particular biblical text is not clear, "we should choose an interpretation in keeping with the context of Scripture and in harmony with our faith."[67] Given the light that historical research has shined upon the intended meaning of Genesis 1–2, can we really take seriously Augustine's effort to find an intelligible pattern, a theological instruction, in the different uses of "day" and the different renderings of the creation of heaven and earth?

In answer, we might recall that in his *Confessions*, Augustine describes Scripture as "a text lowly to the beginner but, on further reading, of mountainous difficulty and enveloped in mysteries."[68] Augustine tells us that as a young man he only saw the lowliness of Scripture; the book of Genesis did not then impress him, and many educated persons of his day had the same response (perhaps like Krauss and Hawking today). To unimpressed readers of Scripture, Augustine's exegesis can shed light on the ways that the words of Genesis open up mountainous "mysteries." Augustine demonstrates that Genesis invites a profound reflection on God's creation of all things and on their spatio-temporal unfolding. At the same time, Augustine makes clear that interpreters of Genesis must not talk foolishly about scientific matters: "it is a disgraceful and dangerous thing for an infidel to hear a Christian, presumably giving the meaning of Holy Scripture, talking nonsense on these topics."[69] There is no reason, Augustine shows, to set up a literalistic reading of Genesis 1–2 against scientific views that are richer and more

---

67. *Gn. Litt.* 1.21.41.
68. *Conf.* 3.5.9.
69. *Gn. Litt.* 1.19.39.

complex. What we find in Augustine's reading of Genesis 1–2—of the "day" and the "days," of the two creation accounts of "heaven and earth" and of human beings—is that these inspired texts are themselves filled with the complexity that we would expect from the mystery of the creation and unfolding of all finite things.

Describing the style and vocabulary of the authors of the Torah (his example is Genesis 1:16), Robert Alter observes, "They revel in repetition, sometimes of a stately, refrainlike sort, sometimes deployed in ingenious patterns through which different meanings of the same term are played against one another."[70] This stately and subtle operation of repetition, in "ingenious patterns," describes not only the style of Genesis but also—as Augustine bears witness—its theology. Put another way, Genesis includes "words that have been written obscurely for the purpose of stimulating our thought."[71] Augustine observes that the price of failing to appreciate Genesis's acuity is to become "like wingless creatures that crawl upon the earth and, while soaring no higher than the leap of a frog, mock the birds in their nests above."[72] Augustine's interpretation of Genesis continues to instruct us, then, not only because of the parallels and cautions that it offers contemporary science, but also because his very mode of exegesis shows us how to read Genesis 1-2 with a fitting appreciation for the "ingenious patterns" of creation through the Word and Spirit of God.

BIBLIOGRAPHY

Alter, Robert. "To the Reader." In *Genesis: Translation and Commentary*, by Robert Alter, ix–xlvii. New York: Norton, 1996.

Augustine. *Confessions*. Translated by Henry Chadwick. Oxford: Oxford University Press, 1991.

———. *The Literal Meaning of Genesis*. Vol. 1. Translated by John Hammond Taylor. ACW 41. New York: Paulist, 1982.

Blowers, Paul M. *Drama of the Divine Economy: Creator and Creation in Early Christian Theology and Piety*. Oxford: Oxford University Press, 2012.

Hart, David Bentley. *The Experience of God: Being, Consciousness, Bliss*. New Haven: Yale University Press, 2013.

Hawking, Stephen, and Leonard Mlodinow. *The Grand Design*. New York: Random House, 2010.

Krauss, Lawrence M. *A Universe from Nothing: Why There Is Something Rather than Nothing*. New York: Free Press, 2012.

70. Alter, "To the Reader," xxvi.

71. *Gn. Litt.* 1.20.40.

72. Ibid.

Lamb, Matthew L. *Eternity, Time, and the Life of Wisdom.* Naples, FL: Sapientia, 2007.

———. "Introduction" to *Commentary on Saint Paul's Epistle to the Romans by St. Thomas Aquinas.* Translated by Matthew Lamb. Albany, NY: Magi, 1966.

McGrath, Alister. *A Fine-Tuned Universe: The Quest for God in Science and Theology.* Louisville: Westminster John Knox, 2009.

McKeough, Michael John. *The Meaning of the* Rationes Seminales *in St. Augustine.* Washington, DC: Catholic University of America Press, 1926.

McMullin, Ernan. "Introduction." In *Evolution and Creation*, edited by Ernan McMullin, 1–58. Notre Dame: University of Notre Dame Press, 1985.

Swift, Louis J. "Basil and Ambrose on the Six Days of Creation." *Augustinianum* 21 (1981) 317–28.

Torchia, N. Joseph. *Creatio ex nihilo and the Theology of St. Augustine: The Anti-Manichaean Polemic and Beyond.* American University Studies Series 7: Theology and Religion 205. New York: Lang, 1999.

Tyson, Neil deGrasse, and Donald Goldsmith. *Origins: Fourteen Billion Years of Cosmic Evolution.* New York: Norton, 2004.

Williams, Rowan. "Creation." In *Augustine through the Ages: An Encyclopedia*, edited by Allan D. Fitzgerald, 251–54. Grand Rapids: Eerdmans, 1999.

Woods, Henry, *Augustine and Evolution: A Study in the Saint's* De Genesi ad Litteram *and* De Trinitate. New York: Universal Knowledge Foundation, 1924.

Zahm, John Augustine. *Evolution and Dogma.* Chicago: McBride, 1896.

4

Biblical Inspiration in the Theology of St. Thomas Aquinas and Fr. Matthew Lamb

Matthew J. Ramage

INTRODUCTION

A BIBLICAL SCHOLAR COMBING through the corpus St. Thomas Aquinas might be disappointed to learn that the saint whom we call Universal Doctor never wrote a distinct treatise on biblical inspiration. This, however, was a conscious move on the part of Thomas, which, if properly understood, could have important implications for Catholic biblical exegesis today. In his erudite translation and commentary on Aquinas's *Commentary on Ephesians*, Fr. Matthew Lamb discusses this decision and the distinctive features of Thomas' theology of biblical inspiration which flow from it. The goal of this paper is to draw out these characteristics and, in so doing, to suggest that a genuine appropriation of Thomas' exegetical principles could be a fecund source of renewal within Catholic biblical theology today.

THE IMPORTANCE OF ARISTOTELIANISM IN ST. THOMAS' EXEGESIS

In his introduction Fr. Lamb sets out to elucidate Aquinas' *begrifflichkeit*, that is, the set of fundamental concepts employed by Aquinas in his questioning of God's word.[1] These unique characteristics of Thomas' thought are what render it so apt for treating the subject of biblical inspiration. Says Lamb, "Here is where St. Thomas marked a notable transition in regard to the Fathers. Before him biblical exegesis in the West has relied mostly on concepts borrowed from a Middle or Neoplatonism ... Aquinas' appropriation of Aristotle introduced a different perspective from which to question God's word."[2] While on the level of techniques Aquinas adhered closely with the conventions of his day, Lamb tells us that "his specific contribution to biblical exegesis" consists in the philosophical horizon from which he approached the sacred page.[3] Specifically, "St. Thomas' unqualified adoption of the Aristotelian doctrine concerning the dependence of the human mind on imagination threw new light on the importance of the literal sense of Scripture ... Aquinas' appropriation of Aristotle introduced a different perspective from which to question God's word. For Thomas human knowing is impossible without sense and imagination. Efficient and formal causality receive greater recognition. The world and history take on their own value, they are not just symbolic of a higher realm."[4] With Aquinas' serious consideration of the role of man's senses and imagination in the composition of the Bible, biblical inspiration became a problem in a way it could not have before: "Prior to St. Thomas, no theologian had felt the necessity of analyzing the exact relationship between the divine and human authors of the Bible ... Following Athenagoras of Athens, the human authors were described as the harp strings played by the Holy Spirit to produce the melody of the Scripture."[5]

While Aquinas by no means abandons the traditional doctrine of the Four Senses, his Aristotelian *begrifflichkeit* sets these senses in a new perspective: "The Origenist and Augustinian view of physical and historical events, along with man's knowledge of them, as symbolic put the

---

1. Lamb, Introduction to *Commentary on Ephesians*, 5.
2. Ibid., 5–6.
3. Ibid., 4.
4. Ibid., 6, 13.
5. Ibid. 6.

stress on the allegorical-anagogical meaning as revealing the Ultimate: God and Christ in glory. Christian interpretation must not remain on the level of literature and history; these are symbols whose transcendent finality must be unfolded. St. Thomas, however, opens the way for a closer analysis of the text and of history as expressing a divinely given meaning. Where the former concentrate on the plus-value of the symbol as pointing beyond itself, Aquinas directs attention to the salvific intelligibility of the sacred text and of history."[6] Unlike many medieval allegorists who, as Lamb indicates, "seemed more interested in detours than in the intended route," Aquinas paid painstaking attention to the literal sense as the one sense which is present in all the verses of Scripture.[7] Lamb affirms in no uncertain terms: "By far, the greatest service which St. Thomas performed in regard to exegetical presuppositions was to assert plainly the sufficiency of the literal meaning. The literal is the only sense on which theological arguments can be based. St. Augustine and others had counseled that arguments must be adduced from 'plain testimonies,' but never would they have dreamt of identifying these exclusively with the literal sense."[8] This move was to have far-reaching consequences for the history of biblical interpretation within the Christian tradition: "The exegetical presuppositions of St. Thomas provided all the elements needed for a theoretical justification of a Christian exegete applying himself wholeheartedly to the interpretation of the literal sense . . . [T]he identification of the literal meaning of the text and the intention of its authors warranted a study of the factors which shaped and influenced their mentality—their languages, cultures, and historical contexts."[9] Without knowing it, modern exegetes may thus owe a significant debt to Thomas who insisted upon the importance of the literal sense some four hundred years before the advent of the historical-critical method. This is but one indication of the enduring influence and potential import of Aquinas' theology for exegesis today.

6. Ibid., 14–15.
7. Ibid., 13.
8. Ibid., 15.
9. Ibid., 16.

THE LITERAL SENSE AND AUTHORIAL ASSERTIONS

A second area of Thomas' thought germane to modern biblical exegesis flows from the emphasis upon the literal sense discussed above. Throughout his corpus we find Aquinas striving diligently to ascertain something which lies at the heart of the modern exegete's task: namely, the intentions of Scripture's various human authors. It is precisely this intention, considered within the context of the particular biblical book within the canon and the context of salvation history, which gives us a text's literal sense. As Lamb puts it, "We tend to regard a truth as either clearly and explicitly revealed or not revealed at all. But for St. Thomas man's knowledge of the faith grows; truths are revealed slowly over a period of time. The Bible communicates this organic development of salvation-history to men up to its definitive apex in the revelation of the Word Incarnate himself. The whole of the Bible must be approached with faith; this does not mean that every sentence is a definable dogma."[10] As Lamb relates, it is not as if one can find a definable dogma in every sentence of Scripture; indeed, Scripture never claims this about itself. The reason for this is that the authors of Scripture understood and taught revealed truth with varying degrees of clarity depending on their place within the course of salvation history. To discern dogmatic content within Scripture thus requires careful attention to the intentions of its authors and to the broader role of a particular text within the development of the canon as a whole. This also requires overcoming the assumption that something is 'revealed' only if it is perfectly reflective of God's own knowledge, or else it is not revealed at all.

Benedict XVI is a stalwart example of a modern exegete who consistently puts into practice these Thomistic principles understood so well by Fr. Lamb. Throughout his corpus one always finds Ratzinger attempting to determine the "essential point," "kernel," or core assertion of concrete biblical texts. He demonstrates keen awareness that certain texts seem plainly to contradict the assertions of other texts, yet this does not cause him to abandon the doctrines of biblical inspiration or inerrancy: "It is because faith is not set before us as a complete and finished system that the Bible contains contradictory texts, or at least ones that stand in tension to each other ... It follows straightaway that neither the criterion of inspiration nor that of infallibility can be applied mechanically. It is quite impossible to pick out one single sentence and say, right, you find this

---

10. Ibid., 256n17. See also Ramage, *Dark Passages*, 133–34.

sentence in God's great book, so it must simply be true in itself."[11] While I have documented elsewhere at length the dependence of Benedict on Aquinas, here it is simply worth noting the above texts as an illustration of how Aquinas' principles as articulated by Lamb have been made relevant within the practice of Catholic exegesis in recent times.[12]

As a final word on this subject, it is worth observing that Benedict's practice of affirming the core assertion of biblical texts while admitting the existence of problems is his way of implementing Vatican II's exegetical principles. In particular, Benedict approaches the issue of biblical inerrancy in light of *Dei Verbum*'s well-known teaching that "everything asserted by the inspired authors or sacred writers must be held to be asserted by the Holy Spirit."[13] As Germain Grisez has noted along the same lines in a helpful essay, it is a great mistake to read *Dei Verbum* as saying that "everything in Scripture is asserted by the Holy Spirit." He elaborates, "Scripture contains not only many sentences expressing no proposition, but many sentences that express propositions not asserted by their human authors."[14] In a helpful footnote in which he offers illustrations from Aquinas to support his claim, Grisez adds that the Council fathers would have been well aware of the difference between a mere statement and an assertion.[15]

While the above distinction is by no means universally accepted as a solution to reconciling problematic biblical texts with the doctrine of inerrancy, a helpful specification is offered by Brian Harrison in an essay which critiques a view similar to that advanced by Grisez. According to the Council *relator* of *Dei Verbum* 11, Harrison notes, the word teach (*docere*) refers to those things which are truly affirmed (*asseruntur*) in Scripture.[16] Harrison cites an important text from Raúl Cardinal Silva

11. Benedict XVI, *God and the World*, 152–53.
12. This has been traced extensively in my work *Dark Passages of the Bible*.
13. *DV* 11.
14. Grisez, "Inspiration and Inerrancy," 186.
15. Ibid., 186n15. Grisez states that "[t]he distinction between what is asserted and what is said without being asserted is one that Thomas uses regularly." Examples he provides from the *Summa Theologiae* include II-II.110.3, ad 1; I.77.5, ad 3; I.100.2, ad 2.
16. *Acta*, 709; Harrison, "Restricted Inerrancy," 244. In another piece, Harrison pointedly criticizes certain "recent Catholic authors" who "have tried to reconcile [the teaching of *Dei Verbum* 11] with the supposed occurrence of errors in Scripture by charging that the errors they have in mind are never in fact *affirmed* by either the divine or human authors." Harrison describes such a maneuver as a "contorted hermeneutic,"

Herínquez to clarify: "[T]he doctrine of biblical inerrancy is better expressed by the formal criterion of *teaching*, since it is according to that criterion that no error can be found. For in another sense, that is, the material sense, it is possible for expressions to be used by the sacred writer which are erroneous in themselves, but which, however, he does not wish to teach."[17] As Harrison proceeds to observe, the *relator* informed the Council fathers that Herínquez's above proposal had been accepted "substantially" by the doctrinal commission. Thus Harrison affirms Herínquez's clarification as "a guide to what the Council means."[18]

In contrast with Grisez, Harrison argues that the key distinction in the cardinal's text is not between "affirmations" and "teachings" on the one hand and "statements" on the other.[19] Rather, for him the dichotomy is to be found in contrasting what is formally taught from what is merely

---

which "unreasonably attempts to determine what is being affirmed in a given text in Scripture by appealing to content rather than form—subject matter rather than syntax ... but this procedure—trying to identify an author's assertions by looking at *what* he is talking about instead of *how* he talks about it—violates basic, common-sense principles of verbal communication." Harrison, "Does Vatican Council II Allow for Errors in Sacred Scripture?," 279–304. The text cited here is from an updated version of the article available at http://www.rtforum.org/lt/lt145-6.html (accessed March 28, 2016). This is a helpful critique, but it does not negate the importance of distinguishing statements from assertions as Grisez does. This fundamental endeavor to distinguish non-affirmed statements from core assertions in the biblical text can be seen in the exegesis of Joseph Ratzinger throughout his career. But unlike the unnamed authors whom Harrison critiques, Ratzinger's exegesis by no means neglects the syntax or *how* a biblical author wishes to assert his point. On the contrary, his patient attentiveness to this reality is what makes his hermeneutic so powerful.

17. *Acta*, 3/3:799.

18. Harrison, "Restricted Inerrancy," 245.

19. It is helpful to compare what Harrison writes in the above piece to another work in which he provides a helpful clarification of his view: "[S]ome biblical affirmations—above all, those that are *per se* less directly concerned with salvation—may be only approximations, or it may be that they express certain truths only in simple, popular language rather than in precise or technical terminology. For since the formal object of Sacred Scripture is to teach us God's plan of salvation for the human race, and not profane history, natural science, or other forms of merely worldly knowledge *for their own sakes*, one should not expect or demand, as a condition of the Bible's freedom from error, when it touches upon these subjects, the same standards of accuracy and clarity in description and terminology as we would expect and demand in works (especially modern academic works) whose formal object is these 'secular' branches of knowledge ... [W]e should not set the bar unreasonably high in deciding what is *to count* as truth, as opposed to error, when the sacred writers make statements about secondary matters that are only indirectly linked to the Bible's principal and overall purpose." Harrison, "Errors in Sacred Scripture?" 303–304.

"used" (*adhiberi*) by the sacred writers in view of making their assertions. The category of what is merely used, Harrison concludes, may include expressions (*locutiones*) that are "materially" erroneous.[20] It is worth noting that here we have a Thomistically-inspired distinction between material and formal error leveraged in order to make sense of the Scriptures. The language of "use" likewise anticipates another area of Aquinas' theology germane to our endeavor.

DONUM AND *USUS* OF PROPHECY

Related to the issue of discerning an author's intention, a third facet of Aquinas' *begrifflichkeit* is particularly helpful for reconciling the presence of apparently erroneous texts within Scripture with the doctrine of biblical inspiration. This involves the discovery that Aquinas' treatment of inspiration takes place within the context of the Holy Spirit's gift of prophecy. As Lamb says of the saint, "He lived in an age when the Bible was still considered within the total context of the prophetic mission exercised by the people of God. Scripture was not seen as the end product of this mission but as a means of continuing it."[21] According to Paul Synave and Pierre Benoit, commentators on Aquinas whom Lamb discusses and at certain points critiques, the Angelic Doctor offers a corrective for the Christian who might otherwise have a one-dimensional understanding of revelation. As I alluded to above, Christians are often tempted to identify "revelation" with "revelations" or discrete infallible propositions channeled to man by God above. In Thomas' view, however, the divine light infused when an inspired prophet receives a revelation does not necessarily involve the perfect communication of a particular supernatural idea. Simply put, due to the limitations inherent within man's darkened intellect and weakened will, not every idea presented on the sacred page reflects God's own knowledge of the universe.

As Lamb explains, the key here rests on Aquinas' distinction between the *donum* and the *usus* of the gift of prophecy. Aquinas writes: "The use of any prophecy is within the power of the prophet . . . Hence, one could prevent himself from using prophecy; the proper disposition

---

20. Harrison, "Restricted Inerrancy," 245. On the distinction between the existence of material error or imperfection in contrast with formal errors in Scripture, see Ramage, *Dark Passages*, 131–46.

21. Lamb, Introduction to *Commentary on Ephesians*, 7.

is a necessary requirement for the correct use of prophecy since the use of prophecy proceeds from the created power of the prophet. Therefore, a determinate disposition is also required."[22] Thus even if the Holy Spirit inspires a prophet, this does not guarantee that a particular author has the requisite *disposition* to use the prophetic gift properly.

This is by no means to say that an error has been committed when a particular sacred author fails to make perfect use of the *donum* he has received from God. On the contrary, when considering questions of biblical inspiration it is critically important that we not isolate individual authors and texts from the entire order of divine revelation wisely established in God's providence. Thus, says Lamb, "[T]he emphasis is shifted from isolated individuals to God's control of the whole process in which the Bible was formed. The pre-required dispositions [of the Bible's authors] were arranged for within the scope of this special Providence."[23] That is to say, the very defects we observe in Scripture turn out to be a most significant clue for grasping its true purpose. If I may indulge for a moment with a quote from C.S. Lewis, "[T]he value of the Old Testament may be dependent on what seems its imperfection."[24]

CONDESCENSION AND THE DIVINE PEDAGOGY

A fourth dimension of Aquinas' theology relevant to our endeavor helps us answer certain questions which arise in light of the foregoing argument: Why did divine providence permit Scripture's authors to sometimes have imperfect dispositions with regard to the gift of prophecy, and how does this imperfection contribute to the value of the Old Testament? The inner intelligibility of God's decision to permit certain defects in Scripture is found within his choice to ennoble human beings as secondary or instrumental causes of its authorship. While God is the primary author of Scripture, *Dei Verbum* affirms the Patristic tradition that he "condescended" so as to achieve his purpose by means of human

---

22. *De Ver.*, 12, 4. Translation by Matthew Lamb in Aquinas, *Commentary on Ephesians*, 8. Lamb provides references to many other places in Aquinas's corpus in which he distinguishes the prophetic *donum* and *usus*; cf. ibid., 258, n. 20. For a more thorough discussion of inspiration and prophecy in Aquinas from which many insights in this paper were drawn, see Ramage, *Dark Passages*, 118–542.

23. Lamb, Introduction to *Commentary on Ephesians*, 9.

24. Lewis, *Reflections on the Psalms*, 114.

instruments who functioned as true authors.[25] Thus the literal—or perhaps better, literary—sense of Scripture is that which was intended by Scripture's human authors by means of their literary craft using various forms and devices within a particular genre.

Yet Aquinas reminds us that the literal sense of Scripture must be approached not only bearing in mind the literary peculiarities of a given work, but also with attention to how this work fits into the canon of Scripture which developed over a period of more than a thousand years. Aquinas' critical insight here lies in his consideration of the divine pedagogy, the gradual teaching method by which God gradually prepared his people over the centuries for the coming of Christ in the flesh. As Lamb observes, for Thomas the Spirit's prophetic gift is likened to divine education: "Aquinas holds that education is a process in which the teacher actualizes the potentialities of the students as regards knowledge and virtue."[26] In *De veritate*, a text referenced by Lamb at various points in his notes, Thomas develops his divine pedagogy hermeneutic by comparing the education of the whole human race in divine things to the education of an individual: "Just as there is a progress in the faith of an individual man over the course of time, so there is a progress in faith for the whole human race. This is why Gregory says that divine knowledge has increasingly grown over the course of time."[27] In the same way that an individual believer slowly appropriates the truths of the faith into his life, so, too, the people of God gradually appropriated divine knowledge over the course of salvation history.

As Aquinas proceeds to explain, God had to hand on the faith to men in piecemeal form, not because he is an inept teacher, but because this is the only way men can digest its content: "Man acquires a share of this learning, not indeed all at once, but little by little, according to the mode of his nature."[28] Israel, God's pupil, could not perfectly appropriate the divine teaching immediately because she assimilated this teaching according to the mode of our weak human nature. As Aquinas astutely observes, Scripture itself likens the people of Israel in the Old Testament to spiritual childhood before God the Father: "The master, who has perfect knowledge of the art, does not deliver it all at once to his disciple

---

25. *DV* 11.
26. Lamb, Introduction to *Commentary on Ephesians*, 261n29.
27. *De Ver.*, 14, 11.
28. *ST* II-II.2.3. See also Ramage, *Dark Passages*, 101.

from the very outset, for he would not be able to take it all in, but he condescends to the disciple's capacity and instructs him little by little. It is in this way that men made progress in the knowledge of faith as time went on. Hence the Apostle (Galatians 3:24)[29] compares the state of the Old Testament to childhood."[30] For Thomas as for St. Paul whose theology he invokes, God's firstborn son Israel gradually made progress in knowledge of him in accordance with the divine Teacher's most wise pedagogy. God condescended and taught man in accordance with the way he learns best, which is "little by little." Ultimately, through the life and ministry of Jesus Christ, man attained the perfection of divine knowledge.

Aquinas explores this divine teaching method elsewhere in commenting on the same text from St. Paul just cited. He argues that God's teaching was perfectly suited to the needs and ability of the people of God at every stage of divine revelation, taking into account the fact that the people would not always fully grasp what he wished to convey. In the words of Thomas, "Nothing prevents a thing being not perfect simply, and yet perfect in respect of time: thus a boy is said to be perfect, not simply, but with regard to the condition of time. So, too, precepts that are given to children are perfect in comparison with the condition of those to whom they are given, although they are not perfect simply. Hence the Apostle says (Gal 3:24): 'The Law was our pedagogue in Christ.'"[31] For Thomas, God was not unable or unwilling to teach Israel himself; rather, it was precisely because of his knowledge of frail human nature that he used tangible and even transitory means like the Law. Thus he is able to say that "nothing prevents a thing being not perfect simply, and yet perfect in respect of time." In other words, the reality is that God knew the Law was imperfect and did not contain the fullness of truth. However, given man's frail intellect and hard heart it was "perfect in respect of time," meaning that God adapted his teaching to the needs of his disciple Israel at every moment throughout the course of divine revelation. Herein lies the import of C.S. Lewis' words cited above: the very value of the Old Testament depends upon a certain imperfection which God permitted within it so as to reveal himself in a way that respects and ennobles our human nature.

---

29. All citations from the Bible in this chapter are from the RSV.
30. Ibid., II-II.1.7, ad 2.
31. Ibid., I-II.98.2, ad 1.

CAUSALITY AND INSTRUMENTALITY IN THE AUTHORSHIP OF SCRIPTURE

Finally, consideration of Scripture's divine and human authorship in the writings of Aquinas and Lamb offers fruitful possibilities for reconciling the presence of defects in Scripture and for dealing with the complexity of the process of inspiration as a whole. On this point, one must begin by recalling that, although the authors of *human* books conceive all the ideas contained therein, this may not be the case when it comes to the divine authorship of Scripture. Aquinas' commentators Synave and Benoit state: "It is certain that, among men, the author of a book must at least have conceived the ideas; this seems to be a minimum requirement . . . But there is another possibility of which human psychology offers no instance, that of one mind causing another to think by communicating an interior light to it: it is this which the doctrine of inspiration teaches us to be the case with God, and which transforms the ordinary meaning of the word 'author.'"[32] As John Henry Newman explains in his work *On the Inspiration of Scripture*, the Latin *auctor* used in the Tradition to describe God's authorship does not primarily refer to "author" in the literary sense of the term most people associate with the term today: "'Auctor' is not identical with the English 'Author.' Allowing that there are instances to be found in classical Latin in which 'auctores' may be translated 'authors,' instances in which it even seems to mean 'writers,' it more naturally means 'authorities.' Its proper sense is 'originator,' 'inventor,' 'founder,' 'primary cause.'"[33] Newman's point is similar to that of Yves Congar when he writes, "An *auctor* is he who is responsible for something because he stands first and decisively at its origin."[34] Thus, as was said above, God remains the author of the Scriptures in their entirety, yet this does not mean that every idea

---

32. Synave and Benoit, *Prophecy and Inspiration*, 102. Benedict XVI also offers some thought-provoking insights on our topic: "The extent of the Word's meaning cannot be reduced to the thoughts of a single author in a specific historical moment; it is not the property of a single author at all; rather, it lives in a history that is ever moving onward and, thus, has dimensions and depths of meaning in past and future that ultimately pass into the realm of the unforeseen. It is only at this point that we can begin to understand the nature of inspiration; we can see where God mysteriously enters into what is human and purely human authorship is transcended." Benedict XVI, *Pilgrim Fellowship*, 32–33.

33. Newman, *On the Inspiration of Scripture*, 10. See also Rahner, *Inspiration in the Bible*; and Congar, *Sainte Église*, 187–88.

34. Congar, *Sainte Église*, 187; translation mine. See also Ramage, *Dark Passages*, 101.

presented on the sacred page is reflective of his own perfect knowledge. Rather, because he condescended to teach mankind gradually and employ humans as true co-authors, the various texts of Scripture are going to reflect certain limitations—limitations which ultimately contribute to the Bible's perfection when seen from a God's-eye point of view in light of the economy of salvation.

Lamb in turn offers a clarification in line with the above observations which helps to make sense of the process of inspiration in general. In particular, a proper grasp of Aquinas' theology enables us to maintain the plenary inspiration of Scripture while also acknowledging the complexity of the Bible's redaction as recognized by scholars today. Lamb argues that, if we are to properly understand the particular kind of instrumental authorship operative in Scripture, it is necessary to recall that it constitutes a special instance of God's "universal instrumentality." He offers a corrective to the work of Synave and Benoit in warning that it is easy to fall into the trap of approaching inspiration as a series of discrete divine impulses upon isolated individual authors. This is important for the simple reason that the genesis of biblical books was highly complex. As Lamb reminds us, the books "were not, for the most part, composed by single authors, as was formerly held, but by various traditions."[35] Divine inspiration worked through tradition within the believing community, and thus a satisfactory account of inspiration cannot isolate individual recipients of this gift without considering their works within divine providence as a whole. Lamb says,

> For Benoit the whole Bible is inspired because the Almighty controlled every single writer and literary piece. St Thomas's concept of instrumentality, as Lonergan has demonstrated, affirms that God controls each event because he controls all. Applied to Scripture, this means that each and every part of it is authored by God because he *originated* the whole process of the Bible's formation ... The difference between the instrumentality operative in the composing of the Scriptures and the Universal

---

35. Lamb, Introduction to *Commentary on Ephesians*, 257n18. It is illuminating to observe how Benedict conceives of inspiration in light of the complexity of biblical authorship noted here by Lamb. The books of Scripture involve "three interacting subjects"—the individual human authors or groups of authors, God, and the "collective subject" the church. Benedict XVI, *Jesus of Nazareth*, xx–xxi. Here the pontiff builds on the traditional model of dual authorship by underscoring that the many individual human authors and redactors of Scripture are best considered as members of the Bible's corporate author, the people of God.

Instrumentality discussed by Lonergan is that the Providence guiding the genesis of the Bible is an essential element in the special Providence concerned with salvation history."[36]

In speaking of God as originator of Scripture, it is interesting also to consider what it is that makes the Scriptures unique if we assume that God originates other works besides them. According to Lamb, it is crucial to grasp that "the Providence guiding the genesis of the Bible is an essential element in the special Providence concerned with salvation history."[37] In other words, God in his eternal providence inspired the Scriptures in order that they could serve a unique role in salvation history and in the formation of the church. At this point Lamb references Karl Rahner, who eloquently summarized this dynamic: "The inspiration of the Scriptures . . . is but simply the causality of God in regard to the Church, inasmuch as it refers to the constitutive element of the Apostolic Church, which is the Bible."[38] The inspiration of Scripture and the causality of the church are inseparable from one another. Inspiration is not an end in itself; the Scriptures were inspired *for the church*.

Lamb also calls on the authority of Yves Congar to clarify this point. In line with Rahner's thesis, Congar states, "Certain writings are inspired because they were integral to the living establishment of the Church not at any moment whatsoever in her history but in the moment of her birth and constitution."[39] This is an important statement because it helps believers answer the age-old challenge of explaining what makes certain books inspired when they are not necessarily any more enlightening or beautiful than other works of the same time period which did not make

---

36. Ibid., 259n22; emphasis added. Lamb is contrasting his view here with the reflections of Synave and Benoit on the possibility of a text having multiple authors and redactors who "share" the charism of inspiration. See their *Prophecy and Inspiration*, 124.Cf. Lonergan, "St. Thomas' Theory of Operation" and "St. Thomas' Thought on *Gratia Operans*," 375–401, 533–78, esp. 391–95. See also Ramage, *Dark Passages*, 120–22.

37. Ibid.

38. Rahner, *Inspiration in the Bible*, 50–51. Benedict XVI speaks in similar terms with regard to the formation of the canon: "The establishment of the canon and the establishment of the early Church are one and the same process but viewed from different perspectives." Benedict XVI, *Principles*, 148.

39. Congar, *Sainte Église*, 188–99; translation mine. See also Thomas Aquinas, *Hic est liber* 1, on the importance of correctly understanding what it means for God to be the "originator" of Scripture. For a more recent discussion of divine providence and inspiration, see Farkasfalvy, *Inspiration and Interpretation*, 217–19.

it into the canon. For Lamb, Rahner, and Congar, the simple answer is that the inspiration of these works lies in the role they played in salvation history and in the constitution of the church. In his eternal wisdom, God willed them to fill a niche that no other sacred writings would fill. As such, they must be approached in light of their role within the "special Providence" of God's saving plan.

CONCLUSION: AQUINAS' EXEGESIS AS AN ANTIDOTE TO SPINOZA

In concluding, I would be remiss not to mention a final feature of Thomas' exegesis which finds an important place in the work of Fr. Lamb. For Aquinas, says, Lamb, "The Bible was not a historical curiosity to be approached like an antiquated museum piece."[40] Rather, for the Common Doctor the Bible was an object of faith and scientific study. In this connection it is worth remarking how much Aquinas' approach as discussed by Lamb differs from that of another thinker whom he critiques at various points in his corpus. Spinoza, who is sometimes referred to as the founder of modern exegesis, consciously parts from the company of Aquinas and the tradition in separating faith from hermeneutics. Lamb says, "Laying the foundations of modern historical-criticism, Spinoza held that no appeal can be made to faith in biblical interpretation. The method of interpreting Scripture does not widely differ from the method of interpreting nature."[41] With faith divorced from biblical exegesis, it follows that the Bible can no longer be treated as if it had a unity in light of God's educational plan. Lamb writes:

> Spinoza set forth the presuppositions of this denigration of revealed truth in his *Theologico-Political Treatise*. Like nature, the Bible can no longer be treated as a whole; it must be broken up into fragmented parts. These isolated texts must then be reinterpreted only by other texts. Because the wise attunement to the whole Bible was lost, Spinoza remarks that one must never raise the truth question, only the meaning question to be answered solely with reference to other fragmented texts. The development of doctrine within the Bible from Old to New Testament

---

40. Lamb, Introduction to *Commentary on Ephesians*, 26.
41. Lamb, "Wisdom Eschatology," 262.

and within the ongoing mission of the Church is rendered impossible. Wisdom is replaced with arbitrary power."[42]

The difference between Aquinas's hermeneutic of faith and Spinoza's hermeneutic of suspicion could hardly be any greater. Yet, as anyone familiar with contemporary biblical scholarship can attest, Spinoza's philosophy remains alive and well within the Christian community today.

As Ratzinger stated in his Erasmus Lecture, however, simply retreating to past thinkers like Aquinas is not a viable path out of our modern exegetical problems. Lest one take away from this chapter an overly romanticized view of Thomas' theology of inspiration, it is worth recalling that Thomas himself did draw out the full implications of his own principles. Lamb observes, "St. Thomas was aware of a certain growth or development in the revelation of supernatural mysteries, even though he could scarcely perceive the historical dimensions of such an evolution. Any reflections on the Bible's inerrancy must take this development into account. Truth in God undergoes no change, but man's apprehension of the truth does."[43] In other words, notwithstanding the integrity of Aquinas' principles, the exegetical horizon of his day did not allow him to perceive the extent of historical development within the Scriptures which we now recognize thanks to modern exegesis. A theology of inspiration grounded in Aquinas alone is thus impossible; the only way out of the modern exegetical quagmire is to march boldly through it. For Pope Benedict XVI, this effort entails synthesizing the tools and findings modern criticism has to offer with the best of the Christian exegetical tradition. Through an examination of Lamb's writings, the goal of this paper has been to show that Aquinas' theology of inspiration contains principles which are able to play an important role in such a synthesis. In Lamb's careful analysis of Aquinas' work, theologians today have a gem of theological wisdom begging to be rediscovered anew in this third Christian millennium.

BIBLIOGRAPHY

Aquinas, Thomas. *Commentary on Saint Paul's Epistle to the Ephesians*. Translated by Matthew Lamb. Albany, NY: Magi, 1966.

---

42. Lamb and Levering, *Vatican II*, 6. See also Lamb, *Eternity, Time, and the Life of Wisdom*, ix–x.

43. Lamb, Introduction to *Commentary on Ephesians*, 10.

———. *De veritate*. Translated by James V. McGlynn. http://dhspriory.org/thomas/english/QDdeVer.htm (accessed March 28, 2016).

———. *Hic est liber*. http://dhspriory.org/thomas/Principium.htm#1 (accessed March 28, 2016).

———. *Summa Theologica*. Translated by the Fathers of the English Dominican Province. Westminster, MD: Christian Classics, 1981.

Benedict XVI. *God and the World*. San Francisco: Ignatius, 2002.

———. *Pilgrim Fellowship of Faith: The Church as Communion*. San Francisco: Ignatius, 2005.

———. *Principles of Catholic Theology*. San Francisco: Ignatius, 1987.

Congar, Yves. *Sainte Église: études et approches ecclésiologiques*. Paris: Cerf, 1963.

Farkasfalvy, Denis. *Inspiration and Interpretation: A Theological Introduction to Sacred Scripture*. Washington, DC: Catholic University of America Press, 2010.

Germain Grisez, "The Inspiration and Inerrancy of Scripture." In *For the Sake of Our Salvation: The Truth and Humility of God's Word*, by St. Paul Center for Biblical Theology, 181–90. Steubenville, OH: Emmaus Road, 2010.

Harrison, Brian. "Does Vatican Council II Allow for Errors in Sacred Scripture?" *Divinitas* 52 (2009) 279–304.

———. "Restricted Inerrancy and the 'Hermeneutic of Discontinuity.'" In *For the Sake of Our Salvation: The Truth and Humility of God's Word*, by St. Paul Center for Biblical Theology, 225–46. Steubenville, OH: Emmaus Road, 2010.

Lamb, Matthew. *Eternity, Time, and the Life of Wisdom*. Naples, FL: Sapientia, 2007.

———. "Wisdom Eschatology in Augustine and Aquinas." In *Aquinas the Augustinian*, edited by Michael Dauphinais, et al., 258–76. Washington, DC: Catholic University of America Press, 2007.

Lamb, Matthew, and Matthew Levering. *Vatican II: Renewal within Tradition*. New York: Oxford University Press, 2008.

Lewis, C.S. *Reflections on the Psalms*. London: Harvest, 1964.

Lonergan, Bernard. "St. Thomas' Theory of Operation." *Theological Studies* 3 (1942) 375–401.

———. "St. Thomas' Thought on *Gratia Operans*." *Theological Studies* 3 (1942) 533–78.

Newman, John Henry. *On the Inspiration of Scripture*. Edited by J. Derek Holmes and Robert Murray. Washington, DC: Corpus, 1967.

Rahner, Karl. *Inspiration in the Bible*. Translated by Charles H. Henkey. New York: Herder, 1964.

Ramage, Matthew. *Dark Passages of the Bible: Engaging Scripture with Benedict XVI and Thomas Aquinas*. Washington, DC: Catholic University of America Press, 2013.

Ratzinger, Joseph/Pope Benedict XVI. *Jesus of Nazareth: From the Baptism in the Jordan to the Transfiguration*. San Francisco: Ignatius, 2008.

Second Vatican Council. *Acta synodalia Sacrosancti Concilii Oecumenici Vaticani II*. Vatican City: Typis polyglottis Vaticanis, 1970.

———. *Dei Verbum*.

Synave, Paul, and Pierre Benoit. *Prophecy and Inspiration: a Commentary on the Summa Theologica II-II, Questions 171-178*. New York: Desclee, 1961.

5

Metaphysics and Paul's Use of the Old Testament

The Impact of a Participatory Ontology

Charles Raith II

PAUL'S "USE" OF THE Old Testament has become a topic of study in its own right within New Testament scholarship with numerous methodological options now being offered.[1] When the scholarship is analyzed, we find that those who adhere strongly to a historical-critical approach to Scripture continue to assume an objective stance to the raw data of the text that yields various scientific results.[2] For others, right method and adequate literary skills alone—and possibly an emphasis on the proper "interpretive community"—are thought to yield an accurate analysis

---

1. A version of this essay was published as Charles Raith II, "Aquinas on Paul's Use of the Old Testament," *Logos* 18 (2015) 66–87. Scholars frequently cite Hays, *Echoes of Scripture in the Letters of Paul*, as a powerful catalyst for stimulating interest in this topic. For summaries of contemporary approaches, see Moyise, *Paul and Scripture*, 111–23; Stanley, "Paul and Scripture," 4–7.

2. Louth captures historical-critical methodology when he states, "The historical-critical method is, on the analogy of the scientific method, a way of reaching objective truth, that is, truth that inheres in the object, independently of the one who knows this truth." *Discerning the Mystery*, 30. The following analysis demonstrates why such historical-critical assumptions need questioning.

of Paul's use of the Old Testament.³ In the main, however, whether the approach is conservative, progressive, or post-modern, *metaphysical* considerations are at best secondary issues to be explored only after the particular method has yielded its results.

But is our attempt to understand Paul's use of the Old Testament a metaphysically neutral inquiry? Or are interpretations affected by one's metaphysical commitments? This essay explores this question through taking up Fr. Lamb's observation found in his introduction to Aquinas's commentary on Ephesians that because the Word of God is mediated by human beings, "the exegete's philosophical horizon is also a determining factor in his interpretations."⁴ Fr. Lamb's observation is no more clearly borne out than on the topic of Paul's use of the Old Testament. Engagements with Paul's use of the Old Testament bring to the surface a number of the scholar's convictions and assumptions, sometimes stated but more often left unstated, pertaining to the doctrine of inspiration, the metaphysical involvement of God in history, the locus of authorial intent, the Christological linking (or lack thereof) of the canonical writings, and the metaphysics (and not merely literary qualities) underlying the doctrine of the different "senses" of Scripture.⁵ When these assumptions are analyzed, it becomes clear that approaches to Paul's use of the Old Testament are in fact deeply impacted by prior philosophical and theological judgments—judgments that do not merely follow one's interpretation but that are intrinsic to the interpretive approach itself.⁶

3. E.g., Beale, *Handbook*, xviii.

4. Lamb, Introduction to *Commentary on Ephesians*, 4. Fr. Lamb claims that this observation is one of St. Thomas's "specific contributions" to biblical exegesis.

5. For an overview of some of these presuppositions, see Moyise, *Evoking Scripture*, 1–5. Tellingly, however, Moyise does not mention the topic of inspiration or the metaphysical involvement of God in history, which, as we shall see, are key components for understanding Aquinas's approach to Paul's use of the Old Testament.

6. Childs observes that "theological" judgments addressing the Bible as a whole impact one's study of the relationship between the Old and New Testaments, and by implication one's interpretation of Paul's use of the Old Testament. For Childs, these theological convictions surrounding the "conceptual framework" employed in reading the text are not at odds with historical research, but they do impact how such research is conducted. Childs, *Biblical Theology*, 7–12. More recently, and for different reasons, Steve Moyise has also affirmed that certain "fundamental commitments" of the interpreter significantly affect one's analysis of Paul's use of the Old Testament. As an example, Moyise contrasts the "agonistic" theory of quotation from Meir Sternberg that leads to claims that Paul "tore a piece of discourse from its original habitat" with the approach of literary theorists, such as Richard Hays, Ross Wagner, and Francis

In what follows, I focus on the basic "fundamental commitments" (to use Steve Moyise's term[7]) about Scripture that inform Aquinas's approach to Paul's use of the Old Testament—most of which revolves around his theology of participation—with an eye toward modern approaches.[8] Not surprisingly, the burgeoning scholarship on Paul's use of the Old Testament has largely avoided pre-modern approaches to Paul's use of the Old Testament; if pre-modern accounts do appear, they do so often only to highlight the superiority of modern exegetical methods.[9] But pre-modern engagements with Paul's use of the Old Testament help reveal the metaphysical and theological commitments implicit (and often undetected) in modern approaches—commitments that are simply assumed by both scholar and reader. Recovering some of the participatory dimensions of pre-modern approaches, moreover, can aid contemporary exegesis in exploring the full depth of Paul's engagement with Old Testament.

What does a participatory approach to biblical exegesis entail? A participatory approach to biblical exegesis understands the spatio-temporal dimensions of created existence not only as the linear unfolding of individual moments—the approach often taken by modern historical-critical methods—but also as an ongoing participation in God's active providence, both metaphysically (i.e., in the order of creation) and Christologically-pneumatologically (i.e., in the order of grace). In the words of Fr. Lamb, "all singular things and events of all the past, all the present,

---

Watson, who speak of an "embedded meaning" or "potential meaning" that is later unfolded in Paul's discourse. See Moyise,"Quotations," 27. Postmodernist accounts of reading Scripture that claim a text's meaning is generated through the dynamic interaction between text and reader (as well as reader and community) also strongly emphasize the impact of prior commitments on how Scripture (or any text for that matter) will be read; see Rodgers, "Virtues of the Interpreter, 4–81; Fowl, *Engaging Scripture*; Young, "From Suspicion and Sociology to Spirituality, 421–35; Meeks, *In Search of Early Christians*; and *Christ Is the Question*.

7. Moyise, "Quotations," 27.

8. For a more detailed study of Aquinas and participation, see Clarke, *The One and the Many*; Bastit, "Le thomisme est-il un aristotélisme?," 101–16; Schenk, "From Providence to Grace," 307–20.

9. This is true even with the ongoing renewal in biblical interpretation to see pre-modern exegesis as having something to offer modern readings of Scripture and in some cases as superior to modern readings. See David Steinmetz's now-famous article, "The Superiority of Pre-Critical Exegesis," 27–38; see also Boersma, *Heavenly Participation*, 137–53.

and all the future exist and are known in the eternal Triune God."[10] This means, as Fr. Lamb argues, that history is fundamentally redemptive history, since "the concrete events of redemption in the Jewish covenant and the new covenant in Christ Jesus are revelatory of the eternal plan of the Triune God."[11] The biblical texts and their authors, then, "are already historically caught up in a participatory relationship, however obscure, with the trans-temporal realities of faith."[12] A participatory approach to Paul's use of the Old Testament therefore must question the naturalist assumptions of most critical scholarship, in which "not only the empirical findings of science have been conflated with metaphysical naturalism, but also . . . historical-critical textual criticism has uncritically assumed naturalism as a *dogma* rather than as a merely abstractive methodological assumption of scientific inquiry."[13] Insensitivity to the metaphysical differences between much of modern exegesis and Aquinas's exegesis has led, as we shall see, to the erroneous claim that Aquinas is a forerunner to modern (and sometimes postmodern) methods of exegesis due to his emphasis on the literal sense and the role that virtue formation plays in his theory of cognition. But Aquinas's emphasis on the literal sense and the role of virtue for proper interpretation presupposes a participatory ontology in which the world is guided through its participation in God's providential activity in a way often bracketed by modern (and postmodern) approaches to Scripture.

In what follows, I take up Fr. Lamb's participatory approach to biblical exegesis and explore its implication for key components to Aquinas's engagement (and really anyone's engagement) with Paul's use of the Old Testament—the spiritual senses, history, and participation in the faith and life of the church—in conversation with modern approaches.

---

10. Lamb, "Eternity and Time in St. Thomas Aquinas's Lectures on St. John's Gospel," 135.

11. Lamb, "Eternity Creates and Redeems Time, 128.

12. Levering, *Participatory Biblical Exegesis*, 5; see also Levering, *Scripture and Metaphysics*.

13. Gregory, *The Unintended Reformation*, 63n116.

THE UNIQUENESS OF SCARED SCRIPTURE
AND THE SPIRITUAL SENSES

For Aquinas, God's unique activity through the authors of Scripture demands that Scripture be judged as unique among all other writings.[14] Yet this raises the question: if the humanity of the authors of Scripture is fully present in the composition of Scripture, in what way is Scripture unique? One way in which this is so corresponds to the presence of multiple meanings in the text.[15] For Aquinas, all other writings possess only the "literal" or "historical" sense, since all other writings reflect only the human author's intention.[16] Aquinas notes that for Aristotle the intention of a human author is able to correspond to only a single meaning.[17] But the case of Scripture differs significantly from all other writings since the

---

14. In his commentary on 2 Tim 3:16, Aquinas acknowledges Ambrose's claim that all truth from whomever it is spoken is ultimately from the Holy Spirit. What, then, is unique about the inspiration of Scripture? The uniqueness lies in the manner in which God operates through Scripture (versus other writings) to instruct his people in the truth. Aquinas posits two ways in which God operates. God operates both "immediately" as a "special work [*proprium opus*]," such as in a miracle; and God operates "mediately" through inferior causes as a "natural work [*opera naturalia*]." See *ST* I-II.113.10. Here Aquinas's understanding of inspiration comes to the fore. For Aquinas, the divine teacher is so connected to the instruction contained in Scripture that Aquinas claims that God works "immediately" through Scripture to instruct his people, while God works "mediately" through the other writings. It is not merely that God has chosen to use the words of Scripture for his purposes. Rather, the immediacy of God's work of instruction through the Scriptures is rooted in inspiration. We should recall that Aquinas is commenting on 2 Tim 3:16, which states, "All Scripture is divinely inspired [*Omnis scriptura divinitus inspirata*]." It is because the Scriptures are inspired that they are "useful for teaching, for reproof," and so on.

15. I will engage the assertions regarding multiple meanings from postmodernist literary theory below and demonstrate the distance between their claims and Aquinas's position.

16. For Aquinas, literary devices such as parable and metaphor are included as part of the literal sense. *In Gal.* 4.7; *Quodl.* 7.6.2. It is for this reason that Aquinas does not attribute spiritual senses to the art of poetry: although poetry designates certain truths by means of imaginary (*fictum*) similitude, the similitudes are not ordered to something other than what is signified, and thus the signification does not transcend the literal sense. *Quodl.* 7.6.2 ad. 1; 7.6.3, ad 2).

17. See *Quodl.* 7.6.1 arg. 5. The point here is simply that when an uninspired human author communicates something through his or her writing, what the author intends to communicate corresponds to a single meaning. This point does not address the meaning arising from the dynamic interaction between speaker and listener, or the phenomena of a text in its ability to convey meanings unintended by the author.

principal author of Scripture is God.[18] God's intellection differs from human intellection in that unlike human beings God comprehends all things in one act of understanding (*omnia simul suo intellectu comprehendit*).[19] Therefore Scripture as his inspired word is able to communicate multiple meanings at once: the literal and the three spiritual meanings (allegorical, moral, and anagogical).[20] For Karl Froehlich, it is significant that Aquinas never discusses the literal sense in isolation; all "hermeneutical" texts, as Froehlich calls them, discuss the fourfold sense together, and clarifications concerning the literal meaning are incidental to that discussion.[21] This means for Froehlich: "Aquinas is not interested in literature but in the Bible."[22]

In order to grasp Scripture's distinct nature, it is important to emphasize that when Aquinas claims that Paul draws out the "allegorical sense" of the Old Testament, he is not claiming that Paul uses the literary device of allegory, or that allegorical interpretation is merely a textual or intertextual matter.[23] The spiritual sense is not a rhetorical strategy but

18. *Quodl.* 7.6.1, ad 5. Aquinas affirms that the prophets were able to understand many meanings in one "word [*verbo*]," but this is a unique case clearly set aside by Aquinas through his qualification of these authors as God's instrumental causes. They obtained a unique grace in order to "so speak [*ita loquebantur*]" about present things that they intended to signify future realities. But their understanding of the spiritual senses does not amount to their being able to establish or constitute those senses, as we shall see. They could only recognize them.

19. *ST* I.1.10.

20. Postmodern literary theory has argued for the presence of multiple meanings as a characteristic inherent in any given text; see Holub, *Reception Theory*. But Aquinas's affirmation of multiple meanings of Scripture rests on the centrality of divine causality, both in inspiring the text to be written and disposing the reality about which the text is written, thereby making the presence of multiple meanings unique to Scripture. For more on Aquinas and the fourfold sense of Scripture, see de Lubac, *Exégèse Médiévale*, 1:668–681; Mailhiot, "La penseé," 613–63.

21. Not all Scripture verses have all four senses. Depending on the content of the verse, which is the literal or historical sense, Aquinas teaches that some verses may have all four, some three, some two, and some only one. *Quodl.* 7.6.2, ad 5.

22. Froehlich, "Christian Interpretation," 546. Childs also provides "discontinuities" between "so-called secular, universal interpretation of ancient texts and the church's Scripture." Childs, *The Church's Guide*, 44–45.

23. This is not to deny Aquinas's awareness of the literary use of allegory. For Aquinas, allegory simply means that one thing is said and another is understood. See *In Gal.* 4.7.253. This definition is strikingly similar to classical understandings of allegory. See Tryphon, *De tropis* 1.1; Heraclitus, *Homeric Allegories* 5.2; both cited in DiMattei, "Paul's Allegory of the Two Covenants, 104–5. Aquinas recognizes Paul's use of literary allegory when Paul states in Eph 2:21, "In whom all the building, being

rather arises out of an historical reality; or put differently, Aquinas sees God's unique rhetorical strategy located not only in a text but in being itself.[24] The spiritual senses of the Old Testament are derived from *facta* ("activities"),[25] *gesta* ("events"),[26] *ipsum cursum rerum* ("the very course of things"),[27] *in rei veritate* ("things that actually existed"),[28] and *res ipsae* ("things themselves").[29] To understand the spiritual senses of Scripture, as Martin highlights, entails "a Spirit-conferred faith *experience of the reality* mediated by the Sacred Text."[30] Aquinas's emphasis on the *res ipsae* implies that multiple meanings of a text are not due to the text's indeterminacy of meaning but rather to the theological depth of the *res ipsae* as participating in divine providence. Brevard Childs observes that Aquinas's attention to "the ontological force exerted by the subject matter itself (its *res*)" contradicts Eugene Rodgers's and Stephen Fowl's claims that for Aquinas a diversity of meanings occurs through the work of

---

framed together, grows into a holy temple of the Lord." Aquinas comments: "Understood allegorically, this signifies the Church." *S. Eph.* 2.6. Aquinas is not interpreting Paul's statement according to the allegorical sense proper, since Paul is not describing a literal building that is further disposed to signify the church. Rather, Aquinas recognizes that the literal sense of Paul's statement is communicated through an allegory. See also Lubac, *Exégèse Médiévale*, 2:131–40, for his distinction between *allegoria facti* and *allegoria verbi*.

24. Moyise demonstrates the common tendency to reduce allegory to an issue of text when he describes the "simple" rationale behind allegorical interpretation as such: "[I]f the divine had inspired these *texts*, then every sentence, word and letter must have profound meaning." Moyise, *Paul and Scripture*, 51; italics added. I find it noteworthy that Moyise only mentions the turn to "literary theory" as the option for the "theological" approach to Paul's citations. See Moyise, "Quotations," 27. DiMattei, possibly drawing from Jean Daniélou, describes the difference between typology and allegory by claiming the former deals with historical persons, institutions and events, while the later deals merely with *words*. DiMattei, "Biblical Narratives," 63; cf. Daniélou, *From Shadows to Reality*, 11–25, 57–65; for a response to Daniélou's connection of allegory with words and typology with events, see Louth, *Discerning the Mystery*, 118–19.

25. *Quodl.* 7.6.2, ad 5; my translation.

26. Ibid., 7.6.3 s.c., quoting Gregory the Great, *Moralia* 20.1 (PL 76.135).

27. Ibid., 7.6.3.

28. Ibid., 7.6.2, ad 1; as opposed to things in the imagination alone. See Martin, *Sacred Scripture*, 265.

29. *ST* I.1.10.

30. Martin distinguishes between *sensus* as "meaning" and as "understanding." *Sensus* as "understanding," states Martin, "helps us avoid one of the pitfalls of modern literary and biblical criticism, which often restricts itself to what George Steiner characterizes as 'words about words.'" See Martin, *Sacred Scripture*, 249–50; Steiner, *Real Presences*.

"communal assent."³¹ Rather than resulting from indeterminacy of meaning, multiple senses arise out of a depth of meaning; it is a meaning not determined by "communal assent" (although the spiritual community, particularly the church and its graces, provides the location for penetrating the deeper meaning)³² but discovered through prayer, contemplation, participation in the liturgical and sacramental life of the church, and rigorous philosophical and theological study.³³ Given the centrality of the *res ipsae* as foundational for the spiritual senses, spiritual meanings do not dispense with the literal reading. But neither do spiritual meanings simply replicate the literal sense in a different context. Spiritual readings have a distinct meaning, but this meaning is already present in the literal sense. The realities that signify and are expressed by the literal sense are understood as already disposed by God's providence so as to contain in their existence the further signification.³⁴

The spiritual senses are therefore not added to the literal sense like layers of a cake but rather are present in the very existence of the realities conveyed by the literal sense. This is an element that I believe the

---

31. Childs, *Struggle*, 165; see Rodgers, "Virtues of the Interpreter," 65–67; Fowl, *Engaging Scripture*, 39; for a similar postmodernist approach, see Young, "From Suspicion and Sociology to Spirituality," 421–35.

32. Levering raises numerous questions surrounding Fowl's ecclesially-centered approach to interpreting Scripture that hinge on the role of ecclesial authority in determining proper scriptural interpretation. Levering, "Ecclesial Exegesis," 440–53. Levering, writing as a Catholic, raises questions that extend beyond proper interpretation of Scripture and touch on important ecumenical issues surrounding the topic of ecclesiology, a topic ecumenists acknowledge to be a central obstacle to embodying visible unity; see Kasper, "'Credo Unam Sanctam Ecclesiam,'" 84; and Kasper, *That They May All Be One*. Levering is aware that his criticisms touch on Protestant-Catholic debates, suggesting that Fowl's proposal "is an effort to reinsert Scripture and scriptural interpretation into these ecclesial, communal modes from which it was extracted when the sacramental understanding of the Church's authority was, during the Reformation, severely challenged." Levering, "Ecclesial Exegesis," 444. Levering's criticisms demonstrate that broader ecclesiological judgments cannot be elided from the conversation surrounding how proper scriptural interpretation occurs.

33. Although in this study I have been largely critical of the postmodern appropriations of Aquinas that emphasize a text's generated meaning through the dynamic interaction of text and reader (and the dynamic of the reader's formation within the community), Aquinas and postmodern accounts do have an important feature in common: proper formation is intrinsic to being a good reader of Scripture. Whether we are speaking of the acquired virtues or (especially) the infused virtues, Aquinas agrees that a person's formation affects how Scripture is read, and the place of proper formation is within the community of the church; cf., *ST* I.1.9.

34. *Quodl.* 7.6.3.

Pontifical Biblical Commission misses when it posits Aquinas's emphasis on the literal sense against patristic exegesis and in continuity with modern exegesis, claiming that Aquinas began the restoration process of giving "a place of honor" to the literal sense that "culminated in the supremacy of the historical-critical method."[35] It is the same weakness that informs R. M. Grant's interpretation of *Summa theologiae* I.1.10 as "theology's declaration of independence from the allegorical method,"[36] and Joseph Fitzmeyer's claim that Aquinas's emphasis on the literal sense enabled Aquinas to "write off the three nonliteral senses, the allegorical, moral, and anagogical."[37] These evaluations fail to appreciate that for Aquinas it is simply not possible to emphasize the literal sense without simultaneously emphasizing the spiritual senses (where they are present), since the *res ipsae* communicated by the literal sense are already disposed to signify their further spiritual meaning. Aquinas's willingness to give "a place of honor" to the literal sense as the point of access into the spiritual senses should not be misunderstood as displacing the spiritual senses, a phenomenon that often occurs in modern historical-critical approaches to Scripture.[38]

The "already" dimension of the disposition of the *res ipsae* is made possible due to their participation in God's providence; God alone has providential ability to dispose these realities to further signify other realities. Since Scripture is the only inspired word of God—it alone contains the God-inspired record of the historical realities that signify further realities—Scripture is unique in its ability to convey both literal and spiritual senses.[39] Only when we approach Scripture do we approach a

---

35. See Pontifical Biblical Commission, "The Jewish People," 20; cf. Farkasfalvy, "The Pontifical Biblical Commission's Document," 715–37; Kereszty, "Jewish-Christian Dialogue," 738–45; Levering, *Participatory Exegesis*, 90–97.

36. Grant, *A Short History*, 90, cited in Goldsworthy, *Gospel-Centered Hermeneutics*, 104.

37. Fitzmyer, "Scripture in the Catholic Tradition, 154; cited in Levering, *Participatory Exegesis*, 226n20.

38. The implausibility of claims like those of Fitzmeyer and the Pontifical Biblical Commission becomes all the more apparent when we observe Aquinas's actual use of the Old Testament in his Pauline commentary corpus.

39. This is not to deny the fact that creation as a whole participates in a transcendent signification. Louth makes the point that Old Testament "types" are not simply events but "the stories of the events and the significance that is attributed to them in their narration," thus linking allegory with the events as they are recorded in Scripture. Louth, *Discerning the Mystery*, 118–19.

text written through the inspiration of God to communicate realities that God has disposed to signify further realties, all of which lead us, God's friends, to the eternal reward, God himself.[40] For this reason, whether Aquinas engages the literal or the spiritual sense of a text, his concern is not to wrestle between the senses but to "encounter the ultimate and greatest mystery of faith, God and the ways in which He reveals Himself to humanity for our salvation."[41]

THEOLOGY, PHILOSOPHY, AND HISTORY

Aquinas's desire to penetrate through the text in order to encounter the *res* communicated by the text has further implications for his engagement with Paul's use of the Old Testament. Aquinas's penetration into the *res* of the text requires employing concepts and formulations not necessarily present in the biblical author's discourse. Although Childs is mostly appreciative of Aquinas's exegesis,[42] his principal criticism surrounds the way Aquinas sometimes "blurs the particular concerns of the biblical

---

40. Even by the fifteenth century, followers of Aquinas's theory of the spiritual senses, such as Italian Dominican Girolamo Savonarola (1452–1498), had to defend the uniqueness of scriptural allegory against those who argued, in an attempt to bolster the value of the poetic art, that allegory was common to both kinds of writing. In fact as we see in "The Letter to Can Grande," the fourfold sense was applied to Dante's *Commedia* either by Dante himself or by a contemporary of Dante. Dante, "Letter to Can Grande," 99. Savonarola claims that the existence of the spiritual sense requires (a) a solid historical foundation and therefore not fable or fiction; (b) the historical event should signify some other event; (c) the other historical event must "have been both foreseen and ordained and arranged with this signification in mind." Savanarola, *Opus perutile*, cited in Minnis, "Thomistic Literalism," 166–67. As Minnis comments, "We are not dealing here with mere inventions of the apostles and other catholic doctors ... God, who is ultimately responsible for all the meanings of Scripture, is the only author who can use not only words but also things to signify." Ibid. Aquinas's view that spiritual meanings are real meanings belonging to the truth of Scripture is illustrated in his condemnation of Theodore of Mopsuestia's claim that most of the Psalms were later "adapted to Christ," although, according to the letter, they were originally about David. See Verger, "L'exégèse," 206–9.

41. Prügl, "Thomas Aquinas as Interpreter of Scripture," 391–92, cited in Keating and Levering, Introduction to *Commentary on the Gospel of John*, xiv. See the comments of Benedict XVI in *Deus Caritas Est* 12: "The real novelty of the New Testament lies not so much in new ideas as in the figure of Christ himself, who gives flesh and blood to those concepts—an unprecedented realism."

42. See also Childs, *Biblical Theology*, 42.

author."⁴³ For Childs, Aquinas, on the one hand, fails to distinguish to a great enough extent "biblical theology (the theology of the biblical writers themselves)" and systematic theology and therefore does not appreciate enough "the range of questions that are in accord with the intention of the biblical author and those that are only indirectly related to the writer's concern."⁴⁴ On the other hand, Aquinas sometimes "blurs or even conceals" the theological role of the Old Testament in distinction from the New Testament as its "goal."⁴⁵ The issues informing these criticisms are too vast to fully discuss here and include the nature of "canon" and "biblical theology." For our purposes, I note that the extent to which one advocates for the biblical author's "distinct" voice vis-à-vis philosophical or theological reflection not necessarily part of the literal sense of the text, or for the Old Testament's "distinct" theological voice apart from the New Testament will be determined in large part by the extent to which one embraces the participatory character of the *res* communicated through Scripture.⁴⁶ Since, as noted above, Childs affirms Aquinas's attempt to penetrate the *res* communicated by the text, we may then ask: if this *res* participates in the single divine being whose unified salvific economy is recorded in the canon of Scripture, should not the *res* of the Old Testament necessarily have an intrinsic connection to the *res* of the New Testament, thus mitigating the extent to which it is legitimate to speak of the

---

43. Childs, *Struggle*, 163. Congar expressed similar critical remarks of Scholastic exegetical work. He asserts that the danger for the Scholastics was "interpreting the words of Scripture, not by an investigation into the genuine sense of the biblical categories, but by finding out what the same words means to other authors, Aristotle, for example, or what it stands for in a medieval Latin context." Congar, *A History of Theology*, 139. For Congar, the Scholastics sometimes erred by importing theoretical ideas that were foreign to the literal and historical sense. Congar provides examples from Aquinas's exegetical work, such as his application of Aristotle's understanding of wisdom, science, and intelligence to the biblical text.

44. Childs, *Struggle*, 161.

45. Ibid., 163; see also *Biblical Theology*, 8, for Childs's affirmation of the Enlightenment's "discovery" of biblical diversity and the "separate" voices of the Old and New Testaments. For engagements with Childs's affirmation of "separation," see Watson, *Text and Truth*, 216; Levering, "Ecclesial Exegesis, 407–67.

46. Greater attention to the *res* communicated by the text in its participatory character would affect the extent to which Watson's dichotomy between "original meaning" and "contemporary experience" is necessary. Watson states, "The function of canonical scripture is to enable the interpreter to make sense of the world of contemporary experience, and not simply to assign an 'original meaning' to a text: in the end, it is the world rather than the text *per se* that is the object of interpretation." Watson, *Paul and the Hermeneutics of Faith*, 5.

"separate" voices of the Old Testament and the New Testament?[47] Aquinas certainly does not deny the legitimacy of the literal sense of the Old Testament in distinction from the sense that unfolds its relation to the New Testament. But if the spiritual senses are real meanings of the Old Testament, the idea of "separate" voices will need serious qualification. James Samuel Preus's criticisms of Aquinas, particularly that Aquinas leaves "no theological value to the situation of living before the time of Christ's grace, under the mere promise, whereby one would really belong to the old age in fact but the new in faith and hope," are largely marred by his displacement of the role of participation as the foundation of all "value." Preus's lack of a participatory viewpoint becomes clear when he creates a dichotomy between the "value" of the *res* in the Old Testament and the figured *res* embodied in the New Testament, complaining that Aquinas's theory of signification leaves no "unique signification" to "historical" events. Preus's criticisms generally stem from a starting point in which history is presented in purely linear terms and the incarnation, death, and resurrection of Christ are understood more extrinsically in relation to God's salvific economy under the Old Testament.[48] Addressing the sacrifice of Isaac and the crucifixion of Christ, Charles Taylor states, "These two events were linked through their immediate contiguous places in the divine plan. They are drawn close to identity in eternity, even though they are centuries (that is, 'aeons' or 'saecula') apart. In God's time there is a sort of simultaneity of sacrifice and crucifixion."[49] For Aquinas, the spiritual senses are already and intrinsically present in the literal sense. Thus, spiritual readings of the Old Testament that highlight meanings pertinent to the New Testament are not instances of imposing the "separate" voice of the New Testament onto the Old Testament.

In terms of philosophical and theological reflection in exegesis, since for Aquinas the meaning communicated by the biblical authors participates in the single divine wisdom that discloses itself through nature and through revelation, penetrating into the *res* of the Old

---

47. Levering is critical of Childs (as well as Fowl, although on other points) precisely on this issue of participation. Levering, "Ecclesial Exegesis," 427–32; 450–51.

48. Preus, *From Shadow to Promise*, 46–60; see Childs, *Struggle*, 163. Childs tempers Preus's claims by affirming that Aquinas "wrestles with the selfsame ontological reality shared by both testaments" but agrees that Aquinas's emphasis on the New Testament as the "goal" of the Old Testament promise "is such that its theological role can become blurred or even concealed."

49. Taylor, *A Secular Age*, 55, cited in Boersma, *Heavenly Participation*, 126.

Testament (and New Testament) requires employing philosophical and theological categories not necessarily present in the immediate discourse of the human authors. This need not be interpreted as a foreign imposition upon Scripture, since, as Levering states, "biblical exegesis requires such metaphysical and theological precisions, once one treats the word 'God' as intelligible and presumes that the *sacra doctrina* in one part of the Bible illumines, rather than contradicts, the true meaning of the *sacra doctrina* in other parts of the Bible. Exegesis, on this view, constitutes an intelligent, doctrinally informed participation in the sacred teaching, and thus cannot be limited to teasing out the sense of the text strictly in terms of the explanatory categories available to the human author of the text."[50] The extent to which one embraces the participatory character of the created order will impact the extent to which one regards the biblical author as having a "separate" voice from philosophical or theological categories employed in understanding the author's discourse.[51] Graeme Goldsworthy's criticisms are representative of those who bifurcate the positive relationship between created reality as a whole and the reality communicated in the Bible through their common participation in God's guiding wisdom—criticisms which lead to an undervaluing of the contribution of philosophy to biblical reflection. He states, "Thomas shows that medieval theological thought had become so intertwined with unbiblical philosophical categories that the resulting hermeneutics was seriously compromised."[52] If by "unbiblical" one simply means that the philosophical categories used in explicating the text are not immediately present in the text, there is no reason to think this *de facto* "seriously compromises" biblical interpretation.[53]

---

50. Levering, "Reading John with St. Thomas Aquinas," 104. Fowl has criticized Childs's approach for what amounts to a layering effect in constructing "Biblical Theology": first, historical-critical research discloses the particular voices of the Bible, and only then comes the canonical synthetic construal of "Biblical Theology." Fowl, *Engaging Scripture*, 25–26.

51. The harmony between the mind's engagement with created reality itself and the reality presented in the biblical witness is essential to Aquinas's theological reflection upon Scripture. Aquinas employed Platonic and Aristotelian propositions while unfolding the biblical text based on the conviction that the truth presented in Scripture harmonizes with the truth discovered about the created order as a whole.

52. Goldsworthy, *Gospel-Centered Hermeneutics*, 108. Goldsworthy's criticisms, and criticisms like Goldworthy's, need further reflection on the positive relationship between created reality as a whole and the reality communicated in the Bible through their participation in God's guiding wisdom.

53. Moreover, sweeping criticisms of Aquinas's "Aristotelianizing" of biblical

By locating the spiritual senses in the signification intrinsic within historical realities (*res*), Aquinas presupposes in his approach to Paul's use of the Old Testament an understanding of history that differs substantially from the presuppositions that largely guide modern biblical studies. Rather than approaching history as a "closed continuum" of cause and effects in which no place is given to the transcendent or supernatural—an approach Brian Daley has termed "methodologically atheistic"[54]—Aquinas approaches history and time as participatory in the eternal presence of God, which opens time and history to embodying "the mystery . . . of the eternally present Christological dimension of the events of salvation history as this moves through the succession of 'before and after.'"[55] From the viewpoint of history as participatory, the historical-critical method does not err in taking history too seriously; rather it does not take history seriously enough. By engaging history in solely linear and atomistic terms, it fails to engage human time as "already metaphysically participatory in God, sharing ever more deeply in the infinite wisdom and love of divine action."[56] For Aquinas, a true historical reading of the Old Testament does not avoid any and all references to the New Testament but rather plumbs the depths of history to discover God's providential disposition of the historical events in their signification of New Testament realities. Again, Aquinas's affirmation of the full presence of the human authors in the composition of Scripture requires an appreciation for all the "messiness" that comes with being time- and space-bound creatures, and tools that assist in understanding these features are welcome. Yet the New Testament writers cannot be understood as separated from the historical realities conveyed in the Old Testament by a linear succession of time; rather, for Aquinas, the New Testament writers also participate in God unfolding the depth contained in the historical realities of the Old Testament through their participation in the divine providence. As Daniel Keating and Matthew Levering observe, the very presence of the "extraordinary profusion" of parallel texts in Aquinas's commentaries demonstrates a freedom to move throughout the Old and New Testa-

---

theology would also do well to reflect on Aquinas's own criticisms of philosophy: "Any philosopher who has said something that belong to the truth has not said it without a mixture of falseness. Just one old woman knows more about the things that pertain to faith than heretofore all philosophers." Aquinas, "Sermon 14," 202.

54. Daley, "Is Patristic Exegesis Still Usable?," 185–216.
55. Martin, *Sacred Scripture*, 240–41; see also von Balthasar, *A Theology of History*.
56. Levering, *Participatory Exegesis*, 7.

ments that is "only possible for one who believes that the realities of faith are present and active throughout history, preparing for and/or fulfilling the work of deification in Christ through the Holy Spirit."[57]

FAITH AND THE LIFE OF THE CHURCH

The inspiration of Scripture, as noted above, pertains principally to God cultivating friendship with human beings. Through the inspired prophets and apostles, God discloses his heart to us, bringing us into a participation in the divine mysteries. As Aquinas states of friendship with God, "Through the Holy Spirit not only is God in us, but also we are in God."[58] The biblical text is therefore never merely raw text to be exploited; rather, it is an invitation to encounter the *res ipsae* communicated principally by God himself. For friendship with God to be established, the Spirit of God must indwell the person, producing within the person faith animated by love. Without the presence of faith, the person cannot encounter the mysteries being revealed in the *sacrae litterae*. The prophets and apostles needed a special light in order to see the mysteries and disclose them to God's people;[59] God's people also need a special light—the light of faith—in order to receive and contemplate those mysteries now revealed.[60] Necessitating the presence of faith for properly engaging the Scriptures is not meant to blind the reader to the messiness of the text and its composition and redaction history. Faith does, however, provide the interpreter a deeper understanding of God, which thus opens the interpreter to trusting the providence of God in ways fitting to a divine Friend ensuring our friendship with him in faith, hope, and love. By penetrating into the mysteries being taught in the sacred scriptures, the person of faith will often find what seem like contradictions and misinterpretations as opportunities for deeper penetration into the *sacra doctrina* of Scripture. Affirming the presence of spiritual senses is in fact an act of faith; it requires belief in God's creative activity and particular providential oversight of the created order. Moreover, Aquinas affirms the intentional obscurity of passages of Scripture in order to protect the truth from the ridicule of the "impious," citing Matthew 7:6, "Do not

---

57. Keating and Levering, Introduction to *Commentary on John*, xvii.
58. *SCG* 4.21.4.
59. *De Ver.* 12.3.
60. *ST* II-II.1.1 and 4. See Nutt, "Things Not Seen," 372–89.

give what is holy to dogs."[61] Without the presence of faith, the reader is unable to penetrate into the knowledge of the truth. Faith animated by love therefore enables the interpreter of Scripture to reach the goal of Scripture: charitable union with God.

Yet we should not understand the need for faith solely in terms of the individual, making interpretation simply the result of the person of faith reading his or her bible. Aquinas looks to the community of faith as an essential part to the proper reading of Scripture. For Aquinas, the same Spirit that inspired the biblical teachers has guided the church to understand this teaching.[62] Christopher Stanley sums up the modern approach to Paul's use of Old Testament passages when he states: "Recent interpreters, in an effort to avoid reading later theological concerns *back into* Paul's argument, have turned their attention to the hermeneutical question of how Paul understood and interpreted the biblical text."[63] A similar concern is reflected in Hays's request that his audience read Paul's letters as "non-Scripture," since, Hays states, Paul did not think of himself as a writer of Scripture.[64] To read Paul as "non-Scripture" is to ignore the church's recognition that his letters are in fact Scripture.[65] Rather than seeking to displace the church's later theological "concerns," Aquinas sees these concerns as part of the church's ongoing participation in the Teacher who inspired Paul's teaching.[66] For Aquinas, the church plays a

---

61. *ST* I.1.9.

62. See *SCG* III.154.19 where Aquinas notes that those who received revelation from God passed along this revelation not only in speech but also in writing in order to instruct those who were to come later. "Thus it was also necessary that there be those who could interpret what was written down. This also must be by divine grace. And so we read in Genesis 40:8, 'Does not interpretation come from God?'"

63. Stanley, *Arguing with Scripture*, 11; italics added. Boersma makes the interesting connection between the modern emphasis on the literal sense (as the expense of the spiritual senses) and the displacement of the church's tradition: "A hermeneutic that limits itself to the literal or historical meaning of the texts tends to coincide with a low view of tradition: the individual reader does not need the church's tradition to find the 'objective' meaning of the text." Boersma, *Heavenly Participation*, 141.

64. Hays, *Echoes*, 5.

65. This is not an insignificant point. If Paul's writings are in fact Scripture, this takes us back to the topic of inspiration and the effects of our understanding of inspiration on our reading of Paul's use of the Old Testament.

66. On the integration of Scripture and the church's teaching, Aquinas states, "The formal objective of faith is the First Truth as this is made known in Sacred Scripture and in the teaching of the Church which proceeds from the First Truth." Aquinas, *ST* II-II.5.3. "The formal *ratio* of the object in faith is the First Truth made known through the teaching of the Church." *De Car.* 13, ad 6.

role in the transmission of Scripture, and therefore there can be "no clear-cut separation between Scripture, on the one hand, and the authoritative documents in the history of the Church on the other . . . The tradition of the Church [is] to a large extent the tradition of explaining Scripture."[67] The "sacramental time" of the church, as Yves Congar describes it, avoids the modern separation and compartmentalization of the various periods within the church's reflection on Scripture and enables the coincidence of past, present, and future.[68] In this light, the *regula fidei* and the tradition of the church are not seen in extrinsic terms of power, merely setting the boundaries of what are acceptable and what are not acceptable readings of Scripture. Rather, the tradition provides the space in which fruitful readings of Scripture may occur.[69] Lamb sums up Aquinas's exegetical approach this way: "Aquinas could not abstract the Book from its living environment within the ecclesial tradition. The generations of Christians stretching from Apostolic times down to their own were not viewed by the medieval mind as *separating* them from the integral Christian message but far more as *uniting* them to it."[70]

It would be a caricature of Aquinas's exegesis, however, to see him as simply synthesizing prior exegesis, as if Aquinas makes no unique contributions of his own. Rather, as demonstrated in his exegetical practice, Aquinas feels free to disagree with certain theological judgments of the Fathers and sets aside erroneous interpretations found in the *glossa*. Aquinas's focus on the divine intention also does not mean that interpretations are left unchecked by the human author's intention in the passage.

67. Valkenberg, *Words of the Living God*, 11; see Elders, "Aquinas on Holy Scripture," 151.

68. Congar, *Tradition and Traditions*, 259–61; Congar, *La Foi et La Théologie*, 43, 99, 105–6; Boersma, *Heavenly Participation*, 122–30, who attributes the modern separation of time into discrete and separated moments to a univocal concept of being.

69. See Louth, *Discerning the Mystery*, 107–12. The role of tradition for Aquinas, however, according to Healy, "does not anticipate the later Roman Catholic doctrine of two sources of revelation, Scripture and Church tradition." Faith rests on the canonical books alone (See *ST* I.1.8 ad.2), and even when Aquinas acknowledges an oral apostolic tradition, "this has no authority with regard to doctrine, but applies only to specific practices." Keating and Levering, Introduction to *Commentary on the Gospel of John*, 18; see *ST* III.64.2, ad 1.

70. Lamb, Introduction to the *Commentary on Ephesians*, 19. Ian Levy notes that, due to the belief that Scripture was ultimately authored by the Spirit, "there was a sense in which the text is never really closed, its meaning never fixed, since the divine author is continually inspiring readers and disclosing as yet undiscovered truths." Levy, *Letter to the Galatians*, 10.

Oftentimes Aquinas appeals to the "author's intent" as he dismisses prior interpretations.[71] Aquinas is true to his methodological principle that understands the authority of Scripture as the sole "incontrovertible proof" in *sacra doctrina* and the authority of the doctors of the church as only "probable."[72] Yet for some contemporary scholars of Paul's use of the Old Testament, Aquinas's reverence for the church's exegetical and theological tradition makes his exegesis suspect.[73] This is the case particularly with those who believe that New Testament interpretation should set out, in the words of John Ashton, "to come up with an idea or an argument that is at the same time fresh, interesting, and not too far-fetched."[74] Aquinas cannot conceive of interpreting Scripture *around* the church's history of interpretation but only *in* and *through* it.[75]

CONCLUSION

The spiritual senses, theology and philosophy, history, faith, and church tradition—each of these areas impacts one's interpretation of Paul's use of the Old Testament, and each of these areas is impacted by a doctrine of participation. Little attention has been given to the implications of a participatory view of the divine-human relationship in studies on Paul's interpretation of the Old Testament. This is unfortunate. In many cases where contemporary exegetes posit a dichotomous relationship between two realities (e.g., Scripture versus the church; revelation versus the text;

---

71. For example, *In Rom.* 2.4.227; 3.1.259; 3.4.320; 4.1.331; 5.4.427; 7.1.520; and 8.1.609.

72. *ST* I.1.8. For more on Aquinas's treatment of the *auctoritas* of the Fathers, see Chenu, *Toward Understanding Saint Thomas*, 139-49.

73. DiMattei, for example, claims that the interpretations of the Fathers "tell us less about what Paul meant than they do about the apologetic and hermeneutical *agenda* of early Christian exegetes as they vied to defend Paul's scriptural hermeneutic from contending 'heretical' positions." DiMattei, "Biblical Narratives," 61; italics added. DiMattei's own approach, however, which emphasizes Paul's "reshaping" of the biblical story in a new context—the "Abraham-Christ" story as opposed to (for DiMattei) the "biblical" story—displays a search for an exegetical practice that could benefit greatly from Aquinas's understanding of the relationship between the literal and spiritual senses of Scripture.

74. Ashton, *Religion of Paul*, 244.

75. In this way, Aquinas has much more in common with the ancient world of the New Testament Scriptures themselves than does much modern exegesis. See Young, "Pastoral Epistles," 114, who comments, "The ancient world was far more interested in tradition than novelty . . . Ancient wisdom was valued rather than creative genius."

the Old Testament versus the New Testament; the literal sense versus the spiritual sense; biblical exegesis versus theological and philosophical reflection), Aquinas's participatory vision embraces each of these realities as mutually informing so as to enable the reader of Scripture to penetrate the divine mysteries and be lead, ultimately, to the beatific end of the wayfarer journey. Aquinas situates Paul's use of the Old Testament within God's cultivation of friendship with his people through disclosing his heart (i.e., the divine mysteries). Such cultivation of friendship imparts to the exegete, in the words of Fr. Lamb, "faith-illuminated knowledge and wisdom about the *telos* or end of the whole of redeemed creation,"[76] which enables the reader of Scripture to have a proper eschatology and thus to contemplate the unified salvific economy of God unfolded throughout the writings of Scripture as part of the believer's *vita gratiae* culminating in the *vita gloriae*.

BIBLIOGRAPHY

Aquinas, Thomas. "Sermon 14: *Attendite a falsis*." Translated by Mark-Robin Hoogland. In *Thomas Aquinas: The Academic Sermons*. Fathers of the Church 11. Washington, DC: Catholic University of America Press, 2010.

———. *Commentary on Saint Paul's Epistle to the Ephesians by St. Thomas Aquinas*. Translated by Matthew Lamb. Albany, NY: Magi, 1966.

———. *Quaestiones quodlibetales*. Corpus Thomisticum: S. Thomae de Aquino Opera Omnia. http://www.corpusthomisticum.org/iopera.html.

———. *Summa Theologiae*. Corpus Thomisticum: S. Thomae de Aquino Opera Omnia. http://www.corpusthomisticum.org/iopera.html.

Ashton, John. *The Religion of Paul the Apostle*. New Haven: Yale University Press, 2000.

von Balthasar, Hans Urs. *A Theology of History*. San Francisco: Ignatius, 1994.

Bastit, Michel. "Le thomisme est-il un aristotélisme?" *Revue Thomiste* 102 (2001) 101–16.

Beale, G. K. *Handbook on the New Testament Use of the Old Testament: Exegesis and Interpretation*. Grand Rapids: Baker Academic, 2012.

Benedict XVI. *Deus Caritas Est*. http://w2.vatican.va/content/benedict-xvi/en/encyclicals/documents/hf_ben-xvi_enc_20051225_deus-caritas-est.html.

Boersma, Hans. *Heavenly Participation: The Weaving of a Sacramental Tapestry*. Grand Rapids: Eerdmans, 2011.

Chenu, M.-D. *Toward Understanding Saint Thomas*. Translated by A.-M. Landry and D. Hughes. Chicago: Regnery, 1964.

Childs, Brevard. *Biblical Theology of the Old and New Testaments: Theological Reflection on the Christian Bible*. Minneapolis: Fortress, 1993.

Clarke, W. Norris. *The One and the Many: A Contemporary Thomistic Metaphysics*. Notre Dame: University of Notre Dame Press, 2001.

---

76. Lamb, "Wisdom Eschatology," 259.

Congar, Yves. *A History of Theology*. Translated and Edited by Hunter Guthrie. Garden City, NY: Doubleday, 1968.

———. *La Foi et la théologie*. Tournai: Desclée, 1962.

———. *Tradition and Traditions: The Biblical, Historical, and Theological Evidence for Catholic Teaching on Tradition*. Translated by Michael Naseby and Thomas Rainborough. San Diego: Basilica, 1966.

Daley, Brian. "Is Patristic Exegesis Still Usable?" *Communio: International Catholic Review* 29 (2000) 185–216.

Daniélou, Jean. *From Shadows to Reality: Studies in the Biblical Typology of the Fathers*. Translated by W. Hibberd. Westminster, MD: Newman, 1960.

de Lubac, Henri. *Exégèse médiévale. Les quatre sens de l'Écriture*. 4 volumes. Paris: Aubier, 1959–1964.

Dante, "The Letter to Can Grande." In *Literary Criticism of Dante Alighieri*, translated and edited by Robert S. Haller, 95–114. Lincoln: University of Nebraska Press, 1973.

DiMattei, Steven. "Paul's Allegory of the Two Covenants (Gal 4.21–31) in Light of First-Century Hellenistic Rhetoric and Jewish Hermeneutics." *NTS* 52 (2006) 102–22.

Elders, Leo. "Aquinas on Holy Scripture as the Medium of Divine Revelation." In *La Doctrine de la révélation divine de saint Thomas d'Aquin*, edited by Leo Elders, 132–52. Città del Vaticano: Libreria Editrice Vaticana, 1990.

Farkasfalvy, Denis. "The Pontifical Biblical Commission's Document on Jews and Christians and Their Scriptures: Attempt at an Evaluation." *Communio* 29 (2002) 715–37.

Fitzmyer, Joseph. "Scripture in the Catholic Tradition." In *Living Traditions of the Bible: Scripture in Jewish, Christian, and Muslim Practice*, edited by James Bowley, 145–62. St. Louis: Chalice, 1999.

Fowl, Stephen. *Engaging Scripture*. Malden, MA: Blackwell, 1998.

Goldsworthy, Graeme. *Gospel-Centered Hermeneutics: Foundations and Principles of Evangelical Biblical Interpretation*. Downers Grove, IL: Intervarsity, 2010.

Grant, R. M. *A Short History of the Interpretation of the Bible*. Philadelphia: Fortress, 1984.

Gregory, Brad S. *The Unintended Reformation: How a Religious Revolution Secularized Society*. Cambridge, MA: Harvard University Press, 2012.

Hays, Richard. *Echoes of Scripture in the Letters of Paul*. New Haven: Yale University Press, 1989.

Holub, Robert C. *Reception Theory*. London: Methuen, 1984.

Kasper, Walter. "'Credo Unam Sanctam Ecclesiam'—The Relationship Between the Catholic and Protestant Principles in Fundamental Ecclesiology." In *Receptive Ecumenism and the Call to Catholic Learning: Exploring a Way for Contemporary Ecumenism*, edited by Paul Murray, 78–88. Oxford: Oxford University Press, 2008.

———. *That They May All Be One: A Call To Unity Today*. New York: Continuum, 2005.

Keating, Daniel, and Matthew Levering. Introduction to *Commentary on the Gospel of John: Chapters 1–5*, by St. Thomas Aquinas. Translated by Fabian Larcher and James A. Weisheipl. Washington, DC: Catholic University of America Press, 2010.

Kereszty, Roch. "The Jewish-Christian Dialogue and the Pontifical Biblical Commission's Document on 'The Jewish People and Their Sacred Scriptures in the Christian Bible,'" *Communio: International Catholic Review* 29 (2002) 738–45.

Lamb, Matthew. "Eternity Creates and Redeems Time: The Theology of History in St. Augustine." In *Divine Creation in Ancient, Medieval, and Early Modern Thought: Essays Presented to the Rev. Robert Crouse*, edited by M. Treschow et al., 117–40. Leiden: Brill, 2007.

———. *Eternity, Time and the Life of Wisdom*. Ave Maria, FL: Sapientia, 2007.

———. "Eternity and Time in St. Thomas Aquinas's Lectures on St. John's Gospel." In *Reading John with St. Thomas Aquinas: Theological Exegesis and Speculative Theology*, edited by Michael Dauphinais and Mathew Levering, 127–39. Washington, DC: Catholic University of America Press, 2005.

———. "Introduction." In *Commentary on Saint Paul's Epistle to the Ephesians by St. Thomas Aquinas*, translated by Matthew Lamb. Albany, NY: Magi Books, 1966.

———. "Wisdom Eschatology in Augustine and Aquinas." In *Aquinas the Augustinian*, edited by Michael Dauphinais et al., 258–76. Washington, DC: Catholic University of America Press, 2007.

Levering, Matthew. "Ecclesial Exegesis and Ecclesial Authority: Childs, Fowl, and Aquinas." *Thomist* 69 (2005) 407–67.

———. *Participatory Biblical Exegesis: A Theology of Biblical Interpretation*. Notre Dame, IN: University of Notre Dame Press, 2008.

———. "Reading John with St. Thomas Aquinas." In *Aquinas on Scripture: An Introduction to His Biblical Commentaries*, edited by Thomas Weinandy et al., 99–126. London: T. & T. Clark, 2005.

———. *Scripture and Metaphysics: Aquinas and the Renewal of Trinitarian Theology*. Malden, MA: Blackwell, 2004.

Levy, Ian. *Letter to the Galatians*. Bible in Medieval Tradition. Grand Rapids: Eerdmans, 2011.

Louth, Andrew. *Discerning the Mystery: An Essay on the Nature of Theology*. Oxford: Clarendon, 1990.

Mailhiot, M. D. "La penseé de saint Thomas sur le sens spirituel." *Revue Thomiste* 59 (1959) 613–63.

Martin, Francis. *Sacred Scripture: The Disclosure of the Word*. Naples, Fl: Sapientia, 2006.

Meeks, Wayne. *Christ Is the Question*. Louisville: Westminster John Knox, 2006.

———. *In Search of Early Christians*. New Haven: Yale University, 2002.

Minnis, J. "Fifteenth-Century Versions of Thomistic Literalism: Girolamo Savonarola and Alfonso de Madrigal." In *Neue Richtungen in der hoch- und spätmittelalterlichen Bibelexegese*, edited by Robert E. Lerner, 163–80. Munich: Oldenbourg, 1996.

Moyise, Steve. *Evoking Scripture: Seeing the Old Testament in the New*. London: T. & T. Clark, 2008.

———. *Paul and Scripture: Studying the New Testament Use of the Old Testament*. Grand Rapids: Baker Academic, 2010.

———. "Quotations." In *As It Is Written: Studying Paul's Use of Scripture*, edited by Stanley Porter and Christopher D. Stanley, 15–28. Atlanta: SBL, 2008.

Nutt, Roger W. "The Proof of Things Not Seen: Thomas Aquinas on the Role of Reason in the Act of Faith." *Josephinum* 15 (2008) 372–89.

Pontifical Biblical Commission. "The Jewish People and Their Sacred Scripture in the Christian Bible." http://www.vatican.va/roman_curia/congregations/cfaith/pcb_documents/rc_con_cfaith_doc_20020212_popolo-ebraico_en.html.

Porter, Stanley, and Christopher D. Stanley. *As It Is Written: Studying Paul's Use of Scripture*. Atlanta: SBL, 2008.

Prügl, Thomas. "Thomas Aquinas as Interpreter of Scripture." In *The Theology of Thomas Aquinas*, edited by Rik Van Nieuwenhove and Joseph Wawrykov, 386-415. Notre Dame, IN: University of Notre Dame Press, 2005.

Preus, James Samuel. *From Shadow to Promise: Old Testament Interpretation from Augustine to the Young Luther.* Cambridge, MA: Belknap, 1969.

Rodgers, Eugene. "How the Virtues of the Interpreter Presuppose and Perfect Hermeneutics: The Case of Thomas Aquinas." *Journal of Religion* 76 (1996) 64-81.

Schenk, Richard. "From Providence to Grace: Thomas Aquinas and the Platonisms of the Mid-Thirteenth Century." *Nova et Vetera* 3 (2005) 307-20.

Steinmetz, David. "The Superiority of Pre-Critical Exegesis." *Theology Today* 37 (1980) 27-38.

Steiner, George. *Real Presences.* Chicago: University of Chicago Press, 1989.

Taylor, Charles. *A Secular Age.* Cambridge, MA: Belknap, 2007.

Valkenberg, Wilhelmus G. B. M. *Words of the Living God: Place and Function of Holy Scripture in the Theology of St. Thomas Aquinas.* Leuven: Peeters, 2000.

Verger, Jacques. "L'exégèse de l'Université." In *Le Moyen Âge et la Bible*, edited by Pierre Riché and Guy Lobrichon, 199-232. Paris: Beauchesne, 1984.

Watson, Francis. *Text and Truth: Redefining Biblical Theology.* Grand Rapids: Eerdmans, 1997.

Young, Francis. "From Suspicion and Sociology to Spirituality: On Method, Hermeneutics and Appropriation with Response to Patristic Material." *Studia Patristica* 29 (1997) 421-35

———. "The Pastoral Epistles and the Ethics of Reading." *Journal of the Study of the New Testament* 45 (1992) 105-20.

6

Monica as Mystagogue
Time and Eternity at Ostia[1]

Gerald Boersma

But to apprehend
The point of intersection of the timeless
With time, is an occupation for the saint—
No occupation either, but something given
And taken, in a lifetime's death in love,
Ardour and selflessness and self-surrender.

T.S. Eliot, *The Dry Salvages*

"Mystagogue" is a term that, in the Christian faith, hearkens back to the patristic world. A μυσταγωγός is one responsible for "initiating into mysteries."[2] It was the role of the bishop to "hand over" the sacred mysteries to the catechumens as his final act in their preparation to receive

---

1. This essay is offered in grateful appreciation of Fr. Matthew Lamb's ministry as priest and scholar. I have been profoundly enriched (and in ways that perhaps I still do not fully realize) by Fr. Lamb's wisdom and guidance.

2. LSJ.

the fullness of the faith at Easter. He would initiate the neophytes into the mysteries in which they were to participate, namely Baptism and Eucharist. Well-known examples include the "Mystagogical Homilies" of Cyril of Jerusalem and Ambrose's *De mysteriis*. Related definitions of μυσταγωγός include "generally, *teacher, guide*" and also, more specifically a *"Christian priest."*[3]

The mystagogue serves especially a *priestly* role in that the mystagogue bears the mystery of God and initiates those entrusted to him into this mystery. As priest he *links* heaven and earth, offering humanity's gifts to the Father and offering God's gift to his people. In this sacred exchange the mystagogue initiates God's people into the very mystery of Being itself. By linking earth with heaven, the finite with the infinite, the mystagogue acts as the instrument of the Spirit who invites a recalibration of vision to see the whole world suffused with the divine presence; to see the Divine who, beguiled by his own goodness, comes to abide in all things.[4] In short, the mystagogue is habitually attentive to the presence of eternity within life's transience; he is attentive to what St. Augustine describes as *totum esse praesens*.[5] The mystagogue draws others into this speculative, contemplative gaze of eternity. In this sense, Fr. Matthew Lamb is a mystagogue. His *Lebenswerk* as a theologian is to invite others to see the interplay of eternity and time; to contemplate the God who at once utterly transcends the diastemic character of time and yet draws time and its manifold goods into his eternal embrace. As a student under Fr. Lamb, I remember well how he would reiterate that our animating Christian hope remains God's eternity, in which nothing is lost, but all is perfected: the immense aspirations and efforts of countless human beings in acquiring skills, developing intellectual and moral virtues—the wisdom of Socrates, Plato, Aristotle—all these noble and godlike achievements are

---

3. LSJ.

4. Cf. Dionysius the *Areopagite*: "And, in truth, it must be said too that the very cause of the universe in the beautiful, good superabundance of his benign yearning for all is also carried outside of himself in the loving care he has for everything. He is, as it were, beguiled by his goodness, by love, and by yearning and is enticed away from the transcendent dwelling place and comes to abide within all things, and he does so by virtue of his supernatural and ecstatic capacity to remain, nevertheless, within himself." Dionysius, *On the Divine Names*, 4.13.

5. *Conf.* 11.11.13: "In the eternal, nothing is transient, but the whole is present" (*totum esse praesens*). I have used the translation by Chadwick and the *CCSL* Latin text.

not destined to end in death and obliteration. The eternal is no apersonal permanence; the eternal is inter-personal presence.[6]

Fr. Lamb recognizes in Augustine's striking exposition of eternity as *totum esse praesens* a uniquely Christian—indeed, a hope-filled—understanding of time and eternity. If the mystagogue draws his *discipuli* into the contemplation of eternal being and its temporal implications, then Fr. Lamb is truly a mystagogue.

In this essay, I will argue that in the riveting scene of mystical ecstasy at Ostia in *Confessions* 9.10.23–26, Augustine presents his mother, Monica, as a mystagogue, who draws in Augustine to share her contemplative gaze of eternity, so that Augustine comes to understand eternity as *totum esse praesens*. The mystical experience at Ostia, in which Augustine recounts, "[o]ur minds were lifted up by ardent affection towards eternal being itself," is an experience of ascent not unique to Book 9 of the *Confessions*. But the fact that Monica is present is unique. What is the significance of her participation in the experience at Ostia? This question becomes more acute when placed in the context of Augustine's previous attempt at ascent in *Confessions* VII, where his mother is notably absent. Monica's presence at Ostia becomes significant when we consider how she is depicted in the only other works where she features prominently, namely, the Cassiciacum dialogues (particularly, *De beata vita* and *De ordine*). As such, we will first consider how Monica is portrayed in the Dialogues, namely, as a true philosopher in possession of eternal wisdom to which she guides her disciples. Second, we will examine how this portrait finds completion at Ostia, in which, at the end of Monica's life, she is united with her son in an experience of the eternity to which her philosophy was consistently ordered.

MONICA AT CASSICIACUM

The dialogues anticipate the presentation of Monica as the *mulier sapiens* at Ostia. Here at Cassiciacum she is the woman endowed with a particular (divine) gift of wisdom, guiding those under her tutelage to eternal wisdom.[7] In the dialogues it is reiterated that Monica does not speak

---

6. Lamb, *Eternity, Time, and the Life of Wisdom*, 52.

7. O'Donnell points to "parallels in antiquity" for Monica's presence in Augustine's writings, especially in Plato's Diotima in the *Symposium*. Cf. O'Donnell, *Confessions*, 123. Cf. O'Farrell, "Monica, the Mother of Augustine," 23–43; Cacciavillani, *Mamma fino a diventare santa*; Lamirande, "Quand Monique," 3–19; Djuth, "Augustine, Monica, and the Love of Wisdom," 237–52.

with an authority derived from an extensive education in the liberal arts, but from an authority grounded in faith, hope, and love whereby she leads, guides, and nurtures her "children" into eternal Wisdom. Her mystagogical vocation finds its culmination at Ostia.

De beata vita is a dialogue that spans a three-day celebration in honor of Augustine's birthday. In each of the three days Monica interjects to offer a decisive contribution to the overarching question about what constitutes the happy life. In the introduction Augustine lists the contributors to the philosophical colloquy. In the first place, he writes, "our mother" (*nostra mater*) was present.[8] The first person plural not only suggests Monica's spiritual motherhood of all present, but also anticipates the ecclesial character she will represent. It is on her account, writes Augustine, that "I owe everything that I live."[9] Augustine inquires whether one who possesses what he wants is happy. Monica answers, "If he wishes and possesses good things, he is happy; if he desires evil things—no matter if he possesses them—he is wretched."[10] At this point Augustine is elated; he smiles and remarks gladly, "Mother, you have really gained the mastery of the very stronghold of philosophy" (*arcem philosophiae*).[11] Augustine continues by saying that his mother has given a definition of philosophy consonant with that offered by Cicero in the *Hortensius*. She has explained that happiness consists not in living according to the dictates of the will, but, rather, according to a will that is rightly ordered. On this account, evil is not the failure to attain what we desire, but consists, rather, in disordered desires. Philosophy is principally concerned with achieving the happy life and, therefore, after taking note of Monica's exposition of *vera philosophia* as rightly ordered love, Augustine remarks, "At these words our mother exclaimed in such a way that we, entirely forgetting her sex, thought we had some great man in our midst, while in the meantime I became fully aware whence and from what divine source this flowed" (*diuino fonte manarent*).[12]

---

8. *beata u.* 1.6 (CCSL 29:68).

9. Ibid.: *in primis nostra mater, cuius meriti credo esse omne, quod uiuo.*

10. Ibid., 2.10 (CCSL 29:70): *Si bona, inquit, uelit et habeat, beatus est, si autem mala uelit, quamuis habeat, miser est.*

11. Ibid.: *ipsam, inquam, prorsus, mater, arcem philosophiae tenuisti.*

12. Ibid.: *In quibus uerbis illa sic exclamabat, ut obliti penitus sexus eius magnum aliquem uirum considere nobis cum crederemus me interim, quantum poteram, intellegente, ex quo illa et quam diuino fonte manarent.*

Although uneducated in the philosophical tradition, Monica offers an account of wisdom comparable to that of Cicero. An infused gift from a "divine source" (*diuino fonte*) allows her to speak as "a great man" (*magnum uirum*). The conversation is steered toward a consideration of what might be a fitting object of rightly ordered love. The nature of happiness entails that our desires not rest in any finite good. After all, the possession of many temporal goods is fraught with the fear of losing them. Again, Monica makes the decisive contribution: happiness, she explains, lies not in the possession of things, but in the moderation of mind.[13] Augustine is, once again, exuberant in his response: "'Very well expressed,' I said. 'No better answer to my question could be expected, and no other one from you.'"[14] Monica has led the colloquy to the conclusion that the appropriate object of love must be "eternal and remaining" (*aeternus et semper manens*), and the conclusion follows that "whoever possess God is happy."[15]

Even a person who has an abundance of temporal possessions but nonetheless lacks eternal wisdom should be considered in want and miserable, remarks Monica.[16] All were amazed and admired Monica's assertion; Augustine himself remarks, "I myself was filled with joy and delight because it was she who had uttered that truth which, as gleaned from the books of the philosophers, I had intended to bring forward as an imposing final argument."[17] Monica's contributions consistently sublimate temporal good to eternal good; happiness consists above all in possessing eternal wisdom. Monica had obtained this wisdom, not "from the books of the philosophers" but as an infused gift from God. This is abundantly clear in the closing scene of *De beata vita*. Monica, brimming with faith and joy, prays the hymn she received from St. Ambrose: *foue precantes, trinitas*.[18] Then she concludes, "Indeed, this is undoubtedly the happy life, that is, the perfect life, which we must assume that we can attain soon

---

13. Ibid., 2.11 (CCSL 29:72): *animi sui moderatione beatus est*.

14. Ibid.: *Optime, inquam, nec huic interrogationi aliud nec abs te aliud debuit responderi*.

15. Ibid.: *Deum igitur, inquam, qui habet, beatus est*.

16. Ibid., 4.27 (CCSL 29:80).

17. Ibid.: *Ubi cum omnes mirando exclamassent me ipso etiam non mediocriter alacri atque laeto, quod ab ea potissimum dictum esset, quod pro magno de philosophorum libris atque ultimum proferre paraueram*.

18. Ibid., 4.35 (CCSL 29:85).

by a well-founded faith, a joyful hope and an ardent love."[19] Monica receives *vera philosophia* as an infused and unmediated gift of the theological virtues directly from the Triune God to whom she has prayed.[20] The theological virtues are ordered to eternity, and this gift allows her to be the mystagogue for the gathered community at Cassiciacum; it is *she* who offers the decisive contribution to the quest for happiness that animates *De beata vita*, namely, that he who possesses eternal wisdom is happy.

The distinct (divine) source of Monica's wisdom comes to the fore again in *De ordine*. This dialogue was penned in the year of Augustine's conversion (386) and deals with the problem of theodicy in light of divine providence. *De ordine* reveals Augustine's early confidence that creation is intelligible and offers a *via* of ascent to the Creator through the study of the seven liberal arts. Augustine's mother comes into the dialogue at the conclusion of the first book. Augustine wants to record her name and contributions for the records. However, Monica objects: it is uncustomary for a woman to be included in a philosophical dialogue. But Augustine insists. He maintains that only proud men who are more concerned with external appearances than with truth would deem it unseemly to have a woman in their dialogues. Besides, Augustine continues, one finds precedent in the writings of ancient philosophers for the appearance of the most surprising characters, including shoemakers and women.[21] This initial exchange regarding Monica's place in the philosophical records is intended to draw attention to a salient theme in the dialogue, namely, Augustine's insistence that his mother, Monica, is a true philosopher, despite the fact that her wisdom issues from a different source than classical philosophy. Augustine tells Monica, "[Y]our philosophy is very pleasing to me,"[22] and so, she acquiesces and allows her name to be recorded in the philosophical records.

Augustine goes on to explain to his mother that the etymological definition of *philosophia* is "love of wisdom." Paul's prohibition against vain philosophy (Col 2:8)[23] is a warning against the philosophy of this world. Augustine writes, "But there is another world utterly remote from these eyes of ours, a world which the intellect of a few sound men

---

19. Ibid.: *haec est nullo ambigente beata uita, quae uita perfecta est, ad quam nos festinantes posse perduci solida fide alacri spe flagranti caritate praesumendum est.*

20. Cf. Djuth, "Augustine, Monica, and the Love of Wisdom," 244.

21. Cf. *ord.* 1.11.31 (CCSL 29:105).

22. Ibid.: *et philosophia tua mihi plurimum placet.*

23. All citations from the Bible in this chapter are from the RSV.

beholds."[24] Love of wisdom is the love of this other world. After all, notes Augustine, Christ did not say, "My kingdom is not of the world," but "My kingdom is not of *this* world."[25] *Vera philosophia* is not the knowledge of the *saeculum*, but the love of eternal wisdom. It is this love that Monica has already cultivated. Indeed, so much so, that Augustine remarks, "[Y]ou love it even more than you love me."[26] Monica no longer fears any of life's perturbations; the prospect of her own death and even that of her son does not trouble her. Augustine tells Monica, "[Y]ou are not frightened by the dread of any chance discomfort or even death itself."[27]

A mainstay of the Platonic philosophical synthesis is that *the* definitive mark of the true philosopher is that he no longer fears death.[28] Augustine notes that even for the greatest philosophers this state is achieved with immense difficulty, and yet, Monica, who does not even know the etymology of the word *philosophia*, has achieved this "greatest stronghold of philosophy" (*summam philosophiae arcem*).[29] Just as in *De beata vita*, Augustine here also uses this phrase—*philosophiae arcem*—to bespeak the height of Monica's philosophical achievement. Both in *De beata vita* and in *De ordine* it is her confidence that happiness does not reside in this world, in what our eyes can see, but is, rather, the possession of eternal wisdom, that marks her off as the true philosopher. Significantly, Augustine concludes the exchange with his mother by recognizing her as a mystagogue and himself as her *discipulus*: "[S]hall I not gladly entrust myself to you even as a disciple?"[30]

After a few days Augustine reconvenes the group at Cassiciacum. Monica is present from the outset of the second book of *De ordine*.

---

24. Ibid.: *Esse autem alium mundum ab istis oculis remotissimum, quem paucorum sanorum intellectus intuetur.*

25. Ibid.: *satis ipse Christus significat, qui non dicit: 'regnum meum non est de mundo', sed: regnum meum non est de hoc mondo.*

26. Ibid.: *Nunc uero cum eam multo plus quam me ipsum diligas.*

27. Ibid.: *cum que in ea tantum profeceris, ut iam nec cuiusuis incommodi fortuiti nec ipsius mortis, quod uiris doctissimis difficillimum est, horrore terrearis.*

28. Djuth writes, "True philosophers, by contrast, search for the truth for its own sake and are not afraid of death because they know that wisdom is eternal and cannot be found in the temporal world." See "Augustine, Monica, and the Love of Wisdom," 240. How love of eternal wisdom overcomes the fear of death in the Platonic tradition is considered by Malingrey, *"Philosophia,"* 104–6; and Courcelle, "Verissima philosophia," 655nn14–15.

29. *ord.* 1.11.32 (CCSL 29:106).

30. Ibid.: *ego ne me non libenter tibi etiam discipulum dabo?*

Indeed, Augustine insists on her presence because of Monica's "burning desire for things divine [and because] . . . her mind had been revealed to me as so rare that nothing seemed more adapted for true philosophy" (*uerae philosophiae*).³¹ The colloquy has arrived at the knotty issue of divine providence in the face of evil. Monica asserts, "I think that nothing could have been done aside from the order of God, because evil itself, what has had an origin, in no way originated by the order of God; but that divine justice permitted it not to be beyond the limits of order, and has brought it back and confined it to an order befitting it."³² Monica enters into the philosophical challenge of theodicy by distinguishing between the good order created by God and the evil that God permits. Monica's consistent contribution is to distinguish between the (ordered) eternity of God and the (disordered) finitude of post-lapsarian created existence; it is this sustained advertence to the order of eternity that marks her off as a true philosopher.

Near the conclusion to *De ordine* Augustine considers how one can begin to understand immaterial and eternal being, that is to say, how might one ascend from "images" to being itself.³³ First, such knowledge cannot be achieved by one "still a slave to his passions" or "desirous of perishable goods."³⁴ Next, one needs to study immaterial concepts such as intelligible numbers. This requires both "good talents" and "leisure" to follow the "order of study."³⁵ The goal of the ascent in the liberal arts, Augustine continues, is to foster precisely such ability, not only to excel in practical skills, but also "for the knowledge and contemplation of things."³⁶ Augustine freely admits that the attainment of such knowledge

31. Ibid., 2.1.1 (CCSL 29:106): *Nobiscum erat etiam mater nostra, cuius ingenium atque in res diuinas inflammatum animum cum antea conuictu diuturno et diligenti consideratione perspexeram tum uero in quadam disputatione non paruae rei, quam die natali meo cum conuiuis habui atque in libellum contuli, tanta mihi mens eius apparuerat, ut nihil aptius uerae philosophiae uideretur.*

32. Ibid., 2.7.23 (CCSL 29:120): *Tum mater: Ego, inquit, non puto nihil potuisse praeter dei ordinem fieri, quia ipsum malum, quod natum est, nullo modo dei ordine natum est, sed illa iustitia id inordinatum esse non siuit et in sibi meritum ordinem redegit et conpulit.*

33. Ibid., 2.16.44 (CCSL 29:131). The motif of ascent from images to being itself in Augustine's early thought is explored in greater detail in Boersma, *The Origins of Augustine's Early Theology of Image.*

34. Ibid.

35. Ibid.

36. Ibid., 2.5.16. For discussion of Augustine's understanding of the ascent *via* the liberal arts in *De ordine*, see Kenney, *Contemplation and Classical Christianity*, 65–74.

is extremely challenging. Then, he turns to his mother. He encourages her not to be alarmed at the difficulty of the rugged ascent to things eternal by way of the liberal arts: "For many persons, to be sure, they are difficult to learn. But for you, whose talents are brought home to me anew every day—and I know your mind, far removed from all frivolity, both by reason of your age and because of your remarkable moderation, and now rising above the abject misery of the body, has already risen to great heights within itself—for you, those matters will be as easy as they are difficult for duller souls who live most wretchedly."[37] Monica's ascent to things eternal will prove a success more on account of her internal disposition of moderation (which is the hallmark of the virtuous soul) than on account of her learning. Again, we are presented with Monica's *vera philosophia*, which is the sublimation of temporal goods to eternal good, as she rises above the "miseries of the body." In her initial foray in the dialogue she earns a place in the records even when prideful philosophers concerned only with appearances would sanction her presence. Here too, Augustine notes that those well trained in the liberal arts would quibble about the pronunciation of this or that word and that Monica might stumble on this score.[38] However, this lack of training does not impair her ascent. She deserves a place at the philosophical table because she has grasped the end goal of philosophy, namely, love of eternal wisdom. Despite her lack of formation in liberal arts such as grammar, Augustine tells her, "[You] grasp the almost heavenly power and nature of grammar, and with so much discernment that you seem to have taken hold of its very soul, and to have left its body for the eloquent."[39] Perhaps, with training, some ascend in the liberal arts from correct grammar to the articulation of wisdom, but Monica, suggests Augustine, knows with a direct and internal élan the true kernel of eternal wisdom apart from the husk of ornate language within which it might be cloaked. One could

---

37. *ord.* 2.17.45 (CCSL 29:131): *cognitione autem multis quidem ardua, tibi tamen, cuius ingenium cotidie mihi nouum est et cuius animum uel aetate uel admirabili temperantia remotissimum ab omnibus nugis et a magna labe corporis emergentem in se multum surrexisse cognosco, tam erunt facilia quam difficilia tardissimis miserrime que uiuentibus.*

38. Cf. Ibid.

39. Ibid.: *Sed tu contemptis istis uel puerilibus rebus uel ad te non pertinentibus ita grammaticae paene diuinam uim naturam que cognosces, ut eius animam tenuisse, corpus disertis reliquisse uidearis.*

say that faith as a form of knowledge allows Monica to short-circuit the ascent laboriously achieved by the few through the liberal arts.[40]

The concluding prayer in the final chapter of *De ordine* points to Augustine's mother as a guide whom the philosophic community at Cassiciacum ought to follow. They are to pray for "a life most virtuous," and ask that they may see not a part of reality, as one does in this world of sense, but may come, instead, to see the whole. This is seen "in the intelligible world, [where] every part is as beautiful and perfect as the whole."[41] They are to pray not for temporal goods ("wealth or honors or any fleeting and changeful things . . . that quickly pass away"), but instead for those things that will make them "virtuous and happy."[42] Then Augustine states, "And, mother, to the end that these petitions be most observantly made, we enjoin the charge on you, through whose prayers I unhesitatingly believe and proclaim that God has given me this resolve: to prize nothing more highly than the finding of truth, to wish for, to think of, to love nothing else. And I furthermore believe that through your petitioning we shall obtain the great blessing which through your meriting we have come to desire."[43] Monica has guided and nurtured Augustine's love of things eternal; she has led him to desire the end of philosophy. Her prayers and witness have cultivated his participation in eternal wisdom.

MONICA AT OSTIA

Now that we have sketched the mystagogical persona of Monica at Cassiciacum, her significance at Ostia becomes more conspicuous. There Augustine and Monica face death unafraid; in fact, they are filled with hope as they touch eternal wisdom itself. In the Dialogues Monica teaches

---

40. Djuth has made a similar claim: "Monica's lack of extensive training in the liberal arts hardly impairs her ability to grasp the fundamental truths of Christianity. If anything, her grasp of these truths is more vital than the abstract knowledge of the academician because her understanding of them has its roots in faith, hope, and charity." "Augustine, Monica and the Love of Wisdom," 246.

41. *ord.* 2.19.51 (CCSL 29:135): *in illo uero mundo intellegibili quamlibet partem tamquam totum pulchram esse atque perfectam.*

42. Ibid., 2.20.52 (CCSL 29:135): *quae nos bonos faciant ac beatos.*

43. Ibid.: *Quae uota ut deuotissime inpleantur, tibi maxime hoc negotium, mater, iniungimus, cuius precibus indubitanter credo atque confirmo mihi istam mentem deum dedisse, ut inueniendae ueritati nihil omnino praeponam, nihil aliud uelim, nihil cogitem, nihil amem, nec desino credere nos hoc tantum bonum, quod te promerente concupiuimus, eadem te petente adepturos.*

Augustine and his friends *vera philosophia*, which is that true happiness consists in the possession of eternal wisdom. Augustine entrusts himself to his mother as a *discipulus*, recognizing that her wisdom is not derived from the study of the liberal arts, but from participation in the "divine source" of Wisdom, from which she receives the infused theological virtues. Monica shows herself to be a true philosopher who, because she has reached the "greatest stronghold of philosophy" (*philosophiae arcem*), no longer fears death. All this finds its culmination at Ostia.[44]

In some sense the ascent in *Conf.* 9.10 is strikingly similar to that in Book 8 of the *Confessions*. In both cases Augustine recounts an ascent of the soul to a mystical, ecstatic experience of eternity. Indeed, much of the phraseology in the two passages is nearly identical with a Plotinian cadence suffusing both passages. Significantly, both texts share the conclusion that eternity is not grasped in this life. Nevertheless, the presence of Monica at Ostia establishes a drastically different spiritual tenor. The Ostian narrative is charged with optimism: Monica leads her son to the awareness that time and its passing do not stand in opposition to eternity. Nor is the effervescence of time to be eventually lost in an anonymous sea of eternal nothingness. Rather, as Fr. Lamb so often reminds his students, time is created by God the Eternal, so that finite being is anchored in eternal being. God's eternal truth and wisdom do not negate contingent reality; rather, a participatory ontology grounds and redeems contingent reality.[45] It is precisely this theological reality that allows Monica and Augustine—finite and contingent as they are—to experience a hope-filled ascent to eternal wisdom that is not present to the same degree in *Conf.* 7.[46]

---

44. My attempt to read the significance of Monica's presence at Ostia in light of how she is presented in the Dialogues builds on the work of Marianne Djuth who maintains, "Augustine's portrait of Monica in the Cassiciacum dialogues and the *Confessions*, then, is a crucial link in understanding what he means by the *vera philosophia* of Christianity." "Augustine, Monica, and the Love of Wisdom," 238. The connection between the stylized portrait of Monica derived from the Dialogues and her presence at Ostia has also been noted by Coyle: "[T]he motive behind the Ostia account is—in part at least—to direct attention to Monica as a true philosopher who has reached the furthest heights to which one can be brought in this life by a philosophy which is true." "In Praise of Monica," 90.

45. Lamb writes, "The spiritual nature of intelligence together with the *Veritas* of true judgment is the ground for understanding God as the Eternal, creating and redeeming the temporal. The transcendence by truth of space and time does not negate space and time, but affirms them." "Temporality and History," 826.

46. Hope is what makes Monica's impending death so much different from that of

The attempt to delineate precise (Plotinian) parallels between the ascents at Milan and Ostia are numerous.[47] Earlier twentieth-century studies of these two experiences in the *Confessions* tended to focus on the shared Neoplatonic language operative in the two narratives and from this premise assert that the experiences at Milan and Ostia are substantially identical. In this vein André Mandouze succinctly remarks, "C'est qu'il n'y a aucune différence de nature entre les deux expériences."[48] James O'Donnell is correct, in my opinion, to dismiss such superficial structural analyses as "hopelessly wrongheaded."[49] Similarities of structure and even of (Platonic) language serve only to accent the *qualitative* difference between Milan and Ostia: at Ostia, with Monica, Augustine has a *Christian* experience.[50] The intervening period between the ascent in Books VII and IX of the *Confessions* entail considerable change. In those sixteen months Augustine has had a heart-rending experience in the Milanese Garden, through which he was converted to the Christian faith and subsequently baptized. The moral regeneration and participation in the sacramental life of the church means that (according to Augustine's theology) the ascents in Milan and Ostia *cannot* find substantially the same theological expression. The faith that Augustine now shares with Monica infuses a deep and abiding eschatological *hope* to the ascent narrative of *Conf.* 9.10. I

Socrates. As Fr. Lamb notes, "The philosophical agnosticism stated by Socrates at the end of the *Apology*: —I go to die, you to live; but which of us goes to a better reality is unknown to all but God"—was no match for the disorder and evil of human history and of Augustine's own wayward living. In the covenant with Israel and the new covenant in Jesus Christ, God has made known to us how death and evil are overcome." "Temporality and History," 821.

47. The most significant studies that advance this analysis are Mandouze, *Saint Augustin*, 685–99; Courcelle, *Recherches sur les Confessions*, 222–24; O'Connell, *Images of Conversion*.

48. Mandouze, *Saint Augustin*, 697. Likewise, Burnaby writes, "There is no ground for the claim that the intervening 'purgation' and reception into the Church gave to the so-called ecstasy at Ostia a 'Christian' quality lacking to the earlier experience . . . Before and after Christian baptism, the method of a pagan philosopher brought to Augustine a moment's immediate sense of the living and changeless God." *Amor Dei*, 32. Henry's influential study, *La Vision d'Ostie*, argues to the same effect: the similarities of Plotinian idiom entail that both books 7 and 9 of the *Confessions* relate a Platonic experience of the vision of God.

49. O'Donnell, *Augustine*, 124.

50. O'Donnell notes that despite "*all the structural parallels*, the substance of the event was different for its Christianization; indeed, the parallels have the effect of calling attention to the differences." O'Donnell, *Augustine*, 124.

am arguing that this hope, to which Monica leads Augustine, sets the Ostian narrative apart from that of Milan. While both ascents are fleeting experiences, that of Ostia is described as a foretaste of heaven, to which they remain bound (*religatas*) in hope even after the conclusion of the experience. In contrast, after the experience in Milan Augustine crashes down, back into the *regio dissimilitudinis*; at Ostia Augustine and Monica experience the *regio ubertatis indeficientis*: the "region of inexhaustible abundance where you feed Israel eternally with truth for food."[51] After this experience they retain the "first fruits of the Spirit."

Along with other significant events in the *Confessions*, the experience at Ostia takes place in a garden (*hortus*). Augustine and his mother are leaning out of a window at a house in Ostia, the port city of Rome where the Tiber flows into the Mediterranean Sea. The context that Augustine establishes in *Conf.* 9.10.23 is significant. Augustine and Monica were alone (*soli*), removed from the crowd (*remoti a turbis*) after an exhausting journey and were in the process of regaining their strength.[52] Their mystical ascent occurs in the context of an intimate conversation (*conloquebamur*) about the nature of eternity: "We asked what quality of life the eternal life of the saints will have."[53] The presence of Monica—who at this point of the *Confessions* is established as an ecclesial symbol, as in *De beata vita*—is the first clear demarcation between this ascent and that in Book VII. Augustine's ascent in *Conf.* 7 follows Plotinus's injunction to ascend alone to the Alone.[54] Here a communal élan replaces the solitary flight to the One. The ecclesial context of the ascent, represented by Monica's presence, is reinforced in the discussion regarding the nature of the eternal life of the saints. ("We asked what quality of life the eternal life of the saints will have."[55]) As such, the substance of their mystical experience is proleptically present already in their conversation: eternal

---

51. *Conf.* 9.10.24 (CCSL 27:147): *ut attingeremus regionem ubertatis indeficientis, unde pascis Israel in aeternum veritate pabulo.*

52. In many ways this scene is the realization of what Augustine and his friends had proposed years earlier in *Conf.* 6.14.24 (CCSL 27:89–90): a communal life devoted to contemplation. The plan, over which Augustine and his friends then conversed (*conloquentes*), was to withdraw from the crowds and storms of human life (*turbulentas humanae vitae*) and to have all things in common while living a life of contemplation. Cf. O'Donnell, *Augustine*, 125.

53. *Conf.* 9.10.23 (CCSL 27:147): *qualis futura esset vita aeterna sanctorum.*

54. Ibid., 7.10.16: "By the Platonic books I was admonished to return into myself."

55. Ibid., 9.10.23 (CCSL 27:147).

life is the communion of the whole temporal, created order redeemed and delighting in God's eternity.[56]

The conversation proceeds to contrast bodily delights with spiritual delights. This was, of course, the heart of Monica's teaching about happiness at Cassiciacum and that which marked her off as a true philosopher: "[T]he pleasure of the bodily senses, however delightful in the radiant light of this physical world, is seen by comparison with the life of eternity to be not even worth considering."[57] At this point Augustine recounts, "Our minds were lifted up by an ardent affection towards eternal being itself (*idipsum*)."[58] In *Conf.* 7 Augustine twice describes catching sight, in a "trembling glance," of that "which is" (*ad id quod est*); similarly, here, too, being itself (*idipsum*) is experienced.[59] Much

---

56. Louth notes that in contrast to the solitary nature of a Plotinian ascent, here at Ostia we see the heartbeat of Augustine's ecclesial and eschatological vision, which is social: "This makes one wonder to what extent friendship, companionship, communion with other human beings, is important for Augustine in his ascent to God... [T]here is a strand—and an important strand—in Augustine's thought that stresses the social nature of final beatitude." *The Origins of the Christian Mystical Tradition*, 136.

57. *Conf.* 9.10.24 (CCSL 27:147): *ut carnalium sensuum delectatio quantalibet, in quantalibet luce corporea, prae illius vitae iucunditate non conparatione, sed ne conmemoratione quidem digna videretur.*

58. *Conf.* 9.10.24 (CCSL 27:147): *erigentes nos ardentiore affectu in idipsum.*

59. In Ibid., 7.10.16 (CCSL 27:103-4) and ibid., 7.17.23 (CCSL 27:107). Augustine ascends to an experience of eternal being. What he comes to realize in these experiences is the difference between time and eternity. It is helpful briefly to sketch both passages. In *Conf.* 7.10.16 Augustine recalls, "By the Platonic books I was admonished to return into myself." Ibid., 7.10.16. The turn within is the first step of the ascent for Plotinus. Finding eternal beauty does not involve the external trappings of flight, but involves turning to something already present to everyone. Plotinus admonishes, "Go back into yourself and look." Plotinus, *Enneads* 1.6.9. So this is precisely what Augustine does. He enters into his most intimate self (*intima mea*). Then, with his soul's eye (*oculo animae*) he sees the radiance of an unchanging light. Augustine emphasizes that this light was a mystical light; it was unlike any material or even intellectual light. In fact, it was this light that created him (*ipsa fecit me*). In this mystical experience Augustine comes to realize the real distinction between participating being and participated being; between the being that creates and the being of the creatures created ([N]*ec ita erat supra mentem meam . . . sed superior, quia ipsa fecit me, et ego inferior, quia factus ab ea*). In short, Augustine comes to grapple with the concept of eternity. He who knows this light, exclaims Augustine, knows eternity (*nouit aeternitatem*), but it is known only in love. This mystical experience causes Augustine to cry out, "O eternal truth and true love and beloved eternity! You are my God, to you I sigh day and night" (*O aeterna ueritas et uera caritas et cara aeternitas! tu es deus meus, tibi suspiro die ac nocte*). This word sigh (*suspiro*) is significant and will appear again when Augustine recounts his mystical experience at Ostia. The ecstasy described in *Conf.* 7.10.16 is

as in *Conf.* 7, created being and eternal being are contrasted: "Step by step we climbed beyond all corporeal objects and the heaven itself."⁶⁰ As in *Conf.* 7, the ascent is initiated by a turn within (*ascendebamus interius*). Monica and Augustine reflect and dialogue as they enter into their own minds (*venimus in mentes nostras*). Then, they ascend even beyond their own mind (*transcendimus eas*). In this way also the ascent at Ostia tracks that of Book VII.

One line, however, gives a decidedly different hue to the Ostian narrative: "We moved up beyond [our minds] so as to attain to the region of inexhaustible abundance where you feed Israel eternally with truth for food."⁶¹ This arresting line captures precisely the qualitative difference be-

---

short lived. Augustine crashes down, unable to sustain the vision of eternal being. He finds himself far from eternity "in the region of dissimilarity" (*regio dissimilitudinis*). It is important, however, to underscore what precisely Augustine came to understand in this experience, namely, the real distinction between temporal being and eternal being: "What I saw is Being, and that I who saw am not yet Being" (*tu adsumpsisti me ut viderem esse quod viderem, et nondum me esse qui viderem*). Ibid., 7.10.16. In his retrospection of this initial ascent in book 7, Augustine writes, "And I considered the other things below you, and I saw that neither can they be said absolutely to be or absolutely not to be. They are because they come from you. But they are not because they are not what you are." Ibid., 7.11.17 (CCSL 27:104).

In many ways the second ascent described in *Confessions* 7 mirrors the first. In fact, many commentators suggest that it is one experience related in two ways. The ascent is initiated with Augustine contemplating the human phenomenon of judgment. Ibid., 7.17.23 (CCSL 27:107). The mind judges that mutable things *ought* to be this way or that way; this suggests an eternal principle upon which the mind bases such judgments. Augustine comes to an awareness that the "eternity of truth" used as the standard of truth is higher even than the mind which judges. He writes, "And so step by step I ascended from bodies to the soul which perceives through the body, and from there to its inward force . . . From there again I ascended to the power of reasoning to which is to be the attribute the power of judging the deliverances of the bodily senses." Ibid. This reasoning and judging power, Augustine discovers, is itself flooded by light. The ascent from the corporeal body to the incorporeal soul that renders judgment on bodily senses by its participation in eternal light leads Augustine to the same conclusion that he came to in the first description of his mystical experience in book 7: "At that point it had no hesitation in declaring that the unchangeable is preferable to the changeable . . . So in the flash of a trembling glance it attained to that which is (*ad id quod est*)." Ibid. Again, Augustine catches sight of being itself. But again he crashes down: "I did not possess the strength to keep my vision fixed. My weakness reasserted itself and I returned to my customary condition." Ibid.

60. Ibid., 9.10.24 (CCSL 27:147): *perambulavimus gradatim cuncta corporalia, et ipsum caelum*.

61. Ibid.: *ut attingeremus regionem ubertatis indeficientis, unde pascis Israel in aeternum veritate pabulo*.

tween the ascent at Ostia and the ascent in Book VII. In Milan Augustine could not sustain the vision of eternal being, as he soon found himself in the "region of dissimilarity" (*regione dissimilitudinis*); now, however, he finds himself in the "region of inexhaustible abundance" (*regionem ubertatis indeficientis*). It is certainly the case that the similarities between the two accounts are pronounced: both ascents lead to an experience of eternal reality resulting in a profound awareness of the difference between temporal being eternal being. Nevertheless, after the experience at Ostia, Monica and Augustine remain "bound to that higher world."[62] It is the *hope* of remaining bound (*religatas*) to eternity, which Monica the philosopher consistently taught is the highest good, that underwrites the rest and joy of the Ostian ascent and ensures its qualitative distinction from that in *Conf.* 7.

The previous ascent in Book 7 left Augustine disappointed. His "sigh" represents a lack of satisfied desire and a sense of incomplete and unsustained participation with the eternal being experienced.[63] Here, at Ostia, the "sigh" (*suspiravimus*) that Augustine and Monica share is different. They are talking and panting after eternal wisdom and then, in an enraptured moment of pure spiritual contemplation (*toto ictu cordis*), they touch it (*attingimus*).[64] Augustine then writes, "And we sighed and left behind us 'the firstfruits of the Spirit'[65] bound to that higher world."[66] This sighing bespeaks a different sentiment from the disappointed sigh in Book 7. This sighing is the sighing of satisfaction; Monica and Augustine have touched eternity. But eternity is not now gone. Rather, Augustine makes clear that his conversion and Monica's tutelage have led him beyond the insights of *Conf.* 7 to understand all time to be created,

---

62. Ibid.: *reliquimus ibi religatas primitias spiritus.*

63. Usually *suspirare* suggests an unfilled and incomplete desire. Cf. O'Donnell, *Augustine*, 130–31; and Courcelle, *Recherches*, 124–25. It is in this sense that Augustine uses the verb in 6.5.8; 6.10.17; 7.10.16; 9.7.16; 9.10.24; and 9.10.25. Cf. O'Donnell, *Augustine*, 130.

64. Augustine presents this moment of ecstasy with the word *ictus* (a blow, strike, or smite). He uses *ictus* elsewhere either to describe a sudden blow or a mystical experience that feels like a sudden blow. Cf. *Conf.* 7.1.1; 7.17.23; 9.8.18. Louth writes, "[T]his ecstasy is sudden and fleeting, and draws out the whole force of the soul (*toto ictu cordis*) with, it would seem, a certain violence." Louth, *The Christian Mystical Tradition*, 137.

65. Rom 8:23.

66. *Conf.* 9.10.24: *attingimus eam modice toto ictu cordis; et suspirauimus et reliquimus ibi religatas primitias spiritus.*

sustained, and taken up by eternal wisdom. The mystic does not leave time behind in his ascent to eternity, but instead comes to realize that the ground of his own temporal being (and all other being) is anchored in eternity.[67] Here we can at last put our finger on the decisive speculative difference between Monica the mystagogue and Plotinus's mystic (and, therefore, on the qualitative difference between the ascent in Milan and that of Ostia). Fr. Lamb explains that for Plotinus, "the task of the true philosopher or mystic is to leave behind all the temporal for the super-intuition of the eternal."[68] What Monica leads Augustine to realize is that eternity does not do away with time, but is the condition of time. Precisely at the apogee of the ascent at Ostia Augustine recalls the material and temporal event in which God provided for the people of Israel. The significance of this historical event Augustine understands to be made intelligible in eternity: "We moved up . . . to the region of inexhaustible abundance where you feed Israel eternally with truth for food."[69] The

---

67. Lamb underscores the philosophical breakthrough that Augustine's exposition of time and eternity represents. The philosophical legacy that Augustine inherited envisioned the Absolute One either as radically transcendent from finite being (à la Plato and Plotinus) or as immanent in finite being in such a way as to insert an "eternal element" into the finite order (as in the νόησις νοήσεως). Lamb writes, "[T]he efforts of philosophers and theologians to understand the divine either made the divine into Absolute Idea, the transcendence of which is the separation from all finite being; or they made the divine into Absolute Intelligence that somehow informs the whole universe, immanent in all that is . . . Where Plato can contrast the eternal and the temporal to the point of opposing them, Aristotelian scholarship has been unable to determine if the master ever decisively differentiated the eternal and the temporal. This has been a philosophical dialectic ever since: transcendence without immanence or immanence with a very questionable transcendence." *Eternity, Time, and the Life of Wisdom*, 38.

68. Ibid., 39.

69. This revelation of eternity in time is part of the broader divine pedagogy of Scripture in which God gradually discloses himself. Lamb writes, "The pedagogy of the Jewish Scriptures reveals an ever-deepening understanding of God from the tribal through the liberating warrior and the protector of the nation to the mysteriously transcendent God of the prophets and the wisdom literature. The transcendent God is immanent in the messianic suffering of Israel." Ibid.

While the descriptions of ascent in *Conf.* 7 are anti-climactic, they also, like the ascent of Ostia, speak to the temporal, material dispensation within which eternity redeems time. After finding himself in the *regio dissimilitudinis*, Augustine hears a voice speaking to him with encouragement from on high: "I am the food of the fully grown; grow and you will feed on me. And you will not change me into you like the food your flesh eats, but you will be changed into me." *Conf.* 7.10.16. The unmistakable eucharistic overtones in this passage invite Augustine to see that although his ascent in "upward participation" to grasp eternity fails, eternity comes in a movement of "downward participation" to his temporal condition to fit him for eternity. This eternity of wisdom is that in which "all creatures come into being, both things which were and which will be."[70] Past, present, and future beings find stable existence in eternal wisdom, which perdures beyond the ravages of time. This is the hope experienced at Ostia. After experiencing—"touching"—eternal wisdom, Monica and Augustine remain "bound to that higher world" (*reliquimus ibi religatas*) in hope, even while they descend back into the distended realm of time "where a sentence has both a beginning and an ending."[71] Hope promises that all time and the many beautiful, good, and true things we make, experience, know, and love in time are taken up into the eternity of God, which never grows old but "gives renewal to all things."[72]

Four significant Pauline quotations frame and explicate the experience at Ostia. All four texts speak to an eschatology of hope. First, the scene unfolds with a reference to Philippians 3. Monica and Augustine are talking intimately, "forgetting the past and reaching forward to what lies ahead (Phil 3:13)."[73] In the letter to the Philippians Paul celebrates the fact that he is "found in Christ" (Phil 3:9). All other fleeting things he counts as nothing compared to knowing Christ and the sure hope that he will be raised with Christ in glory (Phil 3:10). Monica and Augustine's

---

comports with the broader leitmotif of book 7, which contrasts self-assured Plotinian motifs of ascent, tinged as they are with pride, with the descent of grace given through the humility of the incarnation. In the second description of ascent (*Conf.* 7.17.23 [CCSL 27:107]), comfort is again offered after a short-lived experience; this time in the form of memory and desire for "that of which I had the aroma but which I had not yet the capacity to eat." In the retrospection of his ascent Augustine explains that only after he had embraced the God-man, Jesus Christ, could he "enjoy" God. Augustine's successful ascent is predicated on accepting the prior descent of Christ. The experience of Milan, therefore, leans forward to that of Ostia. Augustine writes, "The food which I was too weak to accept he mingled with flesh, in that 'The Word was made flesh' (John 1:14), so that our infant condition might come to suck milk from you wisdom by which you create all things. To possess my God, the humble Jesus, I was not yet humble enough. I did not know what his weakness was meant to teach." Ibid., 7.18.24 (CCSL 27:108). The humility of the incarnation is the *via* of ascent, and its acceptance requires Augustine to renounce his pride. The emphasis in *Conf.* 7 lies in the sacramental means whereby Christ comes into distended time to feed those who are by grace led to ascend to eternity.

70. Ibid., 9.10.24 (CCSL 27:147): *et ibi vita sapientia est, per quam fiunt omnia ista, et quae fuerunt et quae futura sunt.*

71. Ibid.: *remeavimus ad strepitum oris nostri, ubi verbum et incipitur et finitur.*

72. Ibid.: *in se permanenti sine vetustate atque innovanti omnia.*

73. Ibid.: *et praeterita obliviscentes in ea quae ante sunt extenti.* Cf. O'Daly, "Time as *Distentio*," 265–71.

ascent finds its impetus in Paul's admonition to the Philippians to "reach forward," straining ahead in hope, "for the prize of the upward call of God in Christ Jesus" (Phil 3:14). They take Paul's words as their own: "Our commonwealth is in heaven, and from it we await a Savior, the Lord Jesus Christ, who will change our lowly body to be like his glorious body" (Phil 3:20–21). Hope promises that nothing in time, including "our lowly bodies" are lost, but in eternity all is fulfilled.

The second Pauline quotation is in response to Augustine and Monica's question of what the "eternal life" of the saints is like. In answer, Augustine quotes Paul's epistle to the Corinthians: "Neither eye has seen nor ear has heard, nor has it entered into the heart of man (1 Cor 2:9)."[74] The context of Paul's discourse maps perfectly onto the vision experienced at Ostia. Paul is speaking of the "wisdom of God"—"a secret and hidden wisdom" (1 Cor 2:7). Augustine and Monica "touch" this "wisdom by which all creatures come into being,"[75] but they do not yet participate in it fully. It is a wisdom "prepared" by God "for those that love him" (1 Cor 2:9), known only in hope, the substance of which is reserved for the eschatological *parousia*.

Romans 8:23 is the third and axial Pauline quotation. It is situated at the culmination of the ascent: "And while we talked and panted after [eternal wisdom], we touched it in some small degree by a moment of total concentration of the heart. And we sighed and left behind us 'the first-fruits of the spirit' bound to that higher world."[76] In Romans 8 Paul is expressing the hope of future glory that will far surpass present suffering. Along with the rest of creation, maintains Paul, we now groan as "we wait for adoption as sons, the redemption of our bodies," but the "first fruits of the Spirit" have already been given as pledge, "for it is in hope we are saved" (Rom 8:24). We *are* (now, in time!) saved in hope. This hope entails that the stark antithesis between time and eternity that underwrites the Platonic tradition is unsustainable. The "bondage to decay" (Rom 8:21) is not (as it is for Plato) the definitive and final word about temporal existence. Rather, in the words of Jesuit poet, Gerard Manley Hopkins, creation is "never spent"; there always "lives the dearest freshness deep down things."[77] The human person, endowed

---

74. *Conf.* 9.10.23 (CCSL 27:147): *quam nec oculus vidit nec auris audivit nec in cor hominis ascendit.*

75. Ibid., 9.10.24 (CCSL 27:147): *et ibi vita sapientia est, per quam fiunt omnia ista.*

76. Ibid.

77. Hopkins, "God's Grandeur."

with beauty and grace of body as well as intellectual and moral glory, is uniquely made in and for eternity. Time and temporal existence will be "set free from its bondage to decay and obtain the glorious liberty of the children of God" (Rom 8:21). Augustine and Monica experience a pledge of this hope at Ostia.

The final Pauline quotation deployed to relate the Ostian experience expresses what their vision means in relation to eternal life: "And when is that to be? Surely it is when 'we all rise again, but are not all changed' (1 Cor 15:51)."[78] The quote is part of Paul's lengthy treatise on the resurrection of the body in 1 Corinthians 15 and here forms the capstone to the experience of Ostia, anchoring the entire ascent in hope. As with the other Pauline texts, it is not a hope that we see now. ("If for this life only we have hoped in Christ, we are of all men most to be pitied" [1 Cor 15:19]). The hope of the resurrected body remains a mystery beyond our ken (1 Cor 15:51), but hope promises that the mortal will put on immortality (1 Cor 15:54) and that nothing that has being will be annihilated; rather, death, the privation of being, will be swallowed up in victory (1 Cor 15:54).

Paul's theology of hope is the warp and woof on which Augustine weaves the Ostian narrative. Their conversation is initiated with a meditation on Philippians 3 and 1 Corinthians 2. The heart of the mystical ecstasy of Ostia is related through the prism of Paul's paean to the victory of hope in Romans 8. Finally, 1 Cor 15 offers Augustine the language to express that a sure hope remains, in this life, apophatic in character.

Monica is about to die. Her conversation with her son has been focused on eternity and the life of the saints with God. Earthly pleasures, she remarks, are "not even worth considering" with the joy of eternity.[79] Monica is presented as reaching a perfected mystical state. Her heart is set on things above. As in the Cassiciacum dialogues, Monica considers all temporal goods insignificant to "truth which is you yourself,"[80] "eternal being itself,"[81] and "eternal wisdom."[82] She has completed her life's mission: she has led Augustine to participate in eternal wisdom. Thinking back on their last conversation Augustine writes, "Yet, Lord,

---

78. *Conf.* 9.10.25 (CCSL 27:148): *et istud quando? an cum omnes resurgimus, sed non omnes inmutabimur?*

79. Ibid., 9.10.23.

80. Ibid.

81. Ibid., 9.10.24.

82. Ibid.

you know that on that day when we had this conversation . . . this world with all its delights became worthless to us."[83] Monica herself seals their experience, saying, "My son, as for myself, I now find no pleasure in this life . . . My hope in this world is already fulfilled."[84] It is important not to misprize this evaluation; the sustained theological emphasis on hope that underwrites the entire Ostian ascent, suggests that Monica's mystagogy does not devalue temporal existence, but hopes for its fulfillment in eternity. As Fr. Lamb writes so eloquently, "Eternity does not denigrate time, but creates time in order, through intelligent creatures, to invite a return. Augustine presents God as *totum esse praesens*, the fullness of Being as Presence freely creating, sustaining, and redeeming the universe and all of human history in the Triune Presence. All extensions and durations, all past, present, and future events, are present in the immutable and eternal understanding, knowing, and loving who are Father, Word, and Spirit."[85]

BIBLIOGRAPHY

Augustine. *De beata vita*. In *Corpus Christianorum Series Latina*, edited by W. M. Green and K. D. Daur, 29:63–85. Turnhout: Brepols, 1970.
———. *Confessions*. Translated by Henry Chadwick. Oxford: Oxford University Press, 1991.
———. *Confessionum libri tredecim*. Edited by Luc Verheijen. *Corpus Christianorum Series Latina* 27. Turnhout: Brepols, 1981.
———. *The Happy Life*. Translated by Ludwig Schopp. Writings of Augustine 1. Washington DC: Catholic University of America Press, 1948.
———. *De ordine libri duo*. In *Corpus Christianorum Series Latina*, edited by W. M. Green and K. D. Daur, 29:87–137. Turnhout: Brepols, 1970.
———. *On Order*. Translated by Robert Russell. Writings of Augustine 1. Washington DC: Catholic University of America Press, 1948.
Burnaby, John. *Amor Dei: A Study in the Religion of St. Augustine*. Eugene, OR: Wipf and Stock, 2007.
Cacciavillani, Ivone. *Mamma fino a diventare santa. La vicenda umana di Monica alla ricerca del figlio Agostino*. Gregoriana: Padova, 1986.
Courcelle, Pierre. *Recherches sur les Confessions de saint Augustin*. Paris: Boccard, 1968.
———. "Verissima philosophia." In *Epektasis: Mélanges patristiques offerts au cardinal Jean Daniélieu*, edited by Jacques Fontaine and Charles Kannengiesser, 653–59. Paris: Beauchesne, 1972.
Coyle, Kevin. "In Praise of Monica." *Augustinian Studies* 13 (1982) 87–96.
Djuth, Marianne. "Augustine, Monica, and the Love of Wisdom." *Augustinian Studies* 39 (2008) 237–52.

83. Ibid., 9.10.26.

84. Ibid.: *iam consumpta spe huius saeculi*.

85. Lamb, *Eternity, Time, and the Life of Wisdom*, 41–42.

Henry, Paul. *La Vision d'Ostie*. Paris: Vrin, 1938.
Hopkins, Gerard Manley. "God's Grandeur." In *Gerard Manley Hopkins: The Major Works*, 128. Oxford: Oxford University Press, 2009.
Kenney, John Peter. *Contemplation and Classical Christianity*. Oxford: Oxford University Press, 2013.
Lamb, Matthew. "Temporality and History: Reflections from St. Augustine and Bernard Lonergan." *Nova et Vetera* 4 (2006) 815–50.
———. *Eternity, Time, and the Life of Wisdom*. Naples, FL: Sapientia, 2007.
Lamirande, Emilien. "Quand Monique, la mere d'Augustin, prend la parole." In *Signum Pietatis, Festgabe für Cornelius Petrus Mayer OSA zum 60*, edited by Adolar Zumkeller, 3–19. Würzburg: Augustinus, 1989.
Liddell, Henry G., et al., eds. *A Greek-English Lexicon*. Oxford: Clarendon, 1996.
Louth, Andrew. *The Origins of the Christian Mystical Tradition*. Oxford: Oxford University Press, 2007.
Malingrey, Anne-Marie. *"Philosophia"*: Étude d'un groupe de mots dans la littérature grecque, des Présocratiques au IVe siècle après J.-C. Études et commentaires 40. Paris: Klincksieck, 1961.
Mandouze, André. *Saint Augustin: L'Aventure de la raison et de la grâce*. Paris: Études augustiniennes, 1968.
O'Connell, Robert. *Images of Conversion in Augustine's Confessions*. New York: Fordham University Press, 1996.
O'Daly, Gerard. "Time as *Distentio* and St. Augustine's Exegesis of Philippians 3,12–14." *Revue d'Études Augustiniennes* 23 (1977) 265–71.
O'Donnell, James. *Confessions: Commentary on Books 8–13*. Oxford: Clarendon, 1992.
O'Farrell, M. M. "Monica, the Mother of Augustine: A Reconsideration." *Recherches Augustiniennes* 10 (1975) 23–43.

7

Psalm 79:8 and St. Augustine's Vision of Education

Christopher D. Collins

Deus virtutum, converte nos, et ostende faciem tuam, et salvi erimus.[1]

O God of hosts convert us; show us your face and we shall be saved.[2]

IN THE *DE MAGISTRO*, a dialogue with his son, Adeodatus, St. Augustine makes a rather bold argument about the natures of cognition and education. He argues not only that few people can teach well, but also that no one can actually teach someone to know anything.[3] Instead of being taught by other people, it is Christ, the Divine Teacher, who illumines each of our minds to arrive at the knowledge of intelligible but also sensible realities. While we may wish to breathe a sigh of relief

---

1. *ord.* 1.8.22.
2. This is my translation of the text as Augustine presents it. The numbering of the Psalm is from the Latin texts that translated the Septuagint. Bible translations based on the Masoretic Text list this as Psalm 80.8.
3. *mag.* 11.38.

about the lessening of our burden in transforming the minds of today's youth, Augustine's presentation appears to have rather problematic consequences. These consequences are felt both in the field of cognition whereby human instruction might appear to be all but inconsequential when coupled with Augustine's theory of divine illumination. Even Augustine's understanding of himself as a teacher seems to be called into question. However, far from a diminishment of the human role of the teacher, Augustine's view of education is far more satisfying of our desire for authentic human communication. His view alleviates our frustration in attaining to self-disclosure by situating our words and ideas as existent within a metaphysical participation in the created order.

The works that present the most prominent understanding of Augustine's own role as educator are the Cassiciacum Dialogues. These three works written in the winter of 386–387 before Augustine's conversion chronicle the discussions held among Augustine, his pupils, and family as he re-evaluates the philosophic patrimony that he has inherited from Cicero, Plato, and many others. The three dialogues, together with a fourth work, the *Soliloquies*, serve to resuscitate and resituate philosophy by describing the cognitional steps necessary for us to formulate true judgments about reality, thereby allowing for philosophic ideas to be rooted in a realist metaphysic.[4]

After dialogues refuting the probabilism of the Academic Skeptics and recovering an ethical motion toward beatitude, Augustine begins his third Cassiciacum dialogue, the *De ordine*, with the goal of arriving at an understanding of the phenomenal things of the world by a return to the metaphysical foundations of the created order. The most fundamental problem facing Augustine's attempt to understand God's creation as that which roots and supports the entire world is the problem of God's apparent lack of providential care for things.[5] As denying this belief in God's Providence is entirely impious and untenable, Augustine concludes, much like Socrates in the *First Alcibiades*,[6] that the chief problem is not

---

4 Often, listings of the Cassiciacum Dialogues include the *Soliloquies*. Yet, as this work is not a dialogue with another person, I argue against this classification. This final Cassiciacum work differs not only in form, but the change in form denotes a substantively different kind of work. While the three dialogues address key philosophical arguments, the Soliloquies addresses the very nature of philosophy and its role in the life of Christian perfection.

5. *ord.* 1.1.1.

6. Plato, *Alcibiades* 1.129b.

in the world itself, as evidently it could not be, but is in fact our lack of self-knowledge.[7] We, like the foolish Alcibiades, do not even know that we do not know. This self-knowledge is to be arrived at, for Augustine, via a threefold process of self-cultivation: withdrawing himself from the sensible, concentrating his thought on the opinions that he holds, and correcting them via reference to liberal education.[8]

The advertence to the liberal arts is a hallmark of early Augustinian views of the perfection of man's rational capacities. Augustine's appreciation reaches its full defense and proper progressive dynamism through the different liberal studies in an intellectual ascent in a work of the following summer entitled *De quantitate animae*. Yet here in the *De ordine*, Augustine is content to present natural conceptions of human learning as a whole directing us toward the good. This orientation of the liberal arts is testified to by the close of Book 2, where Augustine denominates the arts themselves and describes their necessity. He says, "anyone who does not know these matters, and yet wishes to question and dispute about even his own soul—let alone investigating about the Most High God, who is better known by knowing what He is not—such a one will fall into every possible error."[9] In light of this, perhaps we are tempted to draw a superficial conclusion that while Augustine in 387 supported the liberal arts and the human role in the pursuit of real knowledge, something had happened by 389 when Augustine writes negatively in the *De magistro* of the role of human instrumentality in reaching that which is true. Yet, a conclusion that sees these as opposite positions is false, as regards both the *De magistro* and the change in Augustine. Prior to 389, Augustine does tend to follow the Stoic descriptions of the nature of the perfection of the human will. Yet, the liberal arts were never accounted by Augustine as generating knowledge by their own power, nor did Augustine later reject them as unhelpful in knowing the truth. The change is not a radical departure, but instead is one that moves organically: from liberal arts as absolutely necessary secondary causes, to liberal arts as correlative expression of the process of intellectual conversion, to liberal arts as uniquely helpful in our recollection and retention of knowledge.

To appreciate fully the role of Augustine's understanding of the entirety of human cognitional investigation let us return to the *De ordine*.

---

7. *ord.* 1.1.3.
8. Ibid.
9. *lib. arb.* 2.16.44.

Building up to the theoretical systemization of liberal knowledge let us look at two key moments from earlier in this text. In the first, we have the rather unusual opening story of the dialogue. In it, Augustine retells a certain discussion that took place when he was awake in the middle of the night, as had become his custom in his days lost in philosophic thought. Having heard a rustling sound during the middle of a storm, Augustine wondered what it could be, when his student Licentius volunteered a rather detailed answer of the physical phenomena of a leaf stuck in the drain by way of reference to the idea of a larger metaphysical order.[10]

In the discourse that follows throughout the night, it becomes clear that Augustine's pupil Licentius has had a conversion of mind. Augustine reinforces this change through a second pupil, Trygetius, who rejoices in Licentius's adoption of an orderliness that entails intelligibility and also a rejection of Licentius's earlier Academic Skepticism.[11] Augustine is keen to point out that part of Licentius's struggle with philosophy has been due to his over-attachment to literature. In the *Contra academicos* at a number of junctions, Licentius abandons the discussion and pursuit of truth for the reading of poetry. In these prior moments, Augustine had chided the youthful Licentius for his diversions, but now in the *De ordine*, the relationship has changed. Just as Socrates no longer badgers Alcibiades once Alcibiades realizes that he knows nothing, so Augustine, the patient educator, takes a new tack by way of positive encouragement of Licentius's pursuit of the truth, a pursuit that will ultimately terminate in the discussion of the ends of liberal learning.

Augustine, more so than his interlocutors in the De ordine, is aware of the nature of Licentius's intellectual conversion and the effect that his conversion has on their relationship. By the middle of Book 1, in the wake of a particularly intense discussion, Augustine recalls, "Then, when Trygetius had become silent, and while I could scarce contain myself for joy because I saw that the youthful son of my very dear friend was becoming a son to me as well—and not only this, but he was advancing and strengthening in his friendship also towards me."[12] Augustine is led to marvel at the change that has occurred in his pupil, who is no longer

---

10. *ord.* 1.3.6—1.7.20.

11. *c. acad.* 1.3.7.

12 *ord.* 1.6.16.

simply experiencing the beginning of an intellectual conversion, but is now a real student of philosophy.

In taking up the mantle of philosophy, Licentius has now distinguished himself far beyond what Alcibiades was to become to Socrates, but also beyond that of Theatetus. Unlike Alcibiades, Theatetus was a young man who, like Licentius, had studied the liberal arts and was thus ready for the pursuit of the nature of the truth, as we see in his eponymous Platonic dialogue.[13] However, it is important to note the contrast between how Augustine describes his relationship with Licentius versus the description that we have from Plato. Famously, in the *Theatetus*, Plato couples his defense of friendship in pursuing the truth with his analogous role of midwifery.[14] Socrates argues that he is not the one responsible for the production of the ideas, but simply guides the person bearing the idea to term and tests the viability of the offspring. Although not rejecting the fundamental role of facilitator as suggested by the midwife analogy, Augustine's relationship is far more personal than that of a midwife. Licentius becomes an adopted son, and this term is certainly not accidental to Augustine, as the culmination of the pupil/sonship dynamic presents itself in Adeodatus's role in the *De magistro*. Moreover, while, as with Plato there is a reference to friendship, we can readily grasp that Augustine means a friendship far more complete than the one Plato has in mind, due to the responsibility and love that is invested in rearing children. For Augustine, the intellectual conversion of his pupil allows for friendship not because Licentius has been purified enough to enter a rank or class of scholars, but rather because the intellectual conversion allows for an encounter with creation that is transformative of the pupil and transformative of the teacher. Whereas the midwife is hired simply to aid in the birth of the child, the new father or mother does not merely help to conduct the child into the world well. To be a true educator requires the development of a reciprocal relationship. While the principle conversion to the truth occurs in the mind of the pupil, a real teacher is also jointly conformed more fully to the truth as known in his or her pupils. Because the educator and the pupil contemplate a shared extra-mental reality, the intellectual light that each brings to bear on the respective subject matter illumines more than that which was known simply by the educator.

---

13. Plato, *Theatetus*, 145d.
14. Ibid., 148e–151b.

This brings us to the second major scene from the *De ordine* that regards education. Toward the end of Book I, Licentius tells Augustine of his rejection of his prior disordered fascination with poetry, and dedicates himself to philosophy by way of Christ's grace. Augustine's response to this full conversion is quite powerful: he is moved to tears in his prayer. Licentius, for his part, is eloquently depicted as chanting Psalm 79:8 to himself: "O God of hosts convert us; show us your face and we shall be saved."[15] If we parse this lone biblical attribution within the whole text of the *De ordine*, we can see that what Augustine is trying to do is link the discussion of Providence on the grand scale, with that of the personalized steps by which God leads each individual to come to know Him. Regarding the large-scale depiction of Providence, Psalm 79:8 is certainly fitting for speaking of the nature of how the created order is indeed directed only by God so that it can be redeemed. Yet, I think in the smaller context—the context not of the discussion of the problem of Providence, but of Licentius's conversion—the psalm is all the more important. God is the fundamental agent in our conversion, and who is saved is not the individual simply, but the people of God, completely and irrevocably. Nevertheless, it truly is the individual and all of the dimensions of his personality, who in beholding God face to face, is justified by God. To put the prayer in Augustinian terms, "God of perfect intelligibility and love, restore us; show us thy loving presence and we shall be perfectly ordered to you."

Significantly, immediately after Licentius's prayer, Monica, Augustine's mother, makes her first appearance in this text.[16] In the Cassiciacum Dialogues, Monica is the one who embodies infused theological wisdom, and who thus stands to offer a complement to, and in some sense, a perfection of the formally philosophic discussion. At her introduction, she strikes us as incongruous, given the moods of the other characters, and a bit severe, since as soon as she appears, she chides Licentius for singing the psalm out of its liturgical context. The point of this is not for theological wisdom to act as a nag, but rather that perfect theological wisdom entails not only orthodoxy but also orthopraxy. In this sense, the wisdom of Licentius is clearly shown to be authentic, but is at the same time not the full possession of our earthly knowing of the Divine. His philosophic conversion is that of one who is beginning to take the first steps, of one

15. *ord.* 1.8.22; my translation.
16. Ibid., 1.8.22.

who is begging to see God's face, of one who is becoming rightly ordered to his end.

Monica's intervention has another note to it, which is important for our consideration. While Augustine and Licentius experience this greatly affective moment, Monica's lack of tears and brusqueness at Licentius's prayer indicate that she does not have this same privileged kinship with him. While the salvation offered by Jesus Christ through the church is indeed universal, it also is particularized in the sense of being lived out through the conversion of individuals and embodied in their particular renewed relationships. Universality does not entail invariability. Yet, the path of Licentius's conversion to wisdom did not happen in such a way as to largely exclude Monica; it is rather that the particular philosophic pursuit of Licentius allows for a true intellectual communicability about the order of creation with other persons. This attribute is not part of the wisdom given to Monica.[17]

In the *De Magistro*, the discussion of the nature of education is far more technical. Rather than making the points about the nature of the relationship between God's providential ordering of the whole and of the individual, here Augustine and Adeodatus take up the question of the role of language and communication. Augustine begins the work with a very strong premise: that the sole end of speech is teaching or reminding ourselves and others about the nature of what is true.[18] Thus, speech itself does not disclose the reality, but rather recalls that same reality. All speech is a sign of something else.[19]

Augustine, working with Adeodatus, develops his ideas about the nature of signs. He indicates that these signs are either in reference to other signs, which again may refer to other signs, or they refer to things themselves. Unsurprisingly, this distinction, especially as regards signs of signs, brings about a discussion of grammar via the proper understanding of the parts of speech. In speaking of signs that point to realities or

---

17. This may seem puzzling. If theological wisdom is greater than philosophical, should it not be greater in its communicability? I think that Augustine would answer no. There is a reason that Monica's theological wisdom is always expounded via Augustine, who himself is able to possess both forms of wisdom. While philosophical and theological wisdom are cooperative, there is a distinct role played by philosophy insofar as it is necessarily shareable in its pursuit of the truth via our rational faculty. Wisdom due to theological contemplation is not as shareable insofar as it is a mystical encounter initiated by God's own particular agency in the soul.

18. *mag.* 1.1.

19. Ibid., 1.2.

signifiables, Adeodatus is quick to concede, "I do agree with you that we can't carry on a conversation at all unless the words we hear direct the mind to the things of which they are the signs."[20] In other words, the intelligibility of language is found in the degree to which it allows the mind to encounter that which is. What we come to know are not signs principally speaking, but the realities that are indicated by these very signs.

After a brief excursus on the nature of virtual reality versus things that are really real, which paves the way for St. Anselm's Ontological Argument, Augustine closes the discussion with a shift away from the dialogical format. Significantly, he begins with a kind of Socratic disorientation wherein he argues that in our knowing of signs and things that which is first must necessarily be the thing and to it, our knowledge of the sign is then added. Thus, whatever we learn, we learn the thing itself, by way of our senses and interior attunement to the truth of being, but we use the signs to direct our attention toward the reality that we are encountering. Augustine continues, "Regarding each of the things we understand, however, we don't consult a speaker who makes sounds outside of us, but the Truth that presides within over the mind itself, though perhaps words prompt us to consult Him. What is more, He Who is consulted, He Who is said *to dwell in the inner man*, does teach: Christ—that is, *the unchangeable power and everlasting wisdom of God*, which every rational soul does consult, but is disclosed to anyone to the extent that he can apprehend it, according to his good or evil will."[21]

Augustine sketches this out more explicitly as he argues that it is clearly not the role of humans to impart knowledge, but to bring forth signs that through their sensation the mind of the learner can recall that which truly is.[22] The truth is a good that we cannot commodify, precisely because it is not individuals who possess the truth as a discrete good, but rather human persons can only more or less correctly point to the truth in things by the use of efficacious signs. Augustine states clearly, "Therefore, when I'm stating truths, I don't even teach the person who is looking upon these truths. He's taught not by my words but by the things themselves made manifest within when God discloses them."[23]

---

20. Ibid., 8.22.
21. Ibid., 11.38.
22. Ibid., 12.39.
23. Ibid., 12.40.

Even if we leave aside the questions concerning the nature of this immediate divine disclosure to the particular intellect, we are still left to consider the implications of Augustine's conception of the role of teaching. Here, I think it helpful to return to the *De ordine* and consider anew the question of liberal learning. For, if all we can do is point to signs, more or less well, that tend to be oriented toward the disclosure of truth, does not this signification tend toward utter irrelevancy? Cannot God move the intellect to the truth regardless of the poor or even erroneous human signification? And, if this is so, then why should there be a rehabilitation of the liberal arts or philosophy, when all that we need is God to move us to attain to the truth with or without any signs?

The solution to these problems, of course, must necessarily lie in the fact that while Augustine does hold to a theory of Divine Illumination, he is certainly not a noetic Occasionalist. While we human instructors can only supply the signs, those signs, as participating in the intelligible whole of the created order, are actually indicative of and dispositive toward the things themselves. The clarification Augustine attempts to make between humans as teachers of signs and not things is in no way a diminishment of human agency and therefore responsibility in producing correct waymarkers on the path to knowledge of true things. Such correct way markers are not logical propositions that can be simply memorized and thus understood—although recitation of common sayings by a beloved professor may be helpful—but instead, correct signs are never to be mistaken for what they are not. For Augustine, they are certainly neither the end of our journey, nor are they the impetus that allows us to continue to move toward a life most blessed.

Moreover, as Augustine details in Book 2 of *De ordine*, the signs need to be received well in order to lead adequately to the truth. Before Augustine gives his blessing to a study of liberal learning, he first requires two preconditions. These twin principles comprise one unified approach to advance in the truth: an upright moral life and healthy friendships. He commands that students be "supported by faith, hope, and love, let them have God the object of their worship, their thinking, and their striving. Let them desire tranquility and a definite course for their own studies and for those of all their associates; and for themselves and for whomsoever else such things are possible, a good mind and a quiet life."[24]

---

24. *ord.* 2.9.25.

The striving for learning Augustine speaks of in *De Ordine*, with its proximate goals of virtue and taking God as the object of their investigation, strikes a very similar note to a lecture given by Pope Benedict XVI. In 2008, Benedict traveled to Paris and gave a lecture to ministers of culture at the College of the Bernardines on the topic of the nature of European culture. Benedict gently prods them, "We are in a place that is associated with the culture of monasticism. Does this still have something to say to us today, or are we merely encountering the world of the past? In order to answer this question, we must consider for a moment the nature of Western monasticism itself. What was it about?"[25] Pope Benedict, the willing teacher, leads his audience to see that the essence of the monastic vocation was the search for God. Yet because the creative and redemptive God is intelligible, theirs "was not an expedition into a trackless wilderness, a search leading them into total darkness."[26]

Pope Benedict then elaborates the nature of the monastic journey, an ascent, not of individuals necessarily, but of the entire monastic community and, indeed, Western culture itself from the seeking of God who intelligibly discloses himself to becoming a culture of the Word and therefore a culture of education. This education is not an individualized pursuit; Benedict contends that it does not terminate in a private mystical ascent as it was for the Neo-Platonists, but rather in the sharing of the revealed Word of God. Lastly, this community of reading, this fellowship and friendship centered on the pursuit of the truth, finds its culmination in the production and attention to signs in both the liberal and the fine arts. The development of these arts are not a replacement for the study of the Word of God, but provide the full flowering of philosophically sound seeking of that which is most real through the development of magnificent and lasting signs. As Benedict argues in reference to monastic chant, it was not an individual expression of self, but rather, "about vigilantly recognizing with the 'ears of the heart' the inner laws of the music of creation, the archetypes of music that the Creator built into his world and into men, and thus discovering music that is worthy of God, and at the same time truly worthy of man, music whose worthiness resounds in purity."

Augustine's vision of education as outlined in the *De ordine* and the *De magistro*, consists in three distinct steps. First, it is transformative.

25. Benedict XVI, "Meeting."
26. Ibid.

Augustine, like Plato, understands that true education often begins by way of disorientation. However, through signs that point us toward the God who is Truth and who is working in us, we can come to a correct orientation toward the Good. This transformation is then fundamentally unitive, but not simply as individual co-workers in the service of the Lord. Instead, the pursuit of knowledge takes place within a community of faith, friendship, and filial adoption. Finally, this unitive transformation is productive. The encounter with truth allows for the generation of new signs that point more correctly to the created order that informs our lives, and reduces the errors of our own intellectual grasp. God of hosts convert us; show us your face and we shall be saved.

These marks of authentic educational interaction and formation we can see not only in Augustine or in Pope Benedict XVI, but also in St. Benedict of Nursia. In the Prologue to his famous Rule, he echoes Augustine at Cassiciacum in two profound ways. He treats education directly, as he refers to the establishment of a school not of a purely philosophic investigation, but a "school for the Lord's service."[27] That is to say, Benedict is founding a school, a common fellowship, centered upon a purified seeking of the truth and the correct worship of God. More importantly, however, are the incipient lines of the Prologue, where St. Benedict exhorts the new monks, "Listen carefully, my son, to the master's instructions . . . from a father who loves you."[28] We see the embodiment of this same filial seeking of God, this docility which was found in the relationship between Augustine and Licentius, between Augustine and Adeodatus, here in Benedict's Rule. This is, on the one hand, a kind of culmination of seeking: to have found the one to whom you should listen. And we who have been educated by Father Matthew Lamb should indeed account ourselves blessed. May we grow in our appreciation of all of the fathers and mothers who have loved us as they educated us, and may we recall their words as signs pointing us to the Truth. In our own encounter with the face of Truth, may we generate more perfect signs, thus participating in our own human way in the conversion, the revelation, and the salvation that God offers to all people.

---

27. Benedict, *Rule*, prologue.
28. Ibid.

BIBLIOGRAPHY

Augustine. *The Teacher*. In *Against the Academicians and the Teacher*. Translated by Peter King, 94–146. Indianapolis: Hackett, 1995.

———. *Contra Academicos libri III*. Edited by Jacques-Paul Migne. *Patrologia Latina* 32. Paris: Garnier, 1845.

———. *De Magistro liber unus*. Edited by Jacques-Paul Migne. *Patrologia Latina* 32. Paris: Garnier, 1845.

———. *De Ordine libri II*. Edited by Jacques-Paul Migne. *Patrologia Latina* 32. Paris: Garnier, 1845.

———."Divine Providence and the Problem of Evil." In *The Happy Life; Answer to Skeptics; Divine Providence and the Problem of Evil; Soliloquies*, 227–332. Translated by Robert P. Russell. Fathers of the Church: A New Translation 5. Washington, DC: Catholic University of America Press, 2008.

Benedict. *The Rule of St. Benedict in English*. Translated by Timothy Fry. Collegeville, MN: Liturgical, 1982.

Benedict XVI. "Meeting With Representatives from the World of Culture." http://w2.vatican.va/content/benedict_xvi/en/speeches/2008/september/documents/hf_ben-xvi_spe_20080912_parigi-cultura.html.

Plato. *Theatetus*. Translated by M. J. Levett and Rev. Myles Burnyeat. In *Complete Works*, edited by John M. Cooper, 157–234. Indianapolis: Hackett, 1997.

———. *Alcibiades*. Translated by D. S. Hutchinson. In *Complete Works*, edited by John M. Cooper, 557–95. Indianapolis: Hackett, 1997.

8

The Joy of Christ in Albert the Great's *De corpore domini*

Sr. Albert Marie Surmanski, OP

THE THEME OF JOY should never be far from the surface in theology done by Dominicans. In fact, a few years ago, Fr. Paul Murray, OP wrote a book entitled *The New Wine of Dominican Spirituality: A Drink Called Happiness*. It focused on joy in Dominican life and centered around the themes of studying and sharing the truth, awareness of the gift of Redemption, trust in God's Providence, and rejoicing in the natural goodness of creation, particularly in wine.[1] The work on which I wrote my dissertation, *De corpore domini,* which is attributed to Albert the Great accords well with those joyful aspects of Dominican spirituality, and it is on this theme of joy, especially in its connection with wine, on which I will speak in honor of Fr. Lamb and the graduate program at Ave Maria University.

This is not so because studying under Fr. Lamb involves drinking much wine, or even becoming a Dominican but because Fr. Lamb has internalized the wisdom of Aquinas, the Dominican theologian *par excellence*. Therefore, Fr. Lamb's teaching reflects so much of the wisdom grounded in Aquinas's Dominican view of reality. For example, Fr. Lamb approaches the mystery of God with an enduring awe and joy. He models

---

1. Murray, *New Wine*.

a reverential amazement at the fact that our human minds can know deep truths about God by the light of faith and hope to behold him face to face in the light of glory. Showing his living faith, Father continues to exhibit this deep sense of wonder despite teaching some of the same material every year. The texts taught may be the same, but the approach to the reality of God can grow ever deeper. Fr. Lamb also always brings to his classes a joy in contemplating the truth together with his students which leads him to address his students as "friends" and to genuinely care about their lives. Finally, after studying with Fr. Lamb it is impossible to forget his affirmation of the ordered goodness of creation in his often repeated reminder that "the higher does not negate the lower" and "the universal is known in the particular." This awareness leads Fr. Lamb to illustrate philosophical truths with stories, often from his own experience.

So, in honor of Fr. Lamb and appreciating the universal in the particular, I am going to trace the theme of joy in one particular work, St. Albert's *De corpore domini*. *De corpore domini* is a devotional and scholastic work about the Eucharist, written by Albert the Great or one of his disciples at the end of the 1200s.[2] While making rigorous theological arguments about the nature of the Eucharist, it also contains several sections where the theology is more deliberately clothed in beautiful language and imagery to move the heart of the reader.

Although not well known in the English speaking world today, *De corpore domini* became remarkably popular soon after it was written. It remained well liked, especially in Germany until the Reformation. There are more than 80 manuscripts of this work found in different cities throughout Europe, as well as many instances of partial translations into the vernacular either as free-standing works or worked into collections and commentaries by later authors.[3] You may remember that we date the invention of the printing press to 1440. By 1484, three separate Latin editions of *De corpore domini* had been printed, two of which were the inaugural works on new presses.[4]

---

2. Although the Albertine influence on this work is undisputed, its precise authorship is the subject of debate. In favor of the work's authenticity, see Anzulewicz, "Theology of Albert," 64–66; against, see Fries, *Doppeltraktat*.

3. See Sheeben, "Ecrits d'Albert," 28–34. For further consideration of the manuscripts, see Kolping, "Handschriftliche," 1–39; and Fauser, "Handschriften" (1983), 118; (1984), 147; (1985), 142.

4. Gottschall, "Vernacular Literatures," 743–47; Hawkins, *First Books*, 7.

Clearly, the presentation of the Eucharist at the heart of the Christian life in *De corpore domini* was remarkably attractive to its readers. It is a strongly sapiential and very joyful presentation. The theme of joy mirrors the concern of the author to connect being and experience. In the work, joy is grounded in the metaphysical reality of God's perfect being but through the Eucharist, it becomes a significant element in Christian experience. Within *De corpore domini*, joy even overflows into the style and emphasis of the writing itself.

The fountainhead of joy in *De corpore domini* is within the inner life of God, source of all goodness. Although Albert's main focus in this work is on the Eucharist, he places the Eucharist within the whole saving plan of God which begins in the mystery of the inner goodness of God and finds its final goal there. This means one of the first movements of *De corpore domini* is to describe the goodness of God as the first cause of the Eucharist. Albert uses the imagery of a torrent of water to describe the movement of God's goodness towards his creatures. He says, "For although everything which is given to us is given by the good and gracious will of God, nevertheless, he had the most gracious and kindly intention towards us when he provided this great sacrament for us. For his rushing and melting charity directed his whole sweetness to this."[5] Albert portrays God's goodness as the source of all created goodness, natural and supernatural. The grace given in the Eucharist is the fullest point of contact between God's goodness and humankind. The image is that of a stream flowing downward so that the whole mass of water touches the earth at the Eucharist.

Continuing, Albert elaborates on God's originating goodness with his own "overflowing torrent" of description. He describes God's qualities as "goodness, kindness, piety, sweetness, charity, and readiness to forgive."[6] The first of the descriptors, goodness, is important because Albert understands it as expressing that God is fullness of being and thus the source of the being of all creation. He uses the Platonic maxim received through Dionysius, "the good is diffusive," to express not only that that the natural goodness of all things comes from God, but especially

---

5. Albert, *De corpore domini* 1.1.1.

6. Ibid., 1.1.2. Some of these may seem to be unnecessarily anthropomorphic qualities, but they are all drawn from Scripture and explicated by Albert with the help of Scripture. Later in his work, Albert does mention the basic principle of negative theology—that created limitations should not be predicated of God.

that the higher gift of the divine life given through the Eucharist comes from the same good God.[7]

Among the other names, the etymology for kindness or *benignitas* is particularly expressive of the spirit of the work. While *benignitas* often has the connotations of gentle goodness, or kindness, Albert chooses to give it an etymology based on a contraction of *bonus ignis*, "good fire."[8] He describes this fire not as a gentle warming heat, but as a "burning and rushing goodness" pouring towards mankind. He deliberately chooses a dramatic and dynamic etymology, characterizing God's intense bounty as a movement almost frightening in its power.

Two initial ways in which this active divine charity impacts human experience can be drawn from this group of texts. First, it satisfies the human heart. Varying slightly his image of the river, Albert writes, "This sacrament appeases desire; as a torrent melted by the fire of charity, it fills each of our hearts to overflowing."[9] The warmth of charity melts the frozen stream or glacier of grace, directing it towards the recipient of communion, quieting his desires. Second, Albert implies that even knowledge of God's intense love can become a great source of confidence for the Christian. He writes, "For this strongly burning kindness should by its merit bring all men to conversion."[10] This would be a heartening reflection for one belonging to an Order dedicated to preaching. On this level, knowledge of God's goodness can be a source of comfort. Christian joy, then, is founded on and is a participation in, the goodness of God, which can be relied upon never to run dry.

God's joy is further revealed in the person of Christ. Albert parallels the joyful outpouring of the divine love with an unusual description of Christ's disposition at the Last Supper. Albert describes Christ as "cheerful" or "joyful" in instituting the Eucharist.[11] He uses the word *hilaritate*, which means cheerfulness or good humor, even exhilaration. At first it may seem almost comical to hear the expression "God loves a cheerful giver" applied to Christ instituting the Eucharist—isn't this a

---

7. See Dionysius, *Divine Names* 4.1. This specific quotation is not found in Dionysius, but this chapter is the source for its usage in the Christian tradition, although it also has earlier origins in Plato (see Plato, *Republic* 517d), from whence it was received through the Platonic authors; Albert, *De corpore domini* 1.1.2.

8. Albert, *De corpore domini* 1.1.2.

9. Ibid., 1.1.1.

10. Ibid., 1.1.2.

11. Albert, *De corpore domini* 2.1.2.

solemn moment?[12] But in this instance, joy or cheerfulness is a sign of wholeheartedness. It is a sign that the gift of Christ's life is given completely willingly. Albert writes, "For if any sadness of heart was felt in giving, he did not completely give himself in the gift . . . For that alone is given, which is fully given, since in this giving, Christ held nothing back as private for himself, conferring on us all the gifts of his humanity and divinity."[13] If he gives himself, including his heart, his whole heart must be in the giving. Albert styles Christ as the one Aristotle describes as practicing the virtue of magnificence—a man who gives generously and appropriately but obviously giving a greater gift than Aristotle could envision.[14]

Albert uses language just as striking to make a similar point about Christ's affection in giving the Eucharist. He draws on Luke 22:15, "with desire I have desired to eat this Passover with you."[15] He writes, "For he desired with desire, who communicated himself to his own from the intimate affection of his heart and endured death rejoicing, who in dying did not slip away from his friends but remained with them in the best communion with them in the gift which he gave."[16] The strongest phrase here is "he endured death rejoicing." There seem to be echoes of Heb 12:2 which says that Jesus "for the joy that was set before him endured the cross."[17]

What is this joy, then, that Christ is said to experience? Since the fullness of God is understood as the first source of joy, it would first need to be a rest of Christ's human will in the divine will. This can be assumed to underlie everything else which is said about joy. Yet how Albert expresses the source of Christ's joy is interesting. He puts emphasis on Christ's joy in bringing his followers into communion with him. Thus Christ is said to take joy in bestowing good on his disciples. Perhaps on a human level, this is the joy experienced in friendship—willing both good to a friend and a certain sharing of life with him and being the means by which the friend's good is brought about. Even more, Albert seems to be showing that Christ's human will parallels the overflowing goodness

---

12. 2 Cor 7–9.
13. Albert, *De corpore domini* 2.1.2.
14. See Aristotle, *Nicomachean Ethics* 4.2 (1122a20—1123a30).
15. Translated from the Vulgate.
16. Albert, *De corpore domini* 2.1.3.
17. All citations from the Bible in this chapter are from the RSV.

of the divine will. By referring to the shared proximate object of Christ's human will and the divine will (that is, the intention of bringing human persons into communion with God) the unity in Christ is emphasized. This unity would be either his unified experience, or the way in which his humanity is the perfect instrument of his divinity. Of course this section also serves to remind each reader that he or she is the object of this loving concern of Christ.

It should be noted here that Albert does not, either in general or in this work, tend towards a reductive Christology, collapsing the humanity of Christ into his divinity. In language, he tends in the other direction, sometimes using terminology closer to the *homo assumptus* theory although never actually formally endorsing that view.[18] In *De corpore domini*, he several times speaks about Christ's soul and Christ's virtues, giving weight to the true humanity of Christ. Albert also refers specifically to Damascene's understanding of the divine nature operating in and through the human as an instrument, as when Christ touched a leper and healed him.[19]

The joy revealed in Christ actually begins to come into contact with the misery of human nature through the Incarnation and Redemption. While God is the source of goodness, the disordered wills of human persons introduced sadness and suffering into the world. It is a theme of the work that all that is perfectly good is from God, while because of sin all misery belongs to mankind, so the Christian life is seen as a turning towards being, healing, and joy. This may be part of the reason why Albert wants to emphasize Christ's joy and charity towards mankind even in his suffering. Albert describes sin as bitter, the antithesis of the sweetness of God, the poisoned bite of the serpent, a sickness for which we need a remedy, a weakness and famine in which we are starving and dying for lack of spiritual sustenance. This sin is the source of all distressing experience, both for humanity and for Christ.

Albert writes that Christ was "not only made like us" (that is, in human nature) "but he was made like sinners and was made able to suffer for us." This is a classical explanation of the various human pains or punishments which Christ took on.[20] Christ assumed a passible human

---

18. In 1.1.6, Albert mentions the "man assumed" although he later corrects his language to the "nature assumed." On this theological issue, see Barnes, "Person, Hypostasis, and the Hypostatic Union," 107–46.

19. Albert, *De corpore domini* 3.3.1; Damascene, *De fide orthodoxa* 3.3, 3.5.

20. Cf. *ST* III.14.

nature so as to be able to suffer the punishment for sin although he was not personally guilty. Albert adds, "and he endured all the weariness of human life."[21] This phrase sounds as though it is supposed to resonate with the experience of the reader. Human life certainly can sometimes be characterized as wearying. Yet when Albert does speak about life as wearying he does so here within his description of what humanity gave to Christ. It is balanced, and more than over-balanced by the description of the transforming goodness Christ gave to mankind. Although Christ's sufferings are acknowledged, the emphasis in the work is not on sorrowing with Christ, but on being healed and invigorated by him.

There are a few other places where Albert emphasizes the difficulties and pains of human life, but as above, it is always in the context of the Redemption transforming them. Albert sees the Eucharist as the place where the marvelous exchange between Christ and humanity, begun in the Incarnation, is continued in each human life. Speaking about communion with God in the Eucharist, he describes it as a river on which trade takes place. In commercial trade, what is abundant in one realm is traded for what is abundant in another. Following this principle, in the exchange of the liturgy, humanity offers "poverty of spirit, mourning for sins, tears, fasting, afflictions and chastisements of the body" and receives "joy of heart, and consolation of the Holy Spirit, and the sweetness of the taste of the divine, and a certain taste of the virtues that we may desire them more strongly."[22]

What exactly does Albert mean by this "taste of sweetness"? Taking into account other places where Albert speaks about the divine sweetness either as an attribute of God or in relation to the healing of the bitterness of original sin, this expression seems to combine the ontological and the experiential. Albert many times mentions that the grace which elevates the soul to union with Christ is sustained through the Eucharist. Sanctifying grace in itself, of course, is not directly experienced, although it does modify the soul, beginning to establish a sweet order within it. Albert thus notes that the practice of virtue is strengthened through the grace of the Eucharist. Here is another level of experience. The ability to live in a consistently virtuous way has a divine foundation but is lived humanly. As a sign of grace, it would be recognized as something sustained by God, but it would be "testable" as a fact of experience in the life of the

---

21. Albert, *De corpore domini* 3.1.6.
22. Ibid., 4.1.

Christian. Finally, Albert often speaks of the particular experience of receiving communion as "sweetness." He uses the expression so frequently that it is unlikely that he means only interior order and the ability to live with virtue. He also seems to be pointing to the awareness of God's gracious presence through, perhaps, the action of gifts of the Holy Spirit and the "taste" of his fruits.

Supporting this reading, Albert also speaks about "sweetness" in receiving communion in his *Commentary on the Sentences*.[23] Here he asks a question not included in Aquinas' *Commentary*, nor in Lombard's *Sentences*. Albert asks why the sweetness of the sacrament is not always experienced by those receiving it. An obvious answer might seem to be that those receiving communion are lacking in some virtue. In Albert's *Commentary* this actually is the first objection. He refutes it by saying that really, all those receiving communion worthily have at least some degree of all the virtues since the virtues are connected. His answer is that experience varies because the bread received in communion is "*panis . . . voluntarius*" that is, "bread with a will" and the experience of communion will be in accordance with Christ's will for the one receiving. Christ's will is always a good will, sometimes withholding experience now so it may be greater in the future.[24] This is a remarkably cheerful answer that sees the merciful providence of God's love as primary and human weakness as very much secondary.

Next, the sweetness offered to humanity in the Eucharist is signified by the wine used in the sacrament. The joy-giving qualities of wine constitute a major and rather lively thread in *De corpore domini*, tied, of course, to the naturally pleasant experience of drinking wine. A recurring instance of this thread is the allegorical interpretation in which wine points to the joy which communion with God brings to human life. Albert describes the mixture of water and wine at Mass, noting that the mixing and dissolving of the tasteless water into the delicious wine symbolizes the way that humanity is elevated through Christ. He says:

> Enough water should be added to the chalice not to change the ... taste of the wine into something else, but to signify what must be signified in the sacrament, and this is the union of human nature with Christ, since water because of its insipid taste

---

23. Albert, *Super IV Sent.* 13.36.

24. Afterwards and secondarily, Albert does admit that an imperfect degree of virtue in the one receiving might have some role in the experience of receiving communion.

> signifies insipid man, and there should be a joining of water with wine, which receives the taste of wine by losing its own insipidity, not so that it dilutes the taste of wine to the insipid taste of water, since man receives the flavoring of grace from Christ, and Christ does not suffer loss of grace from man.[25]

Here, there is the notion that in the hypostatic union itself humanity is ennobled by being united to Christ's divinity.

The same principle applies to the members of the church as they come into union with Christ. Albert comments on the good taste of the species of wine in the Eucharist saying, "the taste of water is not perceived in the sacrament, since the people, united to the blood of the Lord does not make the blood insipid, but rather receives the taste of spiritual joys."[26] It is through Christ that human life is made palatable, cheerful, intoxicating with the joy of being called to friendship with Christ.

Albert spends a good deal of time considering the signification of wine as matter for the sacrament. Of first importance is that Christ himself used it at the Last Supper. It was also used by the people of Israel, who appreciated God's goodness in giving man wine as meant to "cheer the heart," which in turn, is founded on the natural qualities of wine itself.[27] This threefold depth of signification is found in the tradition before Albert. Something similar is found in Hugh of St. Victor's *Sacraments of the Christian Faith*.[28] Within the lowest element of this signification, that is, the fact that wine is good for man, Albert finds room to exuberantly indulge his human love of the natural sciences, combining zeal and scientific exactitude to try to prove not only that wine is good and cheering (which is really all that is required theologically) but to try prove that it is absolutely the best drink possible for man.

At this point, the work itself becomes entertaining and even humorous. In *De corpore domini,* wine is portrayed as the most nourishing and best drink of all drinks. It is very good for the digestion of food. It the only proper drink to quench the thirst of mature persons. Just as the human body is composed of many elements, so wine, which has a certain mixed nature, is an appropriate type of drink for mankind. Milk is good for the soft flesh of infants, barley water might help the sick and water the

---

25. Albert, *De corpore domini* 3.2.3.
26. Ibid., 3.1.2.
27. Ps 104:15.
28. Hugh of St. Victor, *De Sacramentis* 9.2.

feverish, but give wine alone to the healthy. And whatever you do, don't even consider lye, beer, mead, spiced vinegar, apple juice, fruit juice, rose water, violet-water, broom-plant water, or other liquid you might choose to press out of any fruit or flower. If you are a rural farmer, you may and probably should use some rich mixed swamp water to nourish your crops, but even though the human body also includes many elements mixed in, don't even think about drinking that or using it for the sacrament either. Use wine.[29]

Of course, Albert is not advocating overindulgence in wine. He quotes Sir 31:35 as a necessary balance to his praise of wine: "Wine was created from the beginning for joyfulness and not for drunkenness." In humorous ridicule he modifies the quote from Ps 42:6, "Deep calls to deep in the roar of your waterfalls," to mock the over indulgent, saying "in gluttons and drunkards deep calls to deep in the voice of the waterfalls of drink and their courses of food."[30] Here, there is not simply a testimony to the presence of Christ's joy in human life, but an example of a zest and joy in study that manifests itself in both intense careful study of detailed questions and balanced ridicule of the truly ridiculous. It takes a grounding in the truly great realities (in God ultimately) to keep recognition of ridiculous sinfulness from becoming bitter anger and for careful study of small details to be saved from weary futility. At this point, the full joy of God has flowed down, through the Eucharist, to permeate even the furthest reaches of human experience.

And this is what we are commemorating today, and what we are grateful for in Father Lamb's example: a commitment to study in order to see the wisdom of God by which all of creation is ordered. A trust in God's sustaining goodness that the task may be carried out with happiness. And a personal love of Christ who calls each one of us to friendship with him, and through him to communion with the Trinity, the source of all good and joy.

BIBLIOGRAPHY

Albert the Great. *Super IV Sententiarum*. Edited by Auguste Borgnet, *Opera Omnia* 30. Paris: L. Vives, 1894.

———. *De corpore domini*. Edited by Auguste Borgnet, *Opera Omnia* 38. Paris: L. Vives, 1899.

29. Albert, *De corpore domini* 3.2.1.
30 Ibid., 3.2.1.

Aquinas, Thomas. *Summa theologiae*. Translated by Fathers of the English Dominican Province. 5 vols. New York: Benziger Bros., 1947.

Aristotle. *The Nicomachean Ethics*. Translated by W. D. Ross. In *Complete Works of Aristotle: The Revised Oxford Translation*, edited by Jonathan Barnes, 2:1729–1867. Princeton: Princeton University, 1984.

Anzulewicz, Henryk. "The Systematic Theology of Albert the Great." Translated by Cornelia Oefelein. In *A Companion to Albert the Great: Theology, Philosophy and the Sciences*, edited by Irven M. Resnick, 15–67. Leiden: Brill, 2013.

Barnes, Cory L. "Albert the Great and Thomas Aquinas on Person, Hypostasis, and the Hypostatic Union." *Thomist* 72 (2008) 107–46.

John Damascene. *De Fide Orthodoxa*. Edited by J. P. Migne. In *Patrologiae Cursus Completus Series Graeca* 94. Paris: Imprimerie Catholique, 1864.

Dionysius. *The Divine Names*. In *Pseudo-Dionysius: The Complete Works*, translated by Colm Luibheid, 47–131. New York: Paulist, 1987.

Fauser, Winfried. "Albertus–Magnus–Handschriften." *Bulletin de philosophie médiévale* 25 (1983) 100–120; 26 (1984) 127–51; 27 (1985) 110–51.

Fries, Albert. *Der Doppeltraktat uber die Eucharistie unter dem Namen des Albertus Magnus*. Munster: Aschendorff, 1984.

Gottschall, Dagmar. "Albert's Contributions to or Influence on Vernacular Literatures." In *A Companion to Albert the Great: Theology, Philosophy and the Sciences*, edited by Irven M. Resnick, 725–57. Leiden: Brill, 2013.

Hawkins, Rush Christopher. *Titles of the First Books from the Earliest Presses Established in Different Cities, Towns, and Monasteries in Europe*. New York: Bouton, 1884.

Hugh of St. Victor. *De Sacramentis Christianae Fidei*. Edited by J. P. Migne. *Patrologiae Cursus Completus Series Secunda Latina* 176. Paris: Imprimerie Catholique, 1854.

Kolping, Adolf. "Die Handschriftliche Verbreitung der Messerklärung Alberts des Grossen." *Zeitschrift für katholische Theologie* 82 (1960) 1–39.

Murray, Paul. *The New Wine of Dominican Spirituality: A Drink Called Happiness*. London: Burns & Oates, 2006.

Plato. *Republic*. Translated by Paul Shorey. In *The Collected Dialogues of Plato, including the Letters*. Edited by Edith Hamilton and Huntington Cairns, 575–844. Princeton: Princeton University Press, 1961.

Sheeben, Matthias. "Les Ecrits d'Albert le Grand apres les Catalogues." *Revue Thomiste* 36 (1931) 28–34.

9

"Scrutinizing the Signs of the Times"
Truth and History in Catholic Social Doctrine

Thomas P. Harmon

POPE BENEDICT XVI HAS recently outlined two ways of interpreting the Second Vatican Council: according to a hermeneutic of reform, that is, of renewal in continuity with prior tradition, and a hermeneutic of discontinuity. The hermeneutic of reform, Pope Benedict says, holds that the church "is a subject that increases in time and develops; yet always remains the same, the one subject of the journeying people of God." On the other hand, the hermeneutic of discontinuity "risks ending in a split between the preconciliar Church and the postconciliar Church. It asserts that the texts of the council as such do not yet express the true spirit of the council. It claims that they are the result of compromises in which, to reach unanimity, it was found necessary to keep and reconfirm many old things that are now pointless. However, the true spirit of the council is not to be found in these compromises but instead in the impulses toward the new that are contained in the texts."[1] Obviously, Pope Benedict favors the former approach. The latter approach is characterized by an abandonment of the church's long tradition in favor of what is new, or putatively new, in the teaching of the Council.

1. Pope Benedict XVI, "A Proper Hermeneutic," x.

But the move to abandon the old and only to hold on to the new pits old against new and divides the church against herself. As Matthew L. Lamb observes,

> No ecumenical council explicates the whole of the Catholic faith tradition. Councils are called to address specific questions and issues in the light of the truths revealed by Jesus Christ and consigned to the apostles and their successors to hand on faithfully until the Lord returns in glory. The council's authoritative documents reflect the way in which the basic principles of the Catholic faith are applied to the variety of historical circumstances at different times. To appreciate the continuity from the first ecumenical council of Nicea in 325 AD through the most recent council one must attend to the sacred mysteries revealed by the Triune God and expressed in the creeds and worship of the Catholic Church.[2]

What both Pope Benedict and Fr. Lamb point out is that the proponents of a hermeneutic of discontinuity, whether they realize it or not, are also advocating the inverse method in approaching the Catholic faith. Instead of attending to the sacred mysteries revealed by the Triune God and expressed in the creeds and worship of the Catholic Church as the necessary context and hermeneutical key to understanding the Church's teaching, proponents of a hermeneutic of discontinuity instead pick what is newest, most familiar, and most to their taste in the Church's teaching, interpret the sacred mysteries revealed by the Triune God in light of those new things, and use their consequent findings to stand in judgment over the creeds and worship of the Church.

Each of the two hermeneutics sketched by Pope Benedict rest on a different, conflicting view of the relationship between the faith of the church and history. *Gaudium et Spes*, the Second Vatican Council's Pastoral Constitution on the Church in the modern world, looms large in the conflict between the two hermeneutics.[3] There is a particular passage in *Gaudium et Spes* that serves as a linchpin for distinguishing them: "[T]he Church has always had the duty of scrutinizing the signs of the times and of interpreting them in the light of the Gospel."[4] Interpreting this passage in one way leads to the hermeneutic of rupture; interpreting it

---

2. Lamb, "Renewal within Catholic Tradition," 440.

3. The document bears historical language even in its title.

4. "Ecclesiae officium incumbit signa temporum perscrutandi et sub Evangelii luce interpretandi." *GS* 4.

in another way affirms the hermeneutic of reform within continuity. It therefore provides a convenient place to examine the differing hermeneutics and their roots and ramifications.

Many have noted that the church's usage of this phrase in *Gaudium et Spes*, which originates in the Gospel of Matthew, departs substantially from its original Scriptural meaning referring to the advent of the Messiah.[5] In the old usage, rooted in Matthew's Gospel, the signs refer to the advent of the Messiah and so the focus is Christological. The new usage is summarized by Peter Bisson, who says that the new understanding of signs of the times are, "the social, political, economic, cultural, religious phenomena that occur so frequently and pervasively in human life that they seem to characterize a given period and seem to express both the needs and aspirations of humankind at the time; these are not simply events or phenomena, but somehow signs of the presence and activity of God in human history, signs that need to be recognized, interpreted, and responded to."[6] The novel usage of the phrase could itself be called a sign of the times, which indicates a shift in the understanding of history. Despite the presence of this shift in documents of the church's social teaching, the old way of understanding history still finds expression in those same documents. Unless the dual usage is itself unwitting, it is surprising that there is no guidance in the document itself about how to understand the phrase. Its meaning is taken to be immediately clear. This situation has led to what Stephen F. Toracco has called a "cacophony"[7] among competing interpretations. Toracco also notes that the original drafts of *Gaudium et Spes* include a footnote to Matthew, but that certain council fathers objected to its use on the grounds that the passage in Matthew has a quite different meaning than what it means in *Gaudium et Spes*. As Toracco points out, this raises serious questions: "Does this mean that the Council is admitting that the meaning given to 'reading the signs of the times' in *Gaudium et Spes* does not have a basis in Scripture? If 'reading the signs of the times' does not have a basis in Scripture, then what is its

---

5. See, *inter alia*, Bisson, "Breaking Open the Mysteries," 12; Elsbernd and Bieringer, "Interpreting the Signs of the Times" 43; Toracco, "From 'Social Justice' to 'Reading the Signs of the Times,'" 252.

6. Bisson, "Breaking Open," 121.

7. Toracco, "From 'Social Justice' to 'Reading the Signs of the Times,'" 256. The phrase's meaning is polyvalent; those on multiple sides of an argument can simultaneously claim that his or her position is based on a reading of the signs of the times.

basis?"[8] What accounts for its appearance in *Gaudium et Spes*, and what accounts for the document's assumption that everyone will already know what it means to read the signs of the times in the light of the Gospel?

In light of the resulting confusion, it is appropriate to examine the two understandings, their origins, and their significance for reading the signs of the times, one of which regards the church's nature and mission to be historically constituted, the other of which regards the church's task to be to read the signs of the times in order to understand the contemporary audience it addresses in order best to preach and adapt a message that is not hers to change. Following Torraco, I will refer to these ways respectively as "Reading the truth in history," and "Reading history in light of the truth."[9] These ways are what give rise, respectively, to the hermeneutic of discontinuity and the hermeneutic of reform. Here is how Torraco explains the distinction:

> On the one hand, 'reading the signs of the times' is said to involve the discernment of the way in which God is at work in history. The implication is that there is something intelligible in history—a truth that one can perceive. Moreover, the suggestion is that there is the possibility of access to specific knowledge of the way in which God is at work in history. On the other hand, imparting the knowledge of the divine and natural law would suggest that 'reading the signs of the times' involves examining the events and features that characterize a given era and applying the divine and natural law to these events and features. In this case, there is no implication that there is a way of perceiving how God is at work in history."[10]

Pope Benedict outlines what is meant by this latter sense. He says that the purpose of examining the signs of the times is "to offer the new generations the possibility of responding adequately to the eternal questions about this life and the life 'to come and about just social relations." He includes a direct reference to *Gaudium et Spes*.[11]

An examination of these two ways of understanding the phrase "reading the signs of the times" will illuminate the grounds of the differences between the hermeneutic of discontinuity and the hermeneutic of reform and also therefore, I hope, possible reasons for the polarized

---

8. Ibid., 252.
9. See ibid., 256.
10. Ibid., 253.
11. Benedict XVI, "Message for the World Day of Migrants and Refugees (2006)."

interpretations of Catholic social teaching and the Second Vatican Council itself.

READING THE SIGNS OF THE TIMES IN CATHOLIC SOCIAL TEACHING

In order to see how the two ways of reading the signs of the times coexist side by side in Catholic social teaching documents, a few examples will help to illustrate. John XXIII in his speech at the opening of the Second Vatican Council says, "In the present course of human events, in which the society of men is seen to enter a new order, the hidden counsels of Divine Providence ought especially to be recognized, which follow their own outcome through successive ages, the deeds of men, and often even beyond their expectations, and which arranges everything wisely, even human adversity, to the good of the church. This is easy to discern, if the quite grave political and economic questions and crises of today are considered by an attentive mind."[12] In the same speech, he also emphasizes that "the deposit of faith, or the truths, which are contained in our venerable doctrine are one thing; the mode by which they are announced are another, nevertheless keeping the same fundamental sense and meaning."[13] *Gaudium et Spes* says, on the one hand, "The people of God believes that it is led by the Lord's Spirit, who fills the earth. Motivated by this faith, it labours to decipher authentic signs of God's presence and purpose in the happenings, needs and desires in which this people has a part along with other men of our age,"[14] and, "Far from thinking that

---

12. "In praesenti humanorum eventuum cursu, quo hominum societas novum rerum ordinem ingredi videtur, potius arcana Divinae Providentiae consilia agnoscenda sunt, quae per tempora succedentia, hominum opera, ac plerumque praeter eorum exspectationem, suum exitum consequuntur, atque omnia, adversos etiam humanos casus, in Ecclesiae bonum sapienter disponunt." Pope John XXIII, "Allocutio." My translation is from the Latin text at http://w2.vatican.va/content/john-xxiii/la/speeches/1962/documents/hf_j-xxiii_spe_19621011_opening-council.html (accessed March 4, 2015). The presence of Pope John's simultaneous statements that God's designs are "hidden" and his claim to be able easily to discern the motions of providence in the world of today are, to say the least, perplexing.

13. "Est enim aliud ipsum depositum Fidei, seu veritates, quae veneranda doctrina nostra continentur, aliud modus, quo eaedem enuntiantur, eodem tamen sensu eademque sententia." Ibid.

14. "Populus Dei, fide motus, qua credit se a Spiritu Domini duci qui replet orbem terrarum, in eventibus, exigentiis atque optatis, quorum una cum ceteris nostrae aetatis hominibus partem habet, quaenam in illis sint vera signa praesentiae vel consilii Dei, discernere satagit." *GS* 11.

works produced by man's own talent and energy are in opposition to God's power, and that the rational creature exists as a kind of rival to the creator, Christians are convinced that the triumphs of the human race are a sign of God's grace and the flowering of his own mysterious design."[15] On the other hand, it also says that "earthly progress must be carefully distinguished from the growth of Christ's kingdom."[16] Even at this early date, the phrase "scrutinizing the signs of the times" has already raised many questions, and Paul VI used a 1969 Angelus address to provide his interpretation. While Matthew's signs refer to the Messiah, Paul VI states, "today the expression has a new meaning of great importance,"[17] namely, "the theological interpretation of contemporary history."[18] The point of this exercise, Pope Paul says, is to detect signs of the working of an "immanent Providence,"[19] or of some connection with the "secret action"[20] of the kingdom of God. This will allow the church to identify "the possibility, the availability, the exigency of an apostolic action."[21] At the same time, Paul warns that "The changeable element of revealed truth should not be subject to the changeability of times."[22] Richard Schenk argues

---

15. "Christiani itaque, nedum arbitrentur opera, quae homines suo ingenio et virtute pepererunt, Dei potentiae opponi, creaturamque rationalem quasi aemulam Creatoris exsistere, potius persuasum habent humani generis victorias signum esse magnitudinis Dei et fructus ineffabilis Ipsius consilii." Ibid., 34.2.

16. "Ideo, licet progressus terrenus a Regni Christi augmento sedulo distinguendus sit." Ibid., 39.

17. "Ha pertanto acquistato un uso corrente e un significato profondo." Pope Paul VI, Wednesday Audience. The English speech was printed in *L'Osservatore romano*, weekly edition in English on April 24, 1969. The English text I am quoting can be found at http://www.ewtn.com/library/PAPALDOC/P6SIGNS.HTM (accessed March 9, 2015).

18. "Interpretazione teologica della storia contemporanea." Ibid. It is worth noting that patristic commentaries on this passage all understand Christ to be referring to signs of the incarnation. See, for example, Jerome, *Commentary on Matthew* 2.16, who says that the signs Jesus speaks of point to "the advent of the Savior." See also John Chrysostom, *Homilies on the Gospel of Saint Matthew* 53.3. A modern commentary identifies the "signs of the times" Christ refers to as his own miracles, in spite of which the Pharisees and Sadducees do not believe. See Davies and Allison, *Matthew: A Shorter Commentary*, 261–63. Likewise, see *The Jerome Biblical Commentary*, ed. Brown, 43: 111. See also Elsbernd and Bieringer, "Interpreting the Signs of the Times," 62.

19. "Immanente Provvidenza." Pope Paul VI, Wednesday Audience.

20. "Azione segreta." Ibid.

21 "Con la possibilità, con la disponibilità, con l'esigenza di un'azione apostolica." Ibid.

22. Cioè l'elemento immutabile della verità rivelata non dovrebbe soggiacere alla mutabilità dei tempi." Ibid.

persuasively that *Gaudium et Spes* is neither a "monolithic affirmation of the precisely 'modern' ideals of its day,"[23] nor is it a root and branch rejection of those ideals. Instead, "the Council, taken as a whole, was as divided as the world it saw around it."[24] That accounts for what could be taken to be the mixed character of its statements about reading the signs of the times. But without more explicit determination such as Pope Benedict's distinction between the hermeneutic of discontinuity and the hermeneutic of reform, "reading the signs of the times" is almost bound to be taken in a historicist fashion, especially in an era like ours plagued by historicism.[25]

Beginning with his 1979 Puebla address, John Paul II inaugurated a shift in Catholic social teaching from reading the signs of the times to a focus on truth ("unity in love, unity in truth"[26]) which continued throughout his own social teaching[27] and, to an even higher degree, that of his successor, Pope Benedict XVI.[28] Of especial concern to John Paul II was to emphasize discernment of the compatibility of historical movements with the Gospel.[29] In December, 2007, Pope Benedict XVI dedicated an Angelus address to the signs of the times, in which he framed the task of the church in scrutinizing the signs of the times primarily in terms of warning against temporal messianism, going so far as to say, "In fact, history must run its course, which includes human tragedies and natural calamities. Within it is situated the plan of salvation which Jesus fulfilled in his incarnation, death and resurrection."[30] This thought was echoed in *Caritas in Veritate,* in which Benedict warns that social action

---

23. Schenk, "Officium Signa Temporum Perscrutandi," 169.
24. Ibid., 172.
25. See John Paul II, *Fides et Ratio*, 54, 86, and 95.
26. John Paul II, "Opening Address at the Puebla Conference," 1.1.
27. See, e.g., John Paul II, *Laborem Exercens*, 4.
28. Following the Puebla address, John Paul II inaugurates a mini-tradition of criticizing the historicism that is at the root of contemporary attempts to read the truth in history. See also John Paul II, "Address to the University Rectors of the Society of Jesus," § 5; *Fides et Ratio*, 54 (which itself follows Pope Pius XII's *Humani Generis*); "Address to the Pontifical Academy of Theology," § 3; and Benedict XVI, "Address at the Meeting of the Roman Clergy," 11.
29. John Paul II, "Opening Address at the Puebla Conference," 3.6. Torraco has argued that this shift has the effect of ruling out the option to read the truth in history. Torraco, "From 'Social Justice' to 'Reading the Signs of the Times,'" 258.
30. Benedict XVI, Angelus Address.

"is always less than we might wish,"[31] countering extreme positions that apply the standards of the heavenly city to the earthly city without recognizing their different scopes and limitations. In addition, *Caritas in Veritate* places front and center the importance of discernment in light of the truth. When the church has attempted to read the signs of the times, the starting point is always to identify the signs.[32] What is not particularly clear in any given case is whether these signs are indications of the way that *modern society* is, or whether they indicate humanly intelligible movements of divine providence that, when interpreted properly, provide instructions for the church's response.[33] There are some indications that Pope Benedixt XVI has judged *Gaudium et Spes*, at least, to be lacking in this area. In a recent *L'Osservatore Romano* article, he said, "Behind the vague expression [of *Gaudium et Spes*] "today's world" lies the question of the relationship with the modern era. To clarify this, it would have been necessary to define more clearly the essential features that constitute the modern era. 'Schema XIII' [or the document out of which *Gaudium et Spes* came] did not succeed in doing this. Although the Pastoral Constitution expressed many important elements for an understanding of the "world" and made significant contributions to the question of Christian ethics, it failed to offer substantial clarification on this point."[34] On the key questions of what it means to scrutinize the signs of the times in the light of the Gospel and of what modernity is, *Gaudium et Spes* is underdetermined, leaving itself open to abuse.

---

31. "Minora sunt quam ea quae optamus." Benedict XVI, *Caritas in Veritate*, 78.

32. To take just a few examples from several documents, some of these signs are: the desire for negotiation rather than military solutions to international conflict, the arms race, improvement in the situation of workers, increasing participation in politics by women, nations achieving independence (*Pacem in Terris*); increasing technological mastery over nature, growing interdependence of men on one another, growing awareness of human dignity, greater awareness of human rights, an increasing autonomy and sense of responsibility (*Gaudium et Spes*); a desire for liberation from oppression and unjust structures ("Instruction on Aspects of the 'Theology of Liberation'"), and increasing globalization (*Caritas in Veritate* 24).

33. See Bisson, "Breaking Open the Mysteries," 122, for the latter option. The difference is not trivial. If the former, then the church must study these signs in order to adapt her transhistorically true teaching in order that it may be understood by her addressees but also so that the adaptation remains in continuity with what came before. If the latter, then the church's social teaching is historically constituted and she must read the tea leaves of history to discover a guide for her preaching and social action.

34. Pope Benedict XVI, "It Was a Splendid Day."

AUGUSTINE ON HISTORY

On the one hand, Torraco argues that John XXIII's use of the "signs of the times" opens the door of Catholic social teaching to historicism.[35] On the other hand, Gustavo Gutierrez, for example, declares, "The function of theology as critical reflection on praxis has gradually become more clearly defined in recent years, but it has its roots in the first centuries of the Church's life. The Augustinian theology of history which we find in *The City of God*, for example, is based on a true analysis of the signs of the times and the demands with which they challenge the Christian community,"[36] assigning the option to read the truth in history a much older pedigree. The question is whether modern historical consciousness is alien to the Christian or Catholic tradition. Gutierrez identifies Augustine as a kindred spirit.[37] Toracco, on the other hand, identifies Augustine as an important representative of non-historicist reflection on the actions of Providence in history.

St. Augustine delineates two kinds of signs in *De Doctrina Christiana*: natural and given.[38] Natural signs have to do with natural cause and effect. Smoke is a sign of fire because fire causes smoke. Given signs are signs "which living things give to each other, in order to show, to the best of their ability, the emotions of their minds, or anything that they have felt or learnt."[39] Given signs are conventional and involve the will of the sign user. The two kinds of signs correspond to the classical distinction between nature and convention. One notes the lack of any kind of historical sign; it is difficult to say where the "signs of the times" identified in Catholic social teaching after John XXIII would fit into Augustine's division. A historical event certainly involves the actions, and therefore the wills, of human beings, so it cannot be a natural sign, that is, a sign flowing out of natural necessity, strictly speaking. On the other hand, it cannot be a given sign because it does not involve the deliberate intention to express what is in one's mind to another. While history is made up of a collection of intentions and actions of intelligent beings, the aggregate of

---

35. Toracco, "From 'Social Justice' to 'Reading the Signs of the Times,'" 251.

36. Gutiérrez, *A Theology of Liberation*, 5.

37. See ibid., xxxiv. Gilkey has called Augustine "the father of historical consciousness." See *Reaping the Whirldwind*, 175.

38. "Signorum igitur alia sunt naturalia, alia data." *doctr. chr.*, 2.1.2.

39. Ibid., 2.2.3.

those intentions and actions is not for the sake of communicating what is in anyone's mind.

Augustine describes "history" among the useful disciplines as distinct from superstitious or indulgent pursuits. History is the useful narration of past events.[40] He says in the same place, "Historical narrative also describes human institutions of the past, but it should not for that reason itself be counted among human institutions. For what has already gone into the past and cannot be undone must be considered part of the history of time, whose creator and controller is God."[41] The study of history is therefore akin to what we might today call "natural history."[42] But history is not useful, according to Augustine, in providing inspired or divine guidance for what must be done. He says, "There is a difference between describing what has been done and describing what must be done. History relates past events in a faithful and useful way, whereas the books of haruspices and similar literature set out to teach things to be performed or observed, and offer impertinent advice, not reliable information."[43] Augustine might classify attempts to read the signs of the times to derive guidance for action with the impious—and false—art of soothsaying.

Augustine's critique of reading the signs of the times, aside from his noting its impiety, is that those who attempt to read the signs of the times either wittingly or unwittingly see what they already want to see. But because of sin, human beings are prone to ignorance and difficulty.[44] They are therefore subject to the deceptions of demons who flatter the disordered desires of sinful human beings in order to dominate them.[45] According to Augustine, there is no discernible, intrinsic principle of meaning for history; instead, meanings "derive their effects on the mind from each individual's agreement with a particular convention."[46] Men

---

40. Ibid., 2.28.44. The two specific uses of history that Augustine mentions are the fixing of Christ's age, which allows the exegete to uncover some of the meaning of biblical numerology, and the refutation of pagan claims that Christ learned all his ideas from Plato by proving that the Old Testament predates Plato, in other words, an apologetic use.

41. Ibid.

42. See Fortin, *Classical Christianity*, 119.

43. *doctr. chr.* 2.28.44.

44. "Ignorantia et difficultas." See *lib. arb.* 3.18.52.

45. *doctr. chr.* 2.24.37.

46. Ibid. Augustine uses agreement on the meaning of words as an example of the agreement people give to any convention, illustrating the way in which people assign meanings to unusual events, such as "a mule giving birth or something being struck by lightning."

assign meanings to unusual events that agree with or justify their disordered desire for temporal things: "They were not observed as a result of their influence, but they gained their influence as a result of being observed and recorded . . . Spirits who wish to deceive someone devise appropriate signs for each individual to match those in which they see him caught up through his speculations and the conventions he accepts."[47] Augustine goes on to refer to dishonest augurs, who deliberately neglect to hear certain birds' cries so as to ensure the agreement of their findings with what they desire to find. It is not hard to see that historians are subject to the same temptations, and indeed there is a parallel passage in the *City of God* dealing with the unreliability of historians, citing their lack of agreement.[48] This is not even to address the tendency of some historians to mislead about history for their own purposes.[49] What is noticeably lacking in Augustine's treatment of history is any reference to the ability of men to uncover an intelligible plan in history. Augustine is in no doubt that there is such an intelligible plan. As Fortin says, "Seen from the perspective of the Bible, human events no doubt form part of a providential order that comprises the whole of history; but in the absence of any specific knowledge of the workings of divine providence, one is at a loss to say how they are related to one another or to the pre-established end to which they supposedly conduce. Anyone contemplating the sequence of these events is struck first and last not by its rationality but by its patent irrationality."[50] The intelligibility of history is in the mind of God, not in history itself. As Fortin continues, "Human acts are used by God for purposes to which they are not intrinsically ordered . . . But to say this is to admit that the rationality of the divine plan is not in the materials used but in the mind of the user, or, less metaphorically stated, that the teleology in question remains extrinsic to the events themselves. No analysis of these events will ever lead to the discovery of an end which is at once present and operative in the process from the beginning and destined to be progressively actualized through it."[51] Human beings are

---

47. Ibid.
48. See *ciu.* 18.40.
49. See Fortin, *Classical Christianity*, 119.
50. Ibid., 120.
51. Ibid. Fortin goes so far as to say that the completion of history is "in no way related to emergent political structures or the general state of human affairs at any given moment." Ibid.

given to know the end of history, which culminates in Christ's victory on the last day, but not the means by which God will bring about the end.

If Augustine would not have approved of reading the signs of the times in the sense of reading the truth in history, it remains to be seen whether the addition of "in the light of the Gospel" would make any difference to his judgment. This is what Eusebius of Caesarea attempts to do: to find in history the gradual triumph of the Kingdom of God. Eusebius's thesis in his *Historia Ecclesiastica* is simple: Christianity has served Rome well. Eusebius presents the earthly city and the Kingdom of God as fully compatible, even perhaps to the point of finally melding. A few examples will illustrate the point. When speaking of the conflicts between the emperors Licinius and Constantine, the loser's defeat is attributed to his impiety and the winner's victory to his embrace of Christianity. Describing Licinius's war against Constantine as treacherous and insane, Eusebius says that "he turned his back on prudence and commonsense, lost his sanity altogether, and determined to match his strength against God Himself, as Constantine's Protector, rather than against the person protected."[52] Licinius's war was not with Constantine, it was with God; whereas his victories before his apostasy were due to his piety, now his impending defeat at the hands of Constantine are due to his impiety. As Eusebius narrates, "Then, taking God the universal King, and God's Son the Saviour of all, as Guide and Ally, [Constantine and his son, Crispus] divided their battle array against God's enemies on every side, and easily carried off the victory: every detail of the encounter was made easy for them by God, in fulfillment of His purpose."[53] God's plan in Constantine's victory and Licinius's defeat are easily discernible by the pious mind. Similar observations could be made about Eusebius's narration of the sufferings of Jerusalem at the hands of the Romans: Jerusalem was preserved as long as there was a large body of pious Christians living there, and it was subject to cruel Roman persecutions when they fled the city, having abandoned it to the impious Jews.[54]

Augustine's most obvious purpose in writing the *City of God* was to refute the fashionable Roman opinion about the cause of Rome's recent decline, punctuated sharply by Alaric's sack of Rome in 410. The Romans discerned in their fatherland's decline signs of the times that they thought

---

52. Eusebius, *Church History* 10.8.
53. Ibid., 10.9.
54. See ibid., 3.5–7.

pointed to an enervation of Rome brought about by Christianity.[55] Augustine, unlike Eusebius, refuses to grant the terms of the argument to the Romans. God does not mete out blessings and curses on the basis of the religious qualities of the denizens of the age in such a way that human beings can discern God's intention. There is no calamity in Christian times that cannot be found in pre-Christian times. On the other hand, Christianity has not necessarily made things better for Rome in temporal matters, at least not in any discernibly certain way. History remains largely inscrutable. Good and evil men alike suffer hardships and are rewarded with temporal benefits. For example, there seems to be no religious reason why certain emperors have long reigns and why others have short reigns, since both good and bad emperors both flourish and founder. On the one hand, God gave the Christian Constantine a long, successful reign. On the other hand, devout Jovian's reign was short.[56] God metes out chastisements so that men might be withdrawn from enslavement to temporal things, and God metes out blessings so that men might not despise temporal things.[57] The huge difference between Augustine and Eusebius on the intelligibility of history can be seen in their different treatments of Constantine. As Fortin points out, "It is significant that the *City of God* devotes barely more than two short chapters (5.25 and 26) to Constantine and Theodosius, the most renowned of the early Christian emperors, and that in reviewing their reigns Augustine stresses their private virtues to the virtual exclusion of their political virtues. The conversion of the Roman Empire, acclaimed by others as a crucial turning point in the history of the church, is dismissed as a mere episode in an ongoing process no single moment of which is to be privileged over any other."[58] For Eusebius, on the other hand, Constantine is hailed as

55. Christianity, which is a transpolitical faith, encourages men to give their ultimate loyalty to a transcendent, heavenly city. It therefore, by their contention, robs Rome of the complete commitment she requires in order to be strong.

56 "On the other hand, so that no emperor should become a Christian in order to earn the good fortune of Constantine (whereas it is only with a view to life eternal that anyone should be a Christian), God removed Jovian more quickly than Julian." *ciu.* 5.25.

57. God's "purpose is that we should not set too much store by earthly felicity, which is often granted to such scoundrels as Marius, and yet should not regard it as an evil, since we observe that many devout and upright worshippers of the one true God are also richly blest." Ibid., 2.23. See also ibid., 4.33.

58. Fortin, Introduction to Augustine, *Political Writings*, xxiii. I am indebted to this essay by Fortin for pointing out Augustine's purpose in contrasting Constantine and Jovian, as well.

virtually a co-savior with Christ.[59] It will always be the case, in Augustine's view, that "because God does not rule there the general characteristic of that [earthly] city is that it is devoid of true justice,"[60] even if there is a particularly virtuous, even saintly, human sovereign.[61] No lessons about God's plan or the Gospel may be derived from the temporal success of Constantine, or from the temporal failures of Jovian. Augustine is in no way friendly to attempts to read the truth in history.

THE SIGNS OF THE TIMES AND MODERN HISTORICAL CONSCIOUSNESS

The question remains, what is the source of St. John XXIII's innovation? As Toracco asks, "How and why, only after several centuries of dormancy, did Matthew 16:3 pop out at Pope John from the pages of Scripture? How and why could he presume that the meaning of Jesus's words was so clear? How and why could Pope John so easily take the phrase, 'reading the signs of the times,' to be a principle for understanding social and political things?"[62] Either Pope John XXIII was deliberately attempting to bring about a transformation in the Catholic Church's understanding of history and revelation, which is implausible at best, or he and those who followed him in his usage did not see anything different in their own usage versus the older usage of reading the signs of the times. Even Eusebius's sub-historicist muddling of the two cities remained a theoretical minority position until relatively recently. So what is the source of the new usage? At the risk of oversimplifying, the answer seems to be, as Toracco indicates, the 18th-century shift from nature to history. This shift finds its origin

---

59. See also Eusebius's *Laus Constantini*, esp. 1.6 and 3.5–6.

60. *ciu.* 19.25.

61. As to what kind of historian Eusebius is, some evidence may be gleaned by his statement that "I shall include in my history only those things from which first we ourselves and then later generations may benefit," this immediately following his statement that he will not discuss certain shameful actions of Christian pastors under the persecution of Diocletian. Eusebius, *Church History* 8.2. Eusebius's intellectual follower and sometime collaborator of Augustine, Orosius, provides an example of the other type of historian: Orosius's *Seven Books of History against the Pagans* evinces no indications that Orosius saw any chinks in his historical argument about the temporal superiority of Christianity to paganism. Fortin attributes this to Orosius's "ignorance or his monumental shallowness." Fortin, *Classical Christianity*, 126. Book 18 of the *City of God* may be seen, at least partially, as Augustine's tacit rebuke of Orosius's project.

62. Toracco, "From 'Social Justice' to 'Reading the Signs of the Times,'" 251.

or, at least, its most outstanding witness, in the thought of Jean-Jacques Rousseau. The shift from nature to history made the temptation to read the truth in history much more pressing and more attractive.[63] A brief glance at the thought of Rousseau on nature and history, therefore, will clarify the reason for the possibility of an altogether new understanding of Matthew 16:3.

Hobbes and Locke, in thinking through the state of nature, had, according to Rousseau, made a crucial mistake: they assumed that natural man would be in most important respects the same as he is *in* political society, except *without* political society. He says, "All of [the philosophers], finally, speaking continually of need, avarice, oppression, desires, and pride, have carried over to the state of nature ideas they have acquired in society: they spoke about savage man and they described civil man."[64] Rousseau claims to reveal what man in the state of nature was really like. In the *Second Discourse,* Rousseau posits that man acquires his humanity by history and not from his nature, which is remarkably malleable and almost indeterminate.[65] Like Hobbes and Locke and against the premodern political philosophers, Rousseau maintains that man is not by nature social. Unlike Hobbes and Locke, Rousseau's natural man is not warlike but rather for the most part content, given over to the sentiment of his existence and having no plans for the future because of his inability to project beyond the present moment,[66] having no speech and no general ideas.[67] Speech and reason only emerge with society in order to serve man's self-preservation,[68] as do the passions that give rise to conflict, such

---

63. Peter Augustine Lawler, e.g., notes the proto-historicism of John Locke's teaching on nature, for example. See Lawler, *Modern and American Dignity,* 39.

64. Rousseau, *Second Discourse,* 102.

65. Ibid., 105. Also see Rousseau's note c on p. 186, where he says, "Man can give his limbs a destination more useful than that of nature," in the context of a discussion of how an armless man can learn to use his feet to do just as well what other men do with their arms. Compare Rousseau to Elsbernd and Bieringer, who say, "Human persons not only receive *everything* from community, but also contribute to the evolving life of community." Elsbernd and Bieringer, "Interpreting the Signs of the Times" 45; my emphasis.

66. Rousseau, *Second Discourse,* 117.

67. Ibid., 122–24.

68. Ibid., 144.

as vainglory and jealousy.[69] The factors that lead man to enter into society and thus undergo such an extraordinary change are chance events.[70]

Rousseau describes the importance of his observations that man's humanity is acquired in history and not given by nature in striking terms:

> It is in this slow succession of things that [my attentive reader] will see the solution to an infinite number of problems of ethics and politics which the philosophers cannot resolve. He will sense that, the human race of one age not being the human race of another, the reason Diogenes did not find a man was that he sought among his contemporaries the man of a time that no longer existed. Cato, he will say, perished with Rome and freedom because he was out of place in his century. . . . In a word, he will explain how the soul and human passions, altering imperceptibly, change their nature so to speak; why our needs and our pleasures change their objects in the long run; why, original man vanishing by degrees, society no longer offers to the eyes of the wise man anything except an assemblage of artificial men and factitious passions which are the work of all these new relations and have no true foundation in nature.[71]

One might say that Rousseau here outlines the very reason why it would be vital for ethics and politics to scrutinize the signs of the times: because only the signs of the times can reveal what kind of being a human being is at that precise stage in history. Only such up-to-date knowledge would be useful in order to gauge what is good for the human being. Attempting to rely on wisdom from the past or to refer to a universal nature that persists through time would be futile.

CATHOLIC SOCIAL TEACHING AND MODERN HISTORICAL CONSCIOUSNESS

Rousseau himself did not think that "the whole of human history is like a word spoken by God to us, with a meaning for us and for salvation," as Peter Bisson puts it.[72] Rousseau lacks a teaching on special Providence. In fact, Rousseau's teaching on history may be understood as a deliberate rejection and replacement of the Christian doctrine of providence,

69. Ibid., 149.
70. Ibid., 140.
71. Ibid., 178.
72. Bisson, "Breaking Open the Mysteries," 146.

as well as a rejection of pre-modern notions of teleology in nature.[73] But Rousseau's teaching on history does open up conceptual space for a resurgence of a peculiarly modern form of Eusebianism, which previously was checked by a robust theory of nature. The Eusebian temptation is exaggerated now, because now man is viewed as unremittingly historical and his historical movements are understood to be guided by Providence.

The fact that there are statements in the authoritative documents of Catholic social teaching that are susceptible to historicism right alongside statements in line with the great part of Christian tradition indicates that the mixture is not intentional. Now, to be clear, I am not saying that Pope St. John or his successors were any kind of deliberate disciples of Rousseau. But Rousseau is one of the great teachers of the modern age and it would be surprising to find that his thought has had no effect on the way Christians understand the world. After all, there are many examples of theologians who have fastened onto the elements in Catholic social teaching that leave themselves open to historicist interpretations and would at least lend themselves to a hermeneutic of discontinuity without taking into account the non-historicist statements. For example, Mary Elsbernd and Reimund Bieringer argue that the signs of the times are "places where the in-breaking of God's future into the world can occur. As such they are constitutively eschatological. The new epochal developments in our world are not just that, but they are at least potentially the tangible representations of how God enters into this world and moves it toward its final destination."[74] The Holy Spirit, whose revelation is an ongoing historical process according to Elsbernd and Bieringer, "provides eschatological criteria for judging any current social, political, religious or economic structure."[75] Peter Bisson says, "The subject must also read itself, in light of the gospels. What is it reading? It is reading its own transformations. If God is at work in the potential signs, and if the faith-filled subject is genuinely engaged, then the transformations produced in the subject by engagement with the signs will be indicators

---

73. See Bloom, "Jean-Jacque Rousseau," 563. Many twentiety-century Catholic theologians seem, however, to have either forgotten the originally anti-Christian reasons for Rousseau's and his followers' reflections on history, or to have deliberately adopted his project as their own. See Torraco, "From 'Social Justice' to 'Reading the Signs of the Times,'" 250–51; 255–56.

74. Elsbernd and Bieringer, "Interpreting the Signs of the Times," 80.

75. Ibid., 56.

of the authenticity of the earlier readings."[76] Bisson admits that this understanding of the signs of the times is "only consistently possible with the advent of modern historical consciousness and theories of history."[77] If Christ is active in history, and history has transformed a Christian or Christian group in a certain way, then it is possible to see Christ's work in that transformation. Missing from this standpoint is the key insight of Augustine, who knew that God was omnipresent in the world by his power, but that, while God can be present to me, I can still be far from God.[78]

It is hard to see how these positions would escape Augustine's charge of soothsaying, especially in light of Augustine's caution that the soothsayer sees what he already desires to see. What is needed is a "critique of the present," as Frederick G. Lawrence has stated it,[79] which can begin the task of philosophic self-understanding and the liberation from the ideological imprisonment that reading the truth in history is incapable of providing.[80] As Bernard Lonergan puts it, "There is needed, then, a critique of history before there can be any intelligent direction of history."[81] That critique needs to begin with the serious study of the history of political philosophy. Historicism short-circuits this task.

Fortunately, Benedict XVI is uncommonly conversant with the tradition of political philosophy. Both the introduction to *Caritas in Veritate* and its final chapter, "The Development of Peoples and Technology"

76. Bisson, "Breaking Open," 145.

77. Ibid.

78. See *Conf.* 10.27.38. See also David A. Tamisiea's contribution to this volume, which explains the conditions for the exercise of the *sensus fidei* that would make possible the reading of the signs of the times in light of the gospel, in the sense of reading history in light of the truth.

79. A large part of Fr. Lamb's teaching and scholarship is dedicated to precisely this aim.

80. Lawrence, "Fourth Wave," 131. I am not qualified to speak on the main contemporary strand of Catholic theology that attempts to do just this, what goes by the name of "political theology," but Lawrence, an astute theologian who himself has written about the problem of historicism, has criticized political and liberation theologians for failing to transcend the limits of the Enlightenment. See Lawrence, "Political Theology," 238. Regardless of whether this is true of political theology or liberation theology, transcending the limitations of the Enlightenment is precisely what is needed for the "critique of the present" Lawrence calls for. Providing a critique of Kant or Hegel is well and good, but is insufficient if one does not recognize their own dependence on or affinity with a prior tradition of modern political philosophy.

81. Lonergan, *Insight*, 265.

recognize the problem with reading the truth in history. Unreflective love is not enough, Benedict says; the purifying discernment[82] of both faith and reason must be brought to bear on history in order to discern what is compatible with the gospel and what is the result of an enthusiastic impulse that might only appear to be compatible with the gospel.[83] In the last chapter of *Caritas in Veritate*, Benedict states explicitly that it is not institutions or history that make men, but men that make institutions or history, which means that what is needed first are "upright men and women."[84] While never abandoning this affirmation, recent Catholic

82. J. Brian Benestad notes that, in the final draft of *Gaudium et Spes*, *discernere* replaces *animadvertere*. The final text says that the church "seeks to discern . . . the true signs of God's presence and purpose." *Gaudium et spes* 11. Benestad comments, "The emphasis on discernment calls to mind the traditional Catholic teaching on discernment of spirits so prominent in the *Spiritual Exercises* of St. Ignatius." Benestad, "Doctrinal Perspectives," 149–50. Discernment of God's presence and purposes takes place in light of the truths contained in the unalterable deposit of faith. This gives the correct sense to the earlier statement in *Gaudium et Spes* that says the church should "scrutinize the signs of the times in the light of the Gospel." After all, the devil can disguise "himself as an angel of light," according to 2 Cor 11:14. All citations from the Bible in this chapter are from the RSVCE2.

83. Drew Christiansen notes that Benedict's reliance on "metaphysics" seems to return to an earlier model, "abandoned by Vatican II's move to the symbolic rhetorical style of positive theology and reading the signs of the times in its social teaching." Christiansen, "Metaphysics and Society," 16. One does not need to agree with Christiansen's judgment of abandonment to appreciate the basic observation that Benedict did emphasize one of the several strands in the history of Catholic social doctrine about reading the signs of the times—that of John Paul II's emphasis on the truth— over other strands possibly more susceptible to historicist interpretations.

84. Benedict XVI, *Caritas in Veritate*, 71. Even *Caritas in Veritate* is not without some ambiguity about reading the signs of the times. The same problem crops up in *Caritas in Veritate*, 67. The sign of the times in question is the felt need among people of our time to strengthen the United Nations so that "the concept of the family of nations can acquire real teeth." Ibid. This remark is preceded in paragraph 42 by the statement, "The truth of globalization as a process and its fundamental ethical criterion are given by the unity of the human family and its development towards what is good." Ibid. Christiansen remarks on paragraph 67, "While social forces promote globalization, world community is the work of grace." Christiansen, "Commentary on *Caritas in Veritate*," 7. Christiansen's interpretation goes a bit further than the encyclical, but the encyclical does leave itself open to, perhaps even welcomes, this interpretation. It is at least an open question whether the actual process of globalization moves people in deed toward the unity of the human family that is understood in thought, or even whether the motivations for globalization have anything to do with the unity of the human family. Nor is it at all clear whether any "world political authority" would be a boon or a threat to that unity. The resulting transnationalism and "breaking-down of borders" might remove important conventional limits to human relations that are

social teaching and, especially, many of the theological and popular interpreters of recent Catholic social teaching, conspicuously focus more attention on the proper arrangements of institutions than on the goodness of souls. Benedict has regained some balance on this matter. As Drew Christianson has noted, the second part of *Deus Caritas Est* places "emphasis on direct service rather than on transformation of societal structures,"[85] and on the virtues that empower direct service.

THE INTELLIGIBILITY OF HISTORY AND THE FULLNESS OF TIME

In this last section before the conclusion, I want to deal very briefly with one possible objection to my argument so far. Due to space constraints, I will only attempt to articulate the objection and then to give the contours of what might be an answer. The objection is simply that there is an intelligibility to history that is knowable by human beings that is acknowledged by both Scripture and Tradition under what has come to be known as the "divine pedagogy." Briefly put, the idea is that God gradually instructs his people until they are ready to receive Christ. The principle is articulated in Gal 3:24, "The law was our custodian [παιδαγωγός] until Christ came," utilized by many Fathers of the Church, including St. Augustine,[86] and summed up by the *Catechism of the Catholic Church*: "The divine plan of Revelation is realized simultaneously 'by deeds and words which are intrinsically bound up with each other' [*DV* 2] and shed light on each another. It involves a specific divine pedagogy: God communicates himself to man gradually. He prepares him to welcome by stages the supernatural Revelation that is to culminate in the person and mission of the incarnate

---

required by humanity's nature as a finite being limited not only by space and time but also by the effects of sin. See Manent, *A World Beyond Politics?*, for an excellent discussion of the moral and political problems associated with the pursuit of transnational or antinational political authority. Augustine, along with the great part of the Christian tradition, warns that only the city of God, and not the earthly city, is capable of supporting and promoting the full unity of the human family. As a sign of the times, the referent of increasing globalization is at least ambiguous. Fortunately, this tendency is balanced in the encyclical by a Johannine recognition that true fraternity "originates in a transcendent vocation from God the Father, who loved us first." Benedict XVI, *Caritas in Veritate*, 19.

85. Christiansen, "Commentary on *Caritas in Veritate*," 6.
86. See, *uera rel*. 17.34.

Word, Jesus Christ."[87] The concept of the divine pedagogy is related to the phrase a little later in Galatians, "The fullness of time" (Gal 4:4). If there is a fullness of time that would seem to indicate that history is intelligible. The intelligibility would be precisely the instruction of the people of God leading up to the advent of the Messiah.

Against this objection, I would refer again to the argument against identifying the meaning of "scrutinizing the signs of the times" as it appears in Matthew 16:3 and *Gaudium et Spes* 4. The former is Christological, the latter is not. The divine pedagogy leads up to the advent of Christ, the fullness of time refers to Christ; the signs of the times refer to Christ, they do not refer to political or cultural developments or general states of human affairs. While it is true that the divine pedagogy can be replicated in each soul, the Incarnation ended the period in which the people of God were under a παιδαγωγός. Nevertheless, if there is to be humanly discernible intelligibility in history, it would have to do with Christ, just as the Law served as a pedagogue until the coming of Christ. There is nothing left to be fulfilled, since Christ is "full of grace and truth" (John 1:14) and "from his fullness have we all received" (John 1:16). Still, while Christ was himself "full of grace and truth," it is true that receiving from his fullness takes time. The reception of the fullness of Christ through the incorporation of human beings in his mystical body, therefore, would constitute the intelligibility of history. But as Augustine points out by reflecting on the mixed character of the church in this age, there are some who are within the visible bonds of the church who are not inwardly united with Christ; and there are some who are outside the visible bonds of the church who will be revealed in the last judgment to belong fully to the church. As Augustine says, "In this world, the two cities are indeed entangled and mingled with one another; and they will remain so until the last judgment shall separate them."[88] The constitution of the body of Christ is something that is begun in history, but does not have its motive force or intelligibility from history, but rather from divine Providence, which is transhistorical; nor is that transhistorical Providence revealed to men in history, according to Augustine, but only upon the last judgment.

There remains still one way in which there could be intelligibility in history. The divine pedagogy in the Old Testament involves gradual revelation. While Jesus Christ is the fullness of revelation, beyond which

---

87. *Catechism of the Catholic Church*, 53.

88. *ciu.* 1.35.

there can be no more or other,[89] the very fullness of revelation in Christ requires a gradual unfolding for it to be understood by human beings with finite minds. The increase in the understanding of revelation or development of doctrine does not involve newness in the object of revelation, in the deposit of faith grounded in the Incarnate Word; but it does involve newness in the subject, the church and her members. The way *Dei Verbum* puts it is that, "For as the centuries succeed one another, the Church constantly moves forward toward the fullness of divine truth until the words of God reach their complete fulfillment in her."[90] This progress, *Dei Verbum* makes clear, "happens through the contemplation and study made by believers, who treasure these things in their hearts (see Luke, 2:19, 51) through a penetrating understanding of the spiritual realities which they experience, and through the preaching of those who have received through Episcopal succession the sure gift of truth."[91] As Bernard Lonergan points out, "Often enough development [of doctrine] is dialectical. The truth is discovered because a contrary error has been asserted."[92] In this case, doctrine develops through a judgment against some error that is asserted in the course of history. When Peter Bisson's historical subject reads himself, or observes "the social, political, economic, cultural, religious phenomena that occur so frequently and pervasively in human life that they seem to characterize a given period," truth cannot be read in history, but rather history must be read in light of the truth. It is in this sense that the intelligibility of history is the development of doctrine.

CONCLUSION

The line from *Gaudium et Spes* about "reading the signs of the times" is a key text for judging between the hermeneutic of discontinuity and the hermeneutic of reform. Studying the signs of the times in light of the truth is always important and necessary for the church's pastoral task: the church must understand the times to know how to express her message, and to know how to apply the Gospel to new historical circumstances.

---

89. See *DV* 4; also see Brague, *On the God of the Christians*, 79–116, for an extended, theological argument as to why this must be so.

90. *DV* 8.

91. Ibid. See also *ST* II-II.1.7.

92. Lonergan, *Method in Theology*, 319.

But, as Augustine and St. Paul might remind us, we are constantly in danger of exchanging the things of God for the image of man. Reading the truth in history, because it is untethered from any decisive judgment by faith or reason, cannot escape ideological imprisonment by the spirit of the age or the attraction of temporal messianism. Nor does the addition of "in the light of the gospel" make historical augury any more palatable, for the Gospel was never meant to be a key to unlocking the historical movements of Providence. That knowledge is reserved for the blessed in heaven. This makes it all the more pressing today that we should undertake the perennially necessary quest to know ourselves and our patterns of thinking. At the very least, the church risks appearing one-sided in its approach to the political and economic questions of the day, in Pope John XXIII's phrasing; a more serious risk is that, by neglecting to clarify what is meant by "reading the signs of the times" the church opens the door to the kind of soothsaying Augustine warned against and which historicism makes so attractive to us. The effort to clarify what that phrase means will also make easier the task of reading Catholic Social Teaching in the light of the long tradition of Catholic reflection on politics and economics, especially since it will help to disambiguate Catholic teaching from strands of thought not at all congenial to the Catholic faith. Pope Benedict's call in *Spe Salvi* for "a self-critique of modernity"[93] is therefore an excellent example of a prudent recommendation based on the scrutiny of the signs of the times.[94]

BIBLIOGRAPHY

Aquinas, Thomas. *Summa theologiae*. Translated by Fathers of the English Dominican Province. 5 vols. New York: Benziger Bros., 1947.

Augustine. *City of God*. Translated by R. W. Dyson. Cambridge: Cambridge University Press, 1998.

———. *Confessionum libri tredecim*. Edited by Luc Verheijen. *Corpus Christianorum Series Latina* 27. Turnhout: Brepols, 1981.

———. *De doctrina christiana libri quatuor*. In *Corpus Christianorum Series Latina* 32, edited by Josef Martin, 1–167. Turnhout: Brepols, 1962.

———. *De libero arbitrio libri tres*. In *Corpus Christianorum Series Latina* 29, edited by W. M. Green, 211–321. Turnhout: Brepols, 1970.

93. Benedict XVI, *Spe Salvi*, 22.

94. Schenk makes the timely observation, "The question is not 'Should the Church adapt or not?.' The more pressing question is: should the Church be assimilated or not?" Schenk, "Officium Signa Temporum Perscrutandi," 200.

———. *On Christian Teaching*. Translated by R. P. H. Green. Oxford: Oxford University Press, 1999.

———. *De uera religione liber unus*. In *Corpus Christianorum Series Latina 32*, edited by Josef Martin, 171–260. Turnhout: Brepols, 1962.

Benedict XVI. "Message of His Holiness Benedict XVI for the 92nd World Day of Migrants and Refugees (2006)." http://w2.vatican.va/content/benedict-xvi/en/messages/migration/documents/hf_ben-xvi_mes_20051018_world-migrants-day.html.

———. "Address at the Meeting of the Roman Clergy." http://w2.vatican.va/content/benedict-xvi/en/speeches/2006/march/documents/hf_ben-xvi_spe_20060302_roman-clergy.html.

———. Angelus Address of November 18, 2007. http://w2.vatican.va/content/benedict-xvi/en/angelus/2007/documents/hf_ben-xvi_ang_20071118.html.

———. *Caritas in Veritate*. Latin text: http://w2.vatican.va/content/benedict-xvi/la/encyclicals/documents/hf_ben-xvi_enc_20090629_caritas-in-veritate.html. English text: http://w2.vatican.va/content/benedict-xvi/en/encyclicals/documents/hf_ben-xvi_enc_20090629_caritas-in-veritate.html.

———. "'It Was a Splendid Day.' Pope pens rare article on his inside view of Vatican II." http://www.news.va/en/news/it-was-a-splendid-day-benedict-xvi-recalls.

———. "A Proper Hermeneutic for the Second Vatican Council." In *Vatican II: Renewal within Tradition*, edited by Matthew L. Lamb and Matthew Levering. Oxford: Oxford University Press, 2008.

———. *Spe Salvi*. http://w2.vatican.va/content/benedict-xvi/en/encyclicals/documents/hf_ben-xvi_enc_20071130_spe-salvi.html.

Benestad, J. Brian. "Doctrinal Perspectives on the Church in the Modern World." In *Vatican II: Renewal within Tradition*, edited by Matthew L. Lamb and Matthew Levering, 147–64. Oxford: Oxford University Press, 2008.

Bisson, Peter. "Breaking Open the Mysteries: Changing Jesuit Practices of Reading the Signs of the Times." In *Scrutinizing the Signs of the Times in the Light of the Gospel*, edited by Johan Verstraeten, 121–50. Bibliotheca Ephemeridum Theologicarum Lovaniensium 208. Leuven: Leuven University Press, 2007.

Bloom, Allan. "Jean-Jacque Rousseau." In *History of Political Philosophy*, edited by Leo Strauss and Joseph Cropsey, 559–80. Chicago: University of Chicago Press, 1987.

Brague, Rémi. *On the God of the Christians (and on One or Two Others)*. Translated by Paul Seaton. South Bend, IN: St. Augustine's, 2013

Brown, Raymond E., et al., eds. *The Jerome Biblical Commentary*. London: Chapman, 1968.

Christianson, Drew. "Metaphysics and Society: A Commentary on *Caritas in Veritate*." *Theological Studies* 71 (2010) 3–28.

Chrysostom, John. *Homilies on the Gospel of St. Matthew*. Vol. 10 of *A Select Library of the Nicene and Post-Nicene Fathers*. Edited by Philip Schaff. Translated by George Prevost. Grand Rapids: Eerdmans, 1984.

Davies, W. D. and Dale C. Allison. *Matthew: A Shorter Commentary*. London: T. & T. Clark, 2004.

Elsbernd, Mary, and Reimund Bieringer. "Interpreting the Signs of the Times in the Light of the Gospel: Vision and Normativity of the Future." In *Scrutinizing the Signs of the Times in the Light of the Gospel*, edited by Johan Verstraeten, 43–98.

Bibliotheca Ephemeridum Theologicarum Lovaniensium 208. Leuven: Leuven University Press, 2007.
Eusebius. *The Church History*. Translated by Paul L. Maier. Grand Rapids: Kregel, 2007.
———. *Oration in Praise of Constantine* (*Laus Constantini*). Translated by Ernest Cushing Richardson. Nicene and Post-Nicene Fathers, Second Series 1. Buffalo, NY: Christian Literature, 1890.
Gilkey, Langdon. *Reaping the Whirlwind*. New York: Seabury, 1956.
Gutiérrez, Gustavo. *A Theology of Liberation*. Translated by Sister Caridad Inda and John Eagleson. Maryknoll, NY: Orbis, 1995.
Fortin, Ernest L. *Classical Christianity and the Political Order*. Edited by J. Brian Benestad. Collected Essays 2. Lanham, MD: Rowman and Littlefield, 1996.
———. Introduction to *Political Writings*, by Augustine. Edited by Ernest L. Fortin and Douglas Kries. Indianapolis: Hackett, 1994.
Jerome. *Commentary on Matthew*. Translated by Thomas P. Scheck. Fathers of the Church 117. Washington, DC: Catholic University of America Press, 2008.
John XXIII. "Allocutio Ioannis PP. XXIII in Solemni SS. Concilii Inauguratione." http://w2.vatican.va/content/john-xxiii/la/speeches/1962/documents/hf_j-xxiii_spe_19621011_opening-council.html.
———. *Pacem in Terris*. http://w2.vatican.va/content/john-xxiii/en/encyclicals/documents/hf_j-xxiii_enc_11041963_pacem.html. Accessed July 21, 2015.
John Paul II. "Opening Address at the Puebla Conference." http://w2.vatican.va/content/john-paul-ii/en/speeches/1979/january/documents/hf_jp-ii_spe_19790128_messico-puebla-episc-latam.html. Accessed March 9, 2015.
———. *Laborem Exercens*. http://w2.vatican.va/content/john-paul-ii/en/encyclicals/documents/hf_jp-ii_enc_14091981_laborem-exercens.html.
———. "Address to the University Rectors of the Society of Jesus." http://w2.vatican.va/content/john-paul-ii/en/speeches/1985/november/documents/hf_jp-ii_spe_19851109_compagnia-gesu.html.
———. *Fides et Ratio*. http://w2.vatican.va/content/john-paul-ii/en/encyclicals/documents/hf_jp-ii_enc_14091998_fides-et-ratio.html.
———. "Address to the Pontifical Academy of Theology." https://www.ewtn.com/library/PAPALDOC/JP2ACTHE.HTM.
Lamb, Matthew L. "The Challenges of Reform and Renewal within Catholic Tradition." In *Vatican II: Renewal within Tradition*, edited by Matthew L. Lamb and Matthew Levering, 439–42. Oxford: Oxford University Press, 2008.
Lawler, Peter Augustine. *Modern and American Dignity*. Wilmington, DE: ISI, 2010.
Lawrence, Frederick G. "Leo Strauss and the Fourth Wave of Modernity." In *Leo Strauss and Judaism*, edited by David Novak, 131–54. Lanham, MD: Rowman and Littlefield, 1996.
———. "Political Theology and 'The Longer Cycle of Decline.'" In *Lonergan Workshop*, edited by Fred Lawrence, 1:223–56. Missoula, MT: Scholars, 1978.
Lonergan, Bernard. *Insight*. Toronto: University of Toronto Press, 2008.
———. *Method in Theology*, Toronto: University of Toronto Press, 2007.
Manent, Pierre. *A World beyond Politics?* Translated by Marc A. LePain. Princeton: Princeton University Press, 2006.
Paul VI. Wednesday Audience, April 16 1969. http://w2.vatican.va/content/paul-vi/it/audiences/1969/documents/hf_p-vi_aud_19690416.html.

Rousseau, Jean-Jacque. *Discourse on the Origins and Foundations of Inequality (Second Discourse)*. Translated by Roger D. and Judith R. Masters. In *The First and Second Discourses*, edited by Roger D. Masters, 77–228. Boston: St. Martin's, 1964.

Schenk, Richard. "Officium Signa Temporum Perscrutandi." In *Scrutinizing the Signs of the Times in the Light of the Gospel*, edited by Johan Verstraeten, 167–205. Bibliotheca Ephemeridum Theologicarum Lovaniensium 208. Leuven: Leuven University Press, 2007.

Vatican Council II. *Gaudium et Spes*. English text: http://www.vatican.va/archive/hist_councils/ii_vatican_council/documents/vat-ii_const_19651207_gaudium-et-spes_en.html. Latin text: http://www.vatican.va/archive/hist_councils/ii_vatican_council/documents/vat-ii_const_19651207_gaudium-et-spes_lt.html.

———. *Dei Verbum*. http://www.vatican.va/archive/hist_councils/ii_vatican_council/documents/vat-ii_const_19651118_dei-verbum_en.html.

Torraco, Stephen F. "From 'Social Justice' to 'Reading the Signs of the Times': the Hermeneutical Crisis of Catholic Social Teaching." In *Faith Seeking Understanding: Learning and the Catholic Tradition*, edited by George C. Berthold, 247–60. Manchester: St. Anselm College Press, 1991.

10

Vatican II, St. Thomas Aquinas, and the *Sensus Fidelium*

David A. Tamisiea

INTRODUCTION

IN A 2012 ARTICLE entitled, "Vatican II after Fifty Years: The Virtual Council versus the Real Council," Fr. Matthew Lamb calls attention to Pope Benedict XVI's impromptu remarks on the Second Vatican Council in his final public address before entering retirement.[1] As Fr. Lamb recounts, Benedict candidly observed that there were "two councils" that emerged out of Vatican II. On the one hand, there was the true Council of the bishops, who sought to renew the church in continuity with the entire faith tradition, and on the other hand, the virtual Council of the mass media, who superficially viewed the Council as an ideological triumph by "liberals" over "conservatives" in breaking with Catholicism's conservative past.[2]

Perhaps one of the most cited teachings of Vatican II by those who see it as an abrupt break with the past concerns the *sensus fidelium*.

1. Matthew Lamb, "Vatican II," 14–19.
2. Benedict XVI, "Proper Hermeneutic," ix–xv.

The *sensus fidelium*, or "sense of the faithful," refers to the supernatural capacity the People of God as a whole have to discern what belongs to the deposit of faith, and what does not. This ability is a property of the intellect perfected by the theological virtue of faith, but is compared to a "sense" or "instinct" because it allows the believer to judge spontaneously whether a particular teaching is in conformity with the true faith.[3] Many advocates of positions opposed to magisterial teaching argue that when the majority, or at least a large number of Catholics, disagrees with the church's official teaching, this is a sign of an emerging *sensus fidelium* that calls for the magisterium to modify its teaching to correspond to the true faith of the church. Thus, the *sensus fidelium* has been invoked in support of artificial contraception,[4] abortion,[5] cohabitation,[6] divorce and

---

3. International Theological Commission, *Sensus Fidei*, 49.

4. See, e.g., American Bishop Robert Lynch's public remarks on the survey taken in his diocese for the 2014 Extraordinary Synod of Bishops on marriage, family life, and evangelization: "On the matter of artificial contraception the responses might be characterized by the saying, 'that train has left the station long ago.' Catholics have made up their minds and the *sensus fidelium* suggests the rejection of Church teaching on this subject." Lynch, "People of God," para. 9, item 8.

5. See, e.g., Catholic theologian Charles Curran's comments reported by McBrien in the *National Catholic Reporter* concerning the public uproar over Phoenix Bishop Thomas Olmsted's condemnation of the decision by a Catholic hospital in his diocese to perform a direct abortion on an unborn child to save the mother's life: "In my judgment, the strong reaction by many Catholics to the action taken by the Bishop of Phoenix could well indicate the *sensus fidelium* . . . It is clear that many theologians and some bishops have come to the conclusion that an abortion to save the life of the mother is a morally good act." McBrien, "The Phoenix Case."

6. See, e.g., Salzman and Lawler, two Catholic theologians who argue in their book on sexual ethics that the church should offer a "nuptial blessing" ceremony for unmarried couples who cohabitate: "The theological fact that after the Second Vatican Council, the Church is seen predominantly as a communion demands critical dialogue and consensus about the *sensus fidei* of the Church rather than uncritical obedience . . . If the first union for some 75–80 percent of Western women and men is cohabitation and not marriage, again a social fact raises questions for theologians about what the communion-Church believes." Salzman and Lawler, *Sexual Ethics*, 226–27.

remarriage,[7] priestly ordination of women,[8] homosexual acts,[9] same sex "marriage,"[10] *in vitro* fertilization,[11] and, most recently, lifting the ban on divorced and remarried Catholics from receiving Holy Communion.[12]

7. See, e.g., Catholic theologian Lawler's argument for changing church teaching on divorce and remarriage based on the *sensus fidelium*. Lawler, *What is and Ought to Be*, 119–42, 143–67. The gist of Lawler's argument in these two chapters is that, since the majority of the faithful reject the official teaching of the church on divorce and remarriage, it is an indication of the *sensus fidelium* and time for the magisterium to change its doctrine to express the true faith of the church.

8. See, e.g., the public statement by Roman Catholic Womenpriests, a group working for the priestly ordination of women, regarding the attempted "ordination" of seven women on the Danube River in 2002: "The voice of the Catholic people—the *sensus fidelium*—has spoken. We women are no longer asking for permission to be priests. Instead, we have taken back our rightful God-given place ministering to Catholics as inclusive and welcoming priests." Roman Catholic Womenpriests, "About RCWP," para. 1.

9. See, e.g., the public statement by DignityUSA, the Catholic gay advocacy group, explaining their rejection of the Congregation for the Doctrine of Faith's 1986 *Letter to the Bishops of the Catholic Church on the Pastoral Care of Homosexual Persons*: "In not receiving this letter we are acting in accord with the *sensus fidelium* as bestowed by the Holy Spirit upon the People of God throughout History." DignityUSA, "Declaration of Non-Reception," 1.

10. See, e.g., Catholic theologian Daniel Maguire's defense of same-sex marriage, and his charge of what he terms "the sin of heterosexism" by those who oppose it: "The Church consists of more than the pope and the bishops. In Catholicism there are three sources of truth, (or three 'magisteria'): the hierarchy, the theologians, and the wisdom and experience of the laity (called in Latin *sensus fidelium*). In Catholic history, each of these sources of truth has at times been right and each of them has at times been wrong . . . Something like that is now going on regarding homosexuality. Many Catholic theologians agree now with Protestant and Jewish theologians that same sex unions can be moral, healthy, and holy." Maguire, "Same Sex Marriage," §§ 16, 18.

11. See, e.g., the argument in the *amicus curiae* brief submitted by Catholics for Choice to the Inter-American Court of Human Rights in 2012 for why Catholic women should have legal access to *in vitro* fertilization in Costa Rica despite the church's opposition: "While no one would suggest that the findings of opinion polls have the moral strength of church teachings, on questions of reproduction such as IVF, the consensus of the faithful, or *sensus fidelium*, cannot be said to support the hierarchy's position. Catholics all over the world have soundly rejected the hierarchy's ban on IVF, such that only a minority of Catholics can be found to agree with church leaders." Catholics for Choice, *Amicus Curiae Brief*, 8.

12. See, e.g., Cardinal Walter Kasper's comments in his 2014 interview with the British Catholic newspaper, *The Tablet*, where he asserts that the church should allow divorced and remarried Catholics to receive Holy Communion based on their collective *sensus fidei*: "Then there are the 'hot-button' issues. Does he [Kasper] think there will be an opening on Communion for divorced and remarried? 'I do not know. I am not a prophet! I hope that bishops will listen to the voice of people who live as divorced

THE TEACHING OF VATICAN II ON THE *SENSUS FIDELIUM*

But is this a correct understanding of the *sensus fidelium*? The frequent invocation of the *sensus fidelium* in support of positions opposed to magisterial teaching calls for a closer examination of the doctrine itself. While the terminology and formulations vary, the notion that the whole body of the faithful can possess a universal sense of the true faith runs deep in the tradition.[13] Nonetheless, the concept of the *sensus fidelium* received a renewed impetus in the developed ecclesiology of the Second Vatican Council.[14] While Vatican II speaks of the *sensus fidelium* in several texts, the most important passage is found in *Lumen Gentium* 12:

> The entire body of the faithful, anointed as they are by the Holy One (Cf. 1 Jn. 2:20, 27), cannot err in matters of belief. They manifest this special property by means of the whole people's supernatural *sensus fidei* in matters of faith when "from the Bishops down to the last of the lay faithful" (St. Augustine, *De praed. sanct.*) they show universal agreement in matters of faith and morals. That discernment in matters of faith is aroused and sustained by the Spirit of truth. It is exercised under the guidance of the sacred teaching authority, in faithful and respectful obedience to which the people of God accepts that which is not just the word of men but truly the word of God (Cf. 1 Thess. 2:13). Through it, the people of God adheres unwaveringly to

and remarried—the *sensus fidei*. They should listen and then next year they should decide what is possible and what is not possible,' he said, adding that his 'impression' is that the Pope also wants an 'opening'. In his address to the cardinals in February, he cited Cardinal Newman's essay 'On Consulting the Faithful in Matters of Faith', which argued it was the faithful, not bishops, who preserved the faith during the controversies of the fourth and fifth centuries. This emphasized a teaching that each Catholic has a sense of faith by virtue of their Baptism. This sense of faith, the cardinal argues, must be taken seriously." Christopher Lamb, "The Case for Mercy."

13. The following are historical surveys of the supernatural *sensus fidei* of the faithful in the church: Thils, *L'infaillibilité*, 1–66; Hammans, *Die neueren Erklärungen*, 242–62; Beinert, "Bedeutung und Begrundung des Glaubenssinnes," 271–303; Beinert, "Der Glaubenssinn der Gläubigen," 66–131; Thompson, "Sensus Fidelium," 450–86; Steinruck, "Die Gläubigen," 25–50; Finucane, *Sensus Fidelium*, 17–210.

14. The relevant texts from Vatican II that directly discuss the *sensus fidelium* include *LG* 12 and 35; *GS* 52; *Apostolicam Actuositatem* 2; and *Presbyterorum Ordinis* 9. The *sensus fidelium* is also implicitly presumed in *DV* 8 as a criterion for the development of dogma. Other conciliar texts that discuss notions closely related to the *sensus fidelium* include *GS* 62 (*sensus Christianus*), *Apostolicam Actuositatem* 30 (*sensus catholicus*), and *Ad Gentes* 19 (*sensus Christi et Ecclesiae*).

the faith given once and for all to the saints (Cf. Jud. 3), penetrates it more deeply with right thinking, and applies it more fully in its life.[15]

Several observations can be made about the *sensus fidelium* based on this important text. First, the Council highlights the primacy of the Holy Spirit in guiding the entire People of God to correctly discern the true faith. As the Council puts it, the *sensus fidelium* is "aroused and sustained by the Spirit of truth."[16] In support of this teaching, the Council cites a passage from the First Letter of John where the Evangelist teaches that believers have been anointed by the Holy Spirit, who instructs them in the truth and keeps them from false teaching: "But you have been anointed by the Holy One, and you all know. I write to you, not because you do not know the truth, but because you know it, and know that no lie is of the truth. . . . I write this to you about those who would deceive you; but the anointing which you received from him abides in you, and you have no need that any one should teach you; as his anointing teaches you about everything, and is true, and is no lie, just as it has taught you, abide in him" (1 John 2:20–21, 26–27).[17] It is ultimately the Holy Spirit at work in believers that gives them the supernatural ability to discern the true faith from a counterfeit.

The second point to make about this passage from *Lumen Gentium* is that the *sensus fidelium* is a supernatural capacity for discernment that belongs to the church as a whole. The baptismal anointing by the

---

15. *LG* 12.1.

16. Without using the actual term *sensus fidei*, the New Testament speaks frequently of the Holy Spirit working in the hearts of believers so that they might understand the revealed Word of God. In the Gospel of John, Jesus himself tells his followers he will not leave them orphans (John 14:18), but promises to send the Spirit of truth who "will teach you all things, and bring to your remembrance all that I have said to you" (John 14:26), and "guide you into all the truth" (John 16:13). John the Evangelist teaches in his First Letter that believers have received an anointing from the Holy Spirit, who instructs them in the truth and keeps them from false teaching (1 John 2:20–21, 26–27). St. Paul in his Letter to the Ephesians prays for the followers of Christ to receive the "Spirit of wisdom and of revelation in the knowledge of him, having the eyes of your hearts enlightened" (Eph 1:17), and in his First Letter to the Corinthians, describes the Holy Spirit as an interior guide who imparts to believers the hidden wisdom of God so that they have the "mind of Christ" (1 Cor 2:6–16). The fact that the Holy Spirit acts as inner guide and teacher of the messianic people of God fulfills the Old Testament prophecies about God pouring out his spirit on his people and writing his law on their hearts (e.g., Ezek 36:27; Jer 31:33–34).

17. All citations from the Bible in this chapter are from the RSVCE.

Spirit confers on all the faithful, regardless of rank or vocation, a share in Christ's prophetic office, enabling each believer to discern the true Word of God from a counterfeit.[18] As Scripture bears witness and the Council confirms, all the faithful have a prophetic sense for revealed truth because the entire church is the subject-bearer of divine revelation.[19] The faithful instinctively recognize the voice of God who loves them, as our Lord teaches in the Gospel of John: "My sheep hear my voice, and I know them, and they follow me" (John 10:27).

The third point to make regarding this passage from *Lumen Gentium* is that it duly emphasizes that the *sensus fidelium* must be exercised "under the guidance of the sacred teaching authority, in faithful and respectful obedience."[20] The Council in no way envisioned the *sensus fidelium* to be a vehicle for challenging or subverting the teaching authority of the bishops. To the contrary, the Council consistently affirms the constant teaching of the church that the bishops as successors to the apostles, and

---

18. "The holy people of God shares also in Christ's prophetic office; it spreads abroad a living witness to Him, especially by means of a life of faith and charity and by offering to God a sacrifice of praise, the tribute of lips which give praise to His name" (Cf. Heb 13:15). *LG* 12.1. In chapter 4 of *Lumen Gentium* on the laity, the Council emphasizes that not only the hierarchy, but lay people also share in Christ's prophetic office, and therefore possess a supernatural *sensus fidei* for the Word of God: "Christ, the great Prophet, who proclaimed the Kingdom of His Father both by the testimony of His life and the power of His words, continually fulfills His prophetic office until the complete manifestation of glory. He does this not only through the hierarchy who teach in His name and with His authority, but also through the laity whom He made His witnesses and to whom He gave understanding of the faith (*sensus fidei*) and an attractiveness in speech (Cf. Acts 2:17–18; Rev 19:10) so that the power of the Gospel might shine forth in their daily social and family life." Ibid., 35.1.

19. "And we also thank God constantly for this, that when you received the word of God which you heard from us, you accepted it not as the word of men but as what it really is, the word of God, which is at work in you believers" (1 Thess 2:13). See also Acts 2:17–18: "And in the last days it shall be, God declares, that I will pour out my Spirit upon all flesh, and your sons and your daughters shall prophesy, and your young men shall see visions, and your old men shall dream dreams; yea, and on my menservants and my maidservants in those days I will pour out my Spirit; and they shall prophesy." The Council confirms in *Dei Verbum* that the whole church is the bearer of divine revelation: "Sacred tradition and Sacred Scripture form one sacred deposit of the word of God, committed to the Church. Holding fast to this deposit the entire holy people united with their shepherds remain always steadfast in the teaching of the Apostles, in the common life, in the breaking of the bread and in prayers (see Acts 2, 42, Greek text), so that holding to, practicing and professing the heritage of the faith, it becomes on the part of the bishops and faithful a single common effort." *DV* 10.1.

20. *LG* 12.1.

the pope as the successor to St. Peter, have received a specific mandate from Christ and a unique charism from the Holy Spirit, that is not given to the church as a whole, to teach and preach the Gospel to the world (Matt 28:18–20; Mark 16:15–16).[21] By its very nature, therefore, the *sensus fidelium* implies a profound agreement with the magisterium of the church, since it is the very same Spirit who awakens the *sensus fidelium* and assists the magisterium.[22] Any appeal to Vatican II's doctrine on the *sensus fidelium* by pressure groups seeking to challenge the hierarchy's teaching authority distorts the teaching, because it would render the Council's doctrine on the relationship between the entire body of the faithful and the hierarchy internally incoherent and self-contradictory.[23]

21. See, e.g., the following representative texts: "Bishops, as successors of the apostles, receive from the Lord, to whom was given all power in heaven and on earth, the mission to teach all nations and to preach the Gospel to every creature, so that all men may attain to salvation by faith, baptism and the fulfillment of the commandments (Cf. Mt. 28:18; Mk. 16:15–16; Acts 26:17 ff.)." *LG* 24.1. "To fulfill this mission, Christ the Lord promised the Holy Spirit to the Apostles, and on Pentecost day sent the Spirit from heaven, by whose power they would be witnesses to Him before the nations and peoples and kinds even to the ends of the earth (cf. Acts 1:8–2:1 ff; 9:15)." Ibid., 24.1. By virtue of this charism, the pope and bishops are authentic teachers "endowed with the authority of Christ, who preach to the people committed to them the faith they must believe and put into practice, and by the light of the Holy Spirit illustrate that faith." Ibid., 25.1. The Council also emphasizes in *Dei Verbum* that, while it is true that the deposit of faith is entrusted to the whole church, "the task of authentically interpreting the word of God, whether written or handed on, has been entrusted exclusively to the living teaching office of the Church, whose authority is exercised in the name of Jesus Christ." *DV* 10.2.

22. As the Council puts it, there should be a remarkable *conspiratio* or harmony between the bishops and the faithful (*singularis fiat Antistitum et fidelium conspiratio*). *DV* 10.1. Blessed John Henry Newman expresses this same conviction in his celebrated essay advocating that the bishops consult the lay faithful in matters of doctrine "because the body of the faithful is one of the witnesses to the fact of the tradition of revealed doctrine, and because their *consensus* through Christendom is the voice of the Infallible Church." As Newman puts it, the magisterium is never subject to the lay faithful in teaching the faith, but there should be a remarkable *conspiratio* between the *ecclesia docens* and the *ecclesia discens*, which together make up "one two-fold testimony, illustrating each other, and never to be divided." Newman, *Consulting the Faithful*, 53–54, 63, 71.

23. Pope Benedict XVI underscored this fact in his 2012 address to the International Theological Commission, in which he pointed out that dissent from magisterial teaching that tries to justify itself by invoking the *sensus fidelium* is "unthinkable, since the *sensus fidei* cannot be authentically developed in believers, except to the extent in which they fully participate in the life of the Church, and this demands responsible adherence to the Magisterium, to the deposit of faith." Benedict XVI, "Address ITC," § 6. Hattrup makes the same point in arguing that, while the teaching of Vatican II in

The final point to stress about this passage from *Lumen Gentium* 12 is that the *sensus fidelium* is a property of the theological virtue of faith, and flows from it. It is, as the Council puts it, the "supernatural sense of faith" (*supernaturalis sensus fidei*) of the people of God, and not an expression of the opinions, advice, or "consent" which the laity gives to the hierarchy on a question of doctrine. This supernatural instinct enables believers to put their faith in what God has truly revealed. Even so, a believer *can* hold erroneous opinions, since all his thoughts and inclinations do not arise from faith. Other factors affect the minds and hearts of the faithful that do not belong to the *sensus fidelium*, such as the weight of public opinion, the influence of the mass media, and the sinful tendencies of our fallen nature.[24] Even believers can be manipulated, misled, corrupted, or tempted to choose to assent to doctrines opposed to faith. Moreover, some baptized members of the church have a weak faith or even dead faith no longer animated by charity due to persistent mortal sin (James 2:14–26). Others, as St. Paul warns in his First Letter to Timothy, "have made shipwreck of their faith" (1 Tim 1:19) so that while formally remaining members of the church, they are not in fact "the faithful." For all these reasons, the *sensus fidelium* cannot be discovered in a simplistic way based merely upon sociological studies, surveys, or public opinion polls.

Despite the difficulties in ascertaining the *sensus fidelium*, the faithful's instinctive grasp for what belongs to the deposit of faith and what

---

Lumen Gentium 12 represented a rediscovery of the important role of the collective *sensus fidei* of the whole body of the faithful, it was never meant to create a separate body of teachers among the laity opposed to the hierarchy's magisterium and agitating for changes in church teaching. Hattrup, "Amt und Volk," 337–64. Along the same lines, Scheffczyk argues that it is an abuse of the principle of *sensus fidelium* to invoke it to drive a wedge of opposition between the laity and the hierarchy, because the sense of faith in the community of the faithful contains within itself a principle of unity. The church by nature is a kind of living, supernatural organism, and a hierarchical, sacramental *communio*, directed by Christ as its head and animated by the Holy Spirit as its soul, in which there should be a remarkable harmony and unity between the "twofold and yet single witness" given by the teaching church and the believing church. Therefore, if the church is true to its nature, it would not be possible for an authentic *sensus fidelium* to contradict magisterial teaching. Scheffczyk, "Sensus Fidelium," 182–98. For a collection of opposed views that in general sees the laity as having a legitimate teaching authority that can legitimately oppose the teaching authority of the hierarchical magisterium, see Metz and Schillebeeckx, *The Teaching Authority of Believers*.

24. Congregation for the Doctrine of the Faith, *Donum Veritatis* 35.2. For discussions of why the *sensus fidelium* cannot be identified with "public opinion" in the church, see Dulles, "Sensus Fidelium," 240–42; Scheffczyk, "Sensus Fidelium," 196–98.

does not can serve as an important index of revealed truth in disputed questions of doctrine. The *sensus fidelium* of the entire body of the faithful can serve a vital role in the development of the church's understanding of revealed truth because the whole church is the bearer of divine revelation.[25] The magisterium can therefore look to the *sensus fidelium* to discern the entire church's faith concerning a particular truth in order to fulfill its teaching function.[26] Indeed, Vatican II implicitly refers to the *sensus fidelium* as a source of doctrinal development in *Dei Verbum*, where the Council teaches that there is a growth in understanding of the realities and words of divine revelation not only through magisterial teaching, but also "through the contemplation and study made by believers, who treasure these things in their hearts (see Luke, 2:19, 51) [and] through a penetrating understanding of the spiritual realities which they experience."[27] As this text suggests, the faithful do not just passively receive divine revelation, but actively grapple with it, because the human mind must "receive" divine revelation in a manner that befits its nature. Because of the very structure of the human mind and human thought, every believer cannot help but strive to some degree to understand better what he has accepted as the formative principle for his life. This active engagement with divine revelation is guided by the Holy Spirit, who not only moves the mind of believers to assent to revealed truth, but also brings about in them a deeper understanding of it. The *sensus fidelium*, therefore, can be a *locus theologicus* for the magisterium and theologians seeking to discover the mind of the church on yet unresolved matters of doctrine.

Two relatively recent historical examples of the magisterium looking to the faithful's actual beliefs to discern and confirm a revealed truth are Pope Pius IX's definition of the Dogma of the Immaculate Conception in 1854, and Pope Pius XII's definition of the Dogma of the Assumption in 1950. In both cases, several years in advance of formulating the dogmas, these two popes asked the bishops of the world to report back about the piety and devotion of the faithful regarding these proposed

---

25. See International Theological Commission, *Sensus Fidei*, 67–73.

26. Blessed John Henry Newman explains in his famous article *On Consulting the Faithful in Matters of Doctrine* that the faithful can and should be consulted by the magisterium to discover their actual beliefs as an indicium of the Apostolic Tradition, much like we would consult a barometer about the weather, a watch for the time, or a physician would check the pulse of his patient to determine the state of their health.

27. *DV* 8.2.

Marian doctrines.[28] In each case, the popes took particular note of the faithful's liturgical devotion to Mary as evidence of the authentic *sensus fidelium*, and explicitly relied upon it in deciding to define these two dogmas as truths contained in the sacred deposit of faith.[29] Nonetheless, while the beliefs of the faithful can be a valuable index of revealed truth, as St. John Paul II points out in his apostolic exhortation on the family, *Familiaris Consortio*, the supernatural *sensus fidei* "does not consist solely or necessarily in the consensus of the faithful."[30] As history shows, the authentic *sensus fidelium* in the church is not always to be identified with the majority, but sometimes with the isolated few who courageously witness to the true faith against the prevailing tide of public opinion, even in the church. Who can forget, for example, Athanasius in his monumental struggle against the Arian heresy that had seduced most of the Christian world?[31]

Because the *sensus fidelium* is invoked so frequently today in favor of modifying the church's doctrine on a variety of issues, it is perhaps more important now than ever that the magisterium possess sound criteria for making judgments about what constitutes an authentic expression of the *sensus fidelium* and what does not. In fact, both Pope Benedict XVI and Pope Francis in recent years have called upon theologians to aid the magisterium in its teaching task by developing solid theological criteria for discerning authentic expressions of the *sensus fidelium*.[32] It is impor-

28. Pius IX, *Ubi Primum* 6; Pius XII, *Deiparae Virginis Mariae* 4.

29. Pius IX, *Ineffabilis Deus* 3, 6, 30–33; Pius XII, *Munificentissimus Dei*, 11–12, 18–20.

30. John Paul II, *Familiaris Consortio*, 5.2.

31. C.S. Lewis comments on the remarkable witness of Athanasius: "His epitaph is *Athanasius contra mundum*, 'Athanasius against the world' . . . He stood for the Trinitarian doctrine, 'whole and undefiled,' when it looked as if all the civilized world was slipping back from Christianity into the religion of Arius . . . It is his glory that he did not move with the times; it is his reward that he now remains when those times, as all times do, have moved away." Lewis, *St. Athanasius*, 8–9.

32. "The *sensus fidei* is a criterion for discerning whether or not a truth belongs to the living deposit of the Apostolic Tradition. It also has a propositional value for the Holy Spirit never ceases to speak to the Churches and to guide them towards the whole truth. Today, however, it is particularly important to explain the criteria that make it possible to distinguish the authentic *sensus fidelium* from its counterfeit." Benedict XVI, "Address ITC," § 6; "Through the gift of the Holy Spirit, the members of the Church possess the '*sense of the faith*.' It is a kind of 'spiritual instinct' which allows them to *sentire cum Ecclesia* and to discern what conforms to the Apostolic faith and to the spirit of the Gospel. Of course, it is clear that the *sensus fidelium* must not be

tant to note in this context that there is both an objective aspect (the objective beliefs of the faithful) and a subjective aspect (the subjective ability of the faithful to discern the true faith) to the *sensus fidelium*. Since Vatican II, most of the theological literature on the *sensus fidelium* has focused on identifying the objective beliefs held by the faithful, but scant attention has been paid to the fundamental basis for the *sensus fidelium*, that is, how the *sensus fidei* operates in believers.[33] This is an unfortunate lacuna because it is the faithful's instinctive grasp of revealed truth that makes it possible for there to be a corporate set of beliefs held in common by the whole church.[34] In my view, therefore, in order to offer theological criteria for discerning the *sensus fidelium*, we should first turn our attention to how the virtue of faith functions in the individual believer, and to do that, we can do no better than look to St. Thomas Aquinas' account of faith in the *Summa theologiae*.[35]

---

confused with the sociological reality of majority opinion. It is something else. It is therefore important—and it is your task—to develop criteria for discerning authentic expressions of the *sensus fidelium*." Francis, "Address ITC," § 5.

33. Rush makes this same observation in a study on how the *sensus fidei* operates in the act of faith of the individual Christian believer, Rush, "Sensus Fidei," 231–61. Rush expounds on his earlier study on the *sensus fidei* in the individual believer in several chapters of a more comprehensive work, the book *The Eyes of Faith*. The paucity of literature on the subjective aspect of the *sensus fidei* in individual Christians is borne out by perusing Burkhard's periodic surveys of the theological literature on the *sensus fidelium* since Vatican II: Burkhard, "Sensus Fidei: 1965–1984," 41–59; Burkhard, "Sensus Fidei: 1985–1989," 123–36; Burkhard, "Sensus Fidei: 1990–2001: Part I," 450–75; and Burkhard, "Sensus Fidei: 1990–2001: Part II," 38–54. Besides Rush's work, a notable exception to this trend is Wagner, "Glaubenssinn," 263–71. For an extensive bibliography on the *sensus fidelium*, see Finucane, *Sensus Fidelium*, 655–89.

34. The Council implies this very thing by referring to the common sense of all the faithful on matters of belief in *LG* 12 as the "*supernaturalis sensus fidei totius populi Dei*," or the "supernatural sense of faith of the whole People of God," rather than employing the abbreviated terms *sensus fidelium* or *consensus fidelium*. The Council's choice of words here highlights the fact that the corporate *sensus fidelium* presupposes that the individual believers who make up "the faithful" have each been moved by the Holy Spirit and by his supernatural gifts to grasp some truth of the faith.

35. Although I am not aware of any in-depth study of St. Thomas's account of faith as a basis for evaluating the *sensus fidelium*, numerous studies of the corporate *sensus fidelium* in the post-conciliar period at least acknowledge the relevance of Aquinas's account of personal faith in relation to the individual's discerning *sensus fidei*. See, e.g., Glaser, "Connatural Knowledge," 748; Tillard, "Sensus Fidelium," 16–18; Thompson, "Sensus Fidelium," 455–57; Dulles, "Sensus Fidelium," 240; Scheffczyk, "Sensus Fidelium," 186; Tillard, *Church of the Churches*, 110; Pié-Ninot, "Sensus Fidei," 992–94; Finucane, *Sensus Fidelium*, 87–89; Rush, "Sensus Fidei," 243; Rush, *Eyes of Faith*, 2–3, 216. Prior to the Council in the early part of the twentieth century, however, there

ST. THOMAS AQUINAS ON HOW FAITH FUNCTIONS AS A DISCERNING POWER IN THE INDIVIDUAL BELIEVER

The *Habitus* of Faith

According to St. Thomas, the theological virtue of faith is a divinely-infused *habitus* that perfects man's intellect so that he can adhere to the mysteries revealed by God that are necessary for him to attain his supernatural end.[36] As St. Thomas explains, the *habitus* of faith not only inclines the believer to assent to revealed truth, but also prevents him from giving his assent to what is false.[37] As St. Thomas makes clear, the reason why faith discerns between the true and the false with respect to divine revelation is because it is a *habitus* or virtue inclined to its proper object.[38] Since faith is a virtue which, by definition, "can never be put to bad use,"[39] it can only assent to what is true and never to what is false.[40]

---

were three important studies on St. Thomas Aquinas's account of faith's capacity to discern revealed truth: Joyce, "La foi qui discerne," 433–55; Harent, "Note," 455–67; de Guibert, "La foi qui discerne," 30–44.

36 *ST* I-II.62.1.

37. "For just as by the habits of the other virtues, man sees what is becoming to him in respect of that habit, so, by the habit of faith, the human mind is directed to assent to such things as are becoming to a right faith, and not to assent to others." Ibid., II-II.1.4, ad 3.

38. Just as one habitually assents to first principles by the natural light of understanding, and the virtuous one habitually makes right judgments regarding things pertaining to that virtue, the one with the divinely infused light of faith habitually "assents to matters of faith and not to those which are against faith." Ibid., II-II.2.3, ad 2.

39. "Virtue implies a perfection of power . . . Now the limit of any power must needs be good: for all evil implies defect; wherefore Dionysius says (Div. Nom. ii) that every evil is a weakness. And for this reason the virtue of a thing must be regarded in reference to good. Therefore, human virtue, which is an operative habit, is a good habit, productive of good works." Ibid., I-II.55.3. For this reason, St. Thomas defines virtue as "a good habit of the mind, by which we live righteously, *of which no one can make bad use.*" Ibid., I-II.55.4.

40. "Since the true is the good of the intellect, but not of the appetitive power, it follows that all virtues which perfect the intellect, exclude the false altogether, because it belongs to the nature of a virtue to bear relation to the good alone." Ibid., II-II.1.3, ad 1. "For the faith of which we are speaking, does not assent to anything, except because it is revealed by God." Ibid., II-II.1.1. "Now it has been stated (A.1) that the formal aspect of the object of faith is the First Truth; so that nothing can come under faith, save in so far as it stands under the First Truth, under which nothing false can stand, as neither can non-being stand under being, nor evil under goodness. It follows therefore that nothing false can come under faith." Ibid., II-II.1.3.

An act of faith that proceeds from the theological virtue of faith, as such, cannot err.[41] It is this infallible character of faith that provides the very basis for looking to the actual beliefs of the faithful as an index of revealed truth.

And yet, St. Thomas warns that not every belief of the faithful stems from the virtue of faith.[42] First, untrained believers may not be able to articulate with precision what they actually believe, since the act of faith terminates not in propositions, but in the realities which they express.[43] Second, simple believers can also be led astray by more learned men who are charged with a duty to teach them.[44] Third, the virtue of faith admits of degrees, so that some men believe matters of faith more explicitly than others, or with greater certitude, or with greater promptitude, devotion, or confidence.[45] Finally, there will also always be believers who obstinately hold to opinions contrary to faith out of pride, covetousness, or distortions rooted in the imagination, and even those believers who abandon their faith altogether.[46] As St. Thomas's account of faith makes clear, there is a need for careful discernment in making judgments about

---

41. "Now it has been stated that the formal aspect of the object of faith is the First Truth; so that as it stands under the First Truth, under which nothing false can stand, as neither can non-being stand under being, nor evil under goodness. It follows therefore that nothing false can come under faith." Ibid., II-II.1.3; "For it is possible for a believer to have a false opinion through a human conjecture, but it is quite impossible for a false opinion to be the outcome of faith." Ibid., II-II.1.3, ad 3.

42. "For it is possible for a believer to have a false opinion through a human conjecture." Ibid., II-II.1.3, ad 3.

43. Ibid., II-II.1.2 ad. 2.

44. "Simple persons should not be put to the test about subtle questions of faith, unless they be suspected of having been corrupted by heretics, who are wont to corrupt the faith of simple people in such questions." Ibid., II-II.2.6, ad 2. "It is not human knowledge, but the Divine truth that is the rule of faith: and if any of the learned stray from this rule, he does not harm the faith of the simple ones, who think that the learned believe aright; unless the simple hold obstinately to their individual errors, against the faith of the universal Church, which cannot err." Ibid., II-II.2.6 ad. 3.

45. Ibid., II-II.5.4.

46. Ibid., II-II.5.3; 11.1; 11.1, ad 2; 11.1, ad 3; 12.1. Cf.: "Faith is an entirely free gift that God makes to man. We can lose this priceless gift, as St. Paul indicated to St. Timothy: 'Wage the good warfare, holding faith and a good conscience. By rejecting conscience, certain persons have made shipwreck of their faith' (1 Tim 1:18–19). To live, grow and persevere in the faith until the end we must nourish it with the word of God; we must beg the Lord to increase our faith (Cf. *Mk* 9:24; *Lk* 17:5; 22:32); it must be 'working through charity,' abounding in hope, and rooted in the faith of the Church (*Gal* 5:6; *Rom* 15:13; cf. *Jas* 2:14–26)." *Catechism of the Catholic Church*, 162.

the faith-beliefs of the baptized because not everything expressed by the baptized is, in fact, an expression of faith.

Faith and the *Instinctus* of the Holy Spirit

What then makes the difference between beliefs that stem from the *habitus* of faith and those that do not? As St. Thomas makes clear, the *habitus* of faith that disposes the intellect to adhere to revealed truth is not by itself sufficient for the actual assent of faith. The believer must also freely *choose* to adhere to what he recognizes ought to be believed, and not to something else.[47] As St. Thomas explains, in the act of faith the intellect assents to what God has revealed *at the command of the will*, without having clear sight of the object to which it assents.[48]

But what moves the will? According to St. Thomas, there is a twofold cause of the will moving the intellect to assent to revealed truth.[49] The first cause is an external inducement, such as seeing a miracle, or being persuaded by another to embrace the faith, neither of which is sufficient, since of those who see the same miracle or hear the same preacher, some believe and some do not. Hence, explains St. Thomas, we must assert another cause that is internal, that moves man inwardly to assent to matters of faith. This inward cause cannot originate from man's natural faculties because, in order to assent to supernatural matters of faith, man must be

---

47. "The intellect of the believer is determined to one object, not by the reason but by the will, wherefore assent is taken here for an act of the intellect as determined to one object by the will." Thomas Aquinas, *ST* II-II.2.1, ad 3.

48. Ibid., II-II.1.4. This is why St. Thomas defines the virtue of faith as "a habit of mind, whereby eternal life is begun in us, *making the intellect assent to what is non-apparent*." Ibid., II-II.4.1. This antecedent priority of the will in every act of faith explains why the sin of infidelity is not caused merely by a mistaken belief held by the intellect, but ultimately rooted in a bad will. "Now dissent, which is the act proper to unbelief, is an act of the intellect, moved, however, by the will, just as assent is. Therefore unbelief, like faith, is in the intellect as its proximate subject. But it is in the will as its first moving principle, in which way every sin is said to be in the will." Ibid., II-II.10.2. "The will's contempt causes the intellect's dissent, which completes the notion of unbelief. Hence the cause of unbelief is in the will, while unbelief itself is in the intellect." Ibid., II-II.10.2, ad 2. "Unbelief includes both ignorance, as an accessory thereto, and resistance to matters of faith, and in the latter respect it is a most grave sin." Ibid., II-II, 10, 3, ad 2. "Unbelief, in so far as it is a sin, arises from pride, through which man is unwilling to subject his intellect to the rules of faith, and to the sound interpretation of the Fathers." Ibid., II-II.10.1, ad 3.

49. Ibid., II-II.6.1.

elevated above his nature. The movement of the will commanding the intellect to assent requires a supernatural principle, that is, God himself moving man inwardly by grace. Thus, we receive from St. Thomas in the *Summa* the classic formulation of the act of faith as "an act of the intellect assenting to the Divine truth at the command of the will *moved by the grace of God.*"[50] Thus, the act of faith that assents to revealed truth is ultimately initiated by God's grace moving man to believe.

Among all the factors leading to the act of faith, St. Thomas gives absolute priority to God and his grace at work in the believer.[51] In the *Summa theologiae*, St. Thomas coins the term *instinctus* to refer to God's acting in the believer to bring about the assent of faith,[52] which for St. Thomas designates the Holy Spirit's promptings, urgings, and suggestions that stir individuals to perform particular actions.[53] By the *instinctus* or

50. Ibid., II-II.2.9. This is the same definition of the act of faith given by the *Catechism of the Catholic Church*: "In faith, the human intellect and will cooperate with divine grace: 'Believing is an act of the intellect assenting to the divine truth by command of the will moved by God through grace.'" *Catechism of the Catholic Church*, 155 (citing St. Thomas).

51. "Two things are requisite for faith. First, that the things which are of faith should be proposed to man: this is necessary in order that man believe anything explicitly. The second thing requisite for faith is the assent of the believer to the things which are proposed to him. Accordingly, as regards the first of these, faith must needs be from God. Because those things which are of faith surpass human reason, hence they do not come to man's knowledge, unless God reveal them . . . As regards the second, viz. man's assent to the things which are of faith, we may observe a twofold cause, one of external inducement, such as seeing a miracle, or being persuaded by someone to embrace the faith: neither of which is a sufficient cause, since of those who see the same miracle, or who hear the same sermon, some believe, and some do not. Hence we must assert another internal cause, which moves man inwardly to assent to matters of faith . . . Since man, by assenting to matters of faith, is raised above his nature, this must needs accrue to him from some supernatural principle moving him inwardly; and this is God. Therefore faith, as regards the assent which is the chief act of faith, is from God moving man inwardly by grace." *ST* II-II.6.1.

52. "The believer has sufficient motive for believing, for he is moved by the authority of Divine teaching confirmed by miracle, and, what is more, by the inward *instinctus* of God inviting [him] (*interiori instinctu Dei invitantis*)." Ibid., II-II.2.9 ad. 3 (my translation into English altered slightly to track the Latin more literally). "Because not only external revelation, or the object [of faith], has the power to draw us, but also an interior *instinctus* (*sed etiam interior instinctus*), impelling and leading to belief. Thus, the Father draws many to the Son by an *instinctus* of divine operation (*per instinctum divinae operationis*), moving the heart of man interiorly to believe." Thomas Aquinas, *Commentary on the Gospel of John* 1.6.5.

53. O'Connor, "*Instinctus* and *Inspiratio*," 131–41. The notion that *instinctus* of the Holy Spirit denotes the "promptings, urgings, suggestions" of the Spirit is implied

prompting of the Holy Spirit, man is interiorly moved in the act of faith to freely give his assent to what God has revealed.[54] Thus, the discerning *habitus* of faith that assents to revealed truth and not its counterfeit is not moved to its proper act by mere human effort, but ultimately by the grace of the Holy Spirit working in the individual believer.

Faith and the Infused Gifts of Understanding, Knowledge, and Wisdom

But how is the will itself moved by the prompting of the Holy Spirit to direct the intellect to assent to revealed truth? Following the principle that whatever is moved must be proportionate to its mover, St. Thomas explains that we need the infused gifts of the Spirit to be amenable to being moved by the Holy Spirit.[55] Like the virtues, the gifts of the Spirit are habits that perfect the powers of the soul, and like the infused virtues, the gifts are not acquired but placed in us by God.[56] But unlike the virtues,

---

by the fact that *instinctus* is derived from the Latin verb *instiguo*, meaning "to instigate" or "to incite." In St. Thomas's works, the term *instinctus* is not only used for the promptings of the Holy Spirit, but also the promptings of the devil—e.g., "When man commits sin without being influenced by the instinct of the devil (*instinctu Diaboli*), he nevertheless becomes a child of the devil thereby, in so far as he imitates him who was the first to sin."

54. In his study of St. Thomas's teaching on the divine *instinctus*, Walgrave explains how the *instinctus* of the Holy Spirit works in man: the instinct (of the Holy Spirit) comes from outside but works from inside: it is *exterior* by its origin, but *interior* by its way of working within us. The more perfect its work, the more interiorized it becomes; and our will and the Holy Spirit work together as if they were forming a unique principle. The growth of the motion received by our spirit does not diminish the very motion of freedom. Indeed, under the New Law, the instinct of the Holy Spirit becomes in us our own instinct. This highlights, in the context of the analogy that regulates the use of the word "instinct," the radical opposition between the highest and the lowest position on the scale of analogates. To be moved by natural instinct is a sign of a lack of freedom; to be moved by an instinct led by the Holy Spirit is a sign of a growing freedom, which belongs to God's children. Walgrave, "*Instinctus Spiritus Sancti*," 430, quoted by Pinckaers, "Morality and Holy Spirit," 386.

55. *ST* I-II.68.1. Servais Pinckaers observes: "As a matter of fact, we find the highest concentration of the word 'instinct' and its more typical use in question 68 of the *prima secundae*, which St. Thomas dedicates to the gifts of the Holy Spirit as *instinctus divinus* and where he exhibits a preference for the expressions '*moveri quodam superiori instinctu Spiritus Sancti*' (a. 2, ad 2), and '*sequi instinctum Spiritus Sancti*.'" Pinckaers, "Morality and Holy Spirit," 388.

56. *ST* I-II.68.3; Ibid., I-II.68.1.

the gifts shape a person's character to be receptive to the prompting of the Holy Spirit.[57] The gifts of the Spirit do not replace the virtues, but rather assist the virtues and remedy defects in them by making us amenable to the influence of the Holy Spirit.[58] As St. Thomas explains, the gifts operate according to a higher mode of action than the virtues.[59] The virtues operate according to a basically human mode of action because, even when infused by God, they are still directed by human reason. But the gifts of the Spirit operate according to a supernatural mode of action because they put the person in a position of perfect docility to the promptings of the Holy Spirit.[60] Indeed, when we are moved by the Holy Spirit to perform virtuous actions, we act in a manner so far above our natural mode of acting that it leads John of St. Thomas to say, "by the virtues we walk, [but] by the gifts we fly."[61]

St. Thomas teaches that every gift of the Spirit is a complement to a particular virtue. For the virtue of faith, St. Thomas associates not one but two gifts, understanding and knowledge. The gift of understanding is a supernatural *habitus* that perfects the intellect so that, under the

---

57. "These perfections are called gifts . . . because by them man is disposed to become amenable to the Divine inspiration." Ibid., I-II.68.1.

58. Ibid., I-II.68.8. "What is perfect in the order of its nature needs to be helped by something of a higher nature; as man, however perfect, needs to be helped by God. And in this way the virtues, which perfect the powers of the soul, as they are controlled by reason, no matter how perfect they are, need to be helped by the gifts, which perfect the soul's powers, inasmuch as these are moved by the Holy Ghost." Ibid., III.7.5, ad 1.

59. "For it must be noted that in man there is a twofold principle of movement, one within him, viz. the reason, the other extrinsic to him, viz. God . . . Now it is manifest that human virtues perfect man according as it is natural for him to be moved by his reason in his interior and exterior actions. Consequently man needs yet higher perfections, whereby to be disposed to be moved by God. These perfections are called gifts, not only because they are infused by God, but also because by them man is disposed to become amenable to the Divine inspiration, according to Isa. 1.5: *The Lord . . . hath opened my ear, and I do not resist; I have not gone back.* Even the Philosopher says in the chapter *On Good Fortune (Ethic. Eudem., loc. cit.)* that for those who are moved by Divine instinct (*moventur per instinctum divinum*), there is no need to take counsel according to human reason, but only that they might follow the interior instinct (*sequantur interiorem instinctum*), since they are moved by a principle higher than human reason. This then is what some say, viz. that the gifts perfect man for acts which are higher than acts of virtue." Ibid., I-II.68.1.

60. Pinckaers explains that the *instinctus* of the Spirit moves humanity from within, but "its origin is nevertheless exterior, or rather superior, to man." Pinckaers, "Morality and Holy Spirit," 389.

61. Quoted in Gilby, "Dialectic of Love," 131.

prompting of the Holy Spirit, it is made apt for a penetrating intuition or grasp of revealed truths.[62] As St. Thomas explains, the gift of understanding perfects the virtue of faith because, while faith assents to revealed truths, understanding under the illuminating action of the Holy Spirit gives to the believer "a certain excellence of a knowledge that penetrates into the heart of things."[63]

The other gift linked to faith, knowledge, is a supernatural *habitus* that perfects the intellect so that, under the prompting of the Holy Spirit, it makes right judgments concerning created things insofar as they relate to eternal life and Christian perfection.[64] According to St. Thomas, the gift of knowledge directly relates to the virtue of faith because it endows the believer with a "sure and right judgment . . . so as to discern what is to be believed from what is not to be believed."[65] Unlike the knowledge produced by natural discursive reasoning, the gift of knowledge from the Holy Spirit participates in God's mode of knowing and therefore operates by simple intuition.[66]

The gift of wisdom is also directly relevant to the virtue of faith, even though St. Thomas pairs it with the virtue of charity.[67] The gift of

---

62. *ST* II-II.8.1; 8.3.

63. Ibid., II-II.8.1, ad 3; "The gift of understanding is about the first principles of that knowledge which is conferred by grace; but otherwise than faith, because it belongs to faith to assent to them, while it belongs to the gift of understanding to pierce with the mind the things that are said." Ibid., II-II, 8, 6, ad 2. "Faith implies merely assent to what is proposed, but understanding implies a certain perception of the truth." Ibid., II-II, 8, 5, ad 3.

64. Ibid., II-II.9.1.

65. Ibid., II-II.9.1. "[K]nowledge of what one ought to believe, by discerning things to be believed from things not to be believed: in this way knowledge is a gift and is common to all holy persons." Ibid., II-II.9.1 ad. 2. "The gift of knowledge also, primarily and principally indeed, regards speculation, in so far as man knows what he ought to hold by faith." Ibid., II-II.9.3. "They alone have the gift of knowledge who judge aright about matters of faith." Ibid., II-II.9.3, ad 3.

66. Ibid., II-II.9.1, ad 1.

67. St. Thomas in several places in the *Summa theologiae* indicates that the gifts of understanding, knowledge, *and* wisdom all perfect the knowledge gained by faith: "If these three [i.e., understanding, knowledge, and wisdom] be taken as gifts received in this present life, they are related to faith as to their principle which they presuppose." Ibid., II-II.4.8. "Accordingly on the part of the things proposed to faith for belief, two things are required on our part: first that they be penetrated or grasped by the intellect, and this belongs to the *gift of understanding*. Secondly, it is necessary that man should judge these things aright, that he should esteem that he ought to adhere to these things, and to withdraw from their opposites: and this judgment, with regard to

wisdom is a supernatural *habitus* seated in the intellect that enables the believer, by the prompting of the Holy Spirit, to make right judgments regarding "divine things" on account of a certain existential affinity or connaturality with them.[68] While the gift of wisdom perfects the intellect, the connatural knowledge it enjoys is caused by the *habitus* of charity in the will, which brings about an intimate union between the believer and God.[69] Unlike the knowledge that comes from rational inquiry, this connaturality with the divine affords the believer a spontaneous, intimate knowledge of divine things,[70] and gives them a keen intuition or perception for discerning genuine revealed truth from a distortion or counterfeit, even without instruction.[71] Taken together, therefore, the infused gifts of understanding, knowledge, and wisdom give the believer more perfect knowledge than faith affords without these gifts, insofar as they

---

Divine things belongs to the *gift of wisdom*, but with regard to created things, belongs to the *gift of knowledge*." Ibid., II-II.8.6.

68. "It belongs to the wisdom that is an intellectual virtue to pronounce right judgment after reason has made its inquiry, but it belongs to wisdom as a gift of the Holy Spirit to judge aright about them on account of connaturality with them: thus Dionysius says (*Div. Nom.* ii) that *Hierotheus is perfect in Divine things, for he not only learns, but is patient of, Divine things.*" Ibid., II-II.45.2.

69. "Now this sympathy or connaturality for Divine things is the result of charity, which unites us to God, according to 1 Cor. Vi, 17: *He who is joined to the Lord, is one spirit*. Consequently, wisdom which is a gift, has its cause in the will, which cause is charity, but it has its essence in the intellect, whose act is to judge aright." Ibid., II-II.45.2. "The wisdom which is a gift of the Holy Spirit, as stated above, enables us to judge aright of Divine things, or of other things according to Divine rules, by reason of a certain connaturalness or union with Divine things, which is the effect of charity, as stated above. Hence, the wisdom of which we are speaking presupposes charity." Ibid., II-II.45.4. "Although wisdom is distinct from charity, it presupposes it." Ibid., II-II.45.4 ad. 3. Consequently, should a person lose the virtue of charity by falling into mortal sin, it necessarily follows that they would lose the gift of wisdom as well. Ibid., II-II.45.4.

70. Elsewhere in the *Summa theologiae*, St. Thomas refers to this mode of knowing divine things as "judgment by inclination" (*iudicare per modum inclinatio*) (I.1.6, ad 3), "affective cognition" (*cognitio affectiva*) (I.64.1; II-II.97.2, ad 2; II-II.162.3, ad 1), "experiential cognition" (*cognitio experimentalis*) (II-II.97.2, ad 2), and, in the same passage, judgment by "connaturality" (*connaturalitas*), "compassion" (*compassio*) and "experiencing" (*patiens*) (II-II.45.2).

71. See, e.g., Congar, *Tradition and Traditions*, 318; Glaser, "Connatural Knowledge," 742–51; Tillard, "Sensus Fidelium," 16–18; Dulles, "Sensus Fidelium," 240; Tillard, *Church of Churches*, 110; Pié-Ninot, "Sensus Fidei," 992–94.

more clearly, firmly, and intuitively manifest to the mind the revealed truths to which faith adheres.[72]

Faith and Charity

The linchpin that holds together the virtue of faith and its related gifts of understanding, knowledge, and wisdom required for the believer to have a keen grasp of revealed truth is the theological virtue of charity. Charity is an infused *habitus* that perfects the will so that man can attain a loving union with God that St. Thomas characterizes as friendship.[73] Following St. Paul, St. Thomas affirms that charity is the most excellent of all the virtues and gifts of the Spirit since by it we actually attain union with God himself.[74] Moreover, whoever has charity possesses all the gifts of the Holy Spirit, but conversely, whoever lacks charity possesses none of them.[75] Therefore, only a person with living faith, that is, faith animated by charity, also possesses the infused gifts of understanding, knowledge, and wisdom. As St. Thomas explains in his *Commentary on the Gospel of John*, the reason why the apostle John was privileged with more intimate knowledge of divine truth was because of his deep loving friendship with the Lord, since "friends reveals secrets to friends."[76] While faith can exist in a person without charity in an imperfect state, faith is not a virtue

---

72. "The gifts of understanding and knowledge are more perfect than the knowledge of faith in the point of their greater clearness (*quantum ad majorem manifestationem*), but not in regard to more certain adhesion: because the whole certitude of the gifts of understanding and knowledge arises from the certitude of faith, even as the certitude of the knowledge of conclusions arises from the certitude of the premises." *ST* II-II.4.8, ad 3. The importance of the gifts of understanding and knowledge to the virtue of faith cannot be overemphasized because, when they are lost due to sin, the believers suffer at a minimum a dullness of mind that weakens their ability to consider spiritual goods, and at worst total spiritual blindness that completely deprives them of the knowledge of spiritual goods. Ibid., II-II.15.1–3.

73. Ibid., II-II.23.1–3.

74. Ibid., II-II.23.6.; I-II.69.8.

75. Ibid., I-II.68.5.

76. "We can see from this that the more a person wants to grasp the secrets of divine wisdom, the more he should try to get closer to Christ, according to: 'Come to him and be enlightened' (Ps 34:5). For the secrets of divine wisdom are especially revealed to those who are joined to God by love: 'He shows his friend that it is his possession' (Job 36:33); 'His friend comes and searches into him' (Prv 18:17)." Thomas Aquinas, *Commentary on the Gospel of John* 2.13.4.

without charity to perfect it.[77] If the intellect has faith but the will lacks charity, any act of faith produced will be imperfect, weak, and unstable because it will not be motivated by the supernatural love of God for his own sake that proceeds from charity.[78]

FOUR THEOLOGICAL CRITERIA FOR JUDGING THE SENSUS FIDELIUM

Since the Second Vatican Council, a great deal of confusion surrounds its teaching on the *sensus fidelium*. Consequently, our recent popes have pointed out that there is a great need for clear theological criteria to identify authentic expressions of the *sensus fidelium*. As the point of departure for this task, we have examined Vatican II's actual teaching regarding the *sensus fidelium* in *Lumen Gentium* 12. This text emphasizes the objective, corporate sense of the church's faith, but presupposes each individual believer's instinctive grasp of revealed truth. For this reason, we next analyzed closely various aspects of St. Thomas Aquinas' account of personal faith, making it now possible to offer theological criteria for the *sensus fidelium* that is grounded in how faith actually operates in the individual believer. Corresponding to the emphasis of Vatican II and St. Thomas Aquinas, what unites the following four proposed criteria is the absolute primacy of the Holy Spirit and his gifts, illuminating and guiding the faithful to discern what is truly of God.

---

77. *ST* I-II.65.4; II-II.4.4 and 5.

78. Charity is therefore referred to as the form of faith because, as with all voluntary acts, the end is what is most formal, and charity directs the act of faith toward its proper end, loving union with God: "Now it is evident from what has been said, that the act of faith is directed to the object of the will, i.e., the good, as its end: and this good which is the end of faith, viz., the Divine Good, is the proper object of charity. Therefore charity is called the form of faith in so far as the act of faith is perfected and formed by charity." Ibid., II-II.4.3. "Charity is called the form of faith because it quickens the act of faith." Ibid., II-II.4.3, ad 1. "The end of faith, even as of the other virtues, must be referred to the end of charity, which is the love of God and our neighbor." Ibid., II-II.3.2, ad 1. And inasmuch as charity is the form of faith directing it to its end, it is also called the mother and root of faith. Ibid., I-II.62.4; II-II.23.8, ad 1–3.

Criterion No. 1: Are the persons expressing their beliefs really members of "the faithful" who are fully participating in the life of grace?

Developing criteria for discerning the *sensus fidelium* begs a preliminary question, "Who are the faithful?" As a threshold criterion, the magisterium should look only to those Christians who actively participate in the life of the church to discover the authentic *sensus fidelium*.[79] As St. Thomas's account suggests, not every baptized member of the church merits the same consideration for determining the instinctive sense the faithful have for revealed truth, because not all the faithful possess the full complement of divine gifts from the Holy Spirit meant to accompany the virtue of faith. Indeed, it is the gifts of the Spirit that always accompany charity that capacitate believers in a state of grace to instinctively grasp what truly belongs to the deposit of faith and what does not. Only those members of the church who regularly avail themselves of the means of grace entrusted to the church by Christ, that is, the liturgy, the sacraments, the life of prayer, ascetical practices, the study of Scripture, and the like, can be trusted to express an authentic *sensus fidelium*. Conversely, those who stand on the margins and only partially identify with the church, who do not avail themselves of the spiritual treasures of the church, who obstinately hold on to their own dissenting opinions, or who remain in a persistent state of mortal sin, are not reliable sources of the *sensus fidelium*. Such persons do not fully participate in the life of the

---

79. For a view opposed to mine, see Burkhard's argument that the church should pay attention to marginalized, dissenting, and non-practicing Catholics and other Christians in discerning the *sensus fidelium*: "I agree that the voice and experience of the former [i.e., 'prophets, saints, and the suffering members of the church], are absolutely necessary in the Church today, but at the same time we must not forget that the SF [i.e., *sensus fidei*] pertains to all the faithful, and that we can learn from the ordinary, distracted, confused, ill-informed, sinful, and ecclesially marginalized members, e.g., the divorced and remarried, homosexual persons, alienated women, etc . . . The teaching of Vatican II on the SF refers to all believers and makes no such distinction among the faithful [i.e., between practicing and non-practicing Catholics]. Obviously, there are real differences of engagement in the faith and in the Church on the part of Christians. However, to insist too much on the differences results in diminishing our appreciation of the bonds of baptism . . . [T]he Spirit can also be addressing the wider Church precisely through the radical questioning, rejection, or indifference toward the Church of the marginally involved—or even by the Church's hostile critics. It is salutary and startling to recall just how appreciative Jesus was of the religiously alienated persons of his day and their conflicts with their religious leaders." Burkhard, "*Sensus Fidei*: Part I," 452, 463–64.

church, and in various ways and degrees, cut themselves off from the Holy Spirit and his gifts at work in the church. To be sure, this is not a form of spiritual elitism, but rather, in full accord with Vatican II and St. Thomas Aquinas, a realistic affirmation of the absolute primacy of the Holy Spirit, his grace, and his gifts in giving believers an instinctive grasp of revealed truth. The bishops should therefore consider commitment and involvement in the life of the church as a necessary, dispositive factor in making judgments about whether the views of individuals or groups should be taken into account in assessing the *sensus fidelium*.

Criterion No. 2: Are the beliefs in question embraced by the most devout, holy, humble, and saintly men and women in the church?

The beliefs of those most devoted to Christ among us are perhaps the most important criteria of all for discerning the authentic *sensus fidelium*. St. Thomas teaches that the beloved disciple, St. John the Evangelist, had intimate knowledge of divine truth because of his deep loving friendship with Jesus, for "friends reveal secrets to friends." Holiness, or the perfection of charity, is produced in the follower of Christ by the Holy Spirit and is always accompanied by an abundance of his spiritual gifts, including infused understanding, knowledge, and wisdom concerning divine truth. It is especially the saints, the friends of God burning with love for him, who know and understand divine truth the best, and have the most discerning *sensus fidei*.[80] Along these lines, Pope St. John Paul II, Pope Benedict XVI, and Pope Francis have all alluded to the relevance of the following biblical passage for discerning the *sensus fidelium*: "I give praise to you, Father, Lord of heaven and earth, for although you have hidden these things from the wise and the learned you have revealed them to the childlike" (Matt 11:25).[81] Holiness, the perfection of charity, is the surest guaranty that Christian believers possess the authentic *sensus fidelium*. The bishops should therefore look above all else to those Christian believers marked by holiness to discover the authentic *sensus fidelium* being expressed in the church.

---

80. Pope John Paul II referred to this intimate knowledge and precious insight that the saints have regarding the mysteries of God as the "lived theology of the saints." John Paul II, *Novo Millennio Ineunte*, 27.

81. John Paul II, "Prophetic Community," 177–78; Benedict XVI, "Homily ITC," §§ 1–9; Francis, "Address ITC," §§ 5–6.

Criterion No. 3: Are the beliefs being expressed by the faithful better characterized as a fruit of the Spirit of truth, or as a manifestation of the spirit of this world?

St. Thomas teaches that the act of faith not only concerns the intellect, but always involves a free choice of the will moved by the grace of the Holy Spirit. While the act of faith as such is inerrant, not every opinion of the faithful is an expression of faith since there are other forces at work on them. Even believers who fully participate in the life of the church and are not cut off from the sources of grace can be manipulated, misled, corrupted, or tempted to choose to assent to doctrines opposed to faith. St. Paul speaks of a battle for the hearts and minds of men between the Spirit of God and the "ruler of this world" (John 12:31; 14:30), "desires of the flesh" (Gal 5:17), and the "spirit of the world" (1 Cor 2:12). For this very reason, public opinion polls and other sociological measures cannot be trusted to disclose the *sensus fidelium* reliably. Because the Catholic faithful are not only prompted by the Holy Spirit, but also beset by "the world, the flesh, and the devil," careful consideration must be given to the origination of their beliefs. As a consequence of their secular character, lay people in particular are understandably expected to be more susceptible to worldly influences. If the faithful are being moved to adopt a certain view by powerful secular forces at work in the world, such as the mass media, pressure groups, popular forms of entertainment, political forces, prevailing majority opinions, and the like that have a clear influence on society, one should be concerned that it is a reflection of the spirit of the world at work in them. On the other hand, if the faithful are expressing a felt conviction in their devotional, sacramental, and liturgical life in the church, such as occurred among the faithful prior to the Marian dogmas of the Immaculate Conception and Assumption being defined, it is much more likely to be the fruit of the Holy Spirit at work in the church. Even more, doctrinal positions that emerge out of the new ecclesial movements that the church recognizes as the work of the Holy Spirit (e.g., Communion and Liberation, Couples for Christ, Focolare, etc.) are also more likely to be a fruit of the Holy Spirit at work in believers. Thus, the bishops should carefully discern whether the beliefs being presented to them as the *sensus fidelium* appear to originate from life in the Spirit or from life in the world.

Criterion No. 4: Are the beliefs in question congruent with the living tradition of the church? Are there elements of it present in the Tradition in seed form?

By the power of the Holy Spirit, the church is able to hand on from generation to generation the deposit of faith entrusted to it by Christ. The *sensus fidelium* cannot only be an expression of the church's faith here and now, but must be an expression of what the church has always believed, even if only implicitly. G.K. Chesterton puts this well in his book, *Orthodoxy*: "Tradition means giving votes to the most obscure of all classes, our ancestors. It is the democracy of the dead. Tradition refuses to submit to the small and arrogant oligarchy of those who merely happen to be walking about."[82] If the belief being expressed is contained in the deposit of faith, then it has always been part of the church's faith, at least in seed form or in some earlier state of development. This criterion corresponds with Blessed John Henry Newman's first note for identifying authentic doctrinal development, that is, preservation of type. One should be able to find an incipient form of the doctrine in the monuments of Tradition, such as the writings of the Fathers, saints, doctors, and councils of the church. After all, the church possesses the fullness of revelation, "the faith which was once for all delivered to the saints" (Jude 1:3), so that when doctrinal development occurs it is nothing other than a growth in understanding of what the church already possesses. The bishops, therefore, should look at the views being proposed as the *sensus fidelium* through a wider lens that considers the church's handing on of the deposit of faith from generation to generation throughout history, seeking to discover if there were already present in earlier times the seeds of what might be a fuller understanding of a revealed truth that appears to be reaching full blossom only now.

CONCLUSION

As we have seen, the Second Vatican Council teaches in *Lumen Gentium* 12 that the *sensus fidelium* gives the faithful a supernatural ability to discern the true faith from a counterfeit, and in *Dei Verbum* 8 that the *sensus fidelium* can be a valuable theological source for doctrinal development. In this study, in order to develop sound theological criteria for the bishops

---

82. Chesterton, *Orthodoxy*, 43.

to identify authentic expressions of the *sensus fidelium*, we have turned to St. Thomas Aquinas' account of faith in the *Summa theologiae* to analyze how the supernatural sense of faith operates in the individual believer. As St. Thomas makes clear, the infused *habitus* of faith not only inclines the believer to assent to revealed truth, but it also prevents him from giving his assent to what is false. In fact, as St. Thomas shows, any act of faith that proceeds from the supernatural virtue of faith cannot err. It is this infallible character of the act of faith that makes the *sensus fidelium* such an invaluable theological resource for the bishops to draw upon in order to carry out their teaching function. And yet, as St. Thomas also makes clear, because of our fallen nature and the influence of various internal and external factors that are not of God, not every belief held by the faithful can be counted upon as proceeding from the virtue of faith. It seems clear, therefore, that only those believers who are in a state of grace, with the virtues of faith and charity, and possessing the full complement of the infused gifts of the Spirit, could possibly surmount the deleterious influences that cloud the understanding of faith and be counted upon to express reliably the authentic *sensus fidelium*. As we have also seen with the assistance of St. Thomas, only those believers in a state of grace, with faith perfected by charity, have the requisite gifts of understanding, knowledge, and wisdom that endows them with a keen perception for what truly belongs to the deposit of faith and what does not.

The bishops should only look to those Christians who are fully engaged in the life of the church and who avail themselves of the means of sanctification and sources of truth found in her as a minimum, threshold criterion for making judgments about the *sensus fidelium*. Moreover, and above all else, the bishops should look to those everyday saints, the holy ones, the friends of God, to discover the *sensus fidelium* for, as St. Thomas puts it so well, "friends reveal secrets to friends." Further, because there are many secular forces at work on the faithful, the bishops should also carefully analyze whether the source of the views being proposed to them as authentic expressions of the *sensus fidelium* originate from the Holy Spirit or the spirit of this world. Finally, the bishops should ensure that the doctrine being proposed as an authentic expression of the *sensus fidelium* has roots in the church's living tradition, since there should be at least in seed form from the beginning some element of the doctrine being proposed only now. This is simply a recognition that while the church's understanding of the deposit of faith grows and develops, the deposit of faith itself is set and has been given "once and for all" to the faithful.

By giving due attention to these criteria, the bishops can engage in their own discernment of what truly constitutes an authentic expression of the *sensus fidelium* in order to carry out faithfully their teaching function in the church.

BIBLIOGRAPHY

Aquinas, Thomas. *Commentary on the Gospel of John* (Latin and English text). Part I. Chapter 6. Translated by James A. Weisheipl. http://dhspriory.org/thomas/SSJohn.htm.

———. *Commentary on the Gospel of John* (Latin and English text). Part II. Chapter 13. Translated by Fabian R. Larcher. http://dhspriory.org/thomas/John13.htm.

———. *Summa Theologica*. Translated by the English Dominican Province. 5 vols. Notre Dame: Christian Classics, 1981.

Beinert, Wolfgang. "Bedeutung und Begrundung des Glaubenssinnes (Sensus Fidei) al seines dogmatischen Erkenntniskriteriums." *Catholica* 25 (1971) 271–303.

———. "Der Glaubenssinn der Gläubigen in Theologie- und Dogmengeschichte: Ein Überblick." In *Der Glaubenssinn des Gottesvolkes: Konkurrent oder Partner des Lehramts?*, edited by Dietrich Wiederkehr, 66–131. Questiones Disputatae 151. Freiburg: Herder, 1994.

Benedict XVI. "Address to the International Theological Commission." http://w2.vatican.va/content/benedict-xvi/en/speeches/2012/december/documents/hf_ben-xvi_spe_20121207_cti.html.

———. "Homily at Holy Mass with the Members of the International Theological Commission." http://www.vatican.va/holy_father/benedict_xvi/homilies/2009/documents/hf_ben-xvi_hom_20091201_cti_en.html.

———. "A Proper Hermeneutic for the Second Vatican Council." In *Vatican II: Renewal within Tradition*, edited by Matthew Lamb and Matthew Levering, ix–xv. Oxford: Oxford University Press, 2008.

Burkhard, John. "*Sensus Fidei*: Theological Reflection Since Vatican II: I. 1965–1984." *Heythrop Journal* 34 (1993) 41–59.

———. "*Sensus Fidei*: Theological Reflection Since Vatican II: II. 1985–1989." *Heythrop Journal* 34 (1993) 123–36.

———. "*Sensus Fidei*: Recent Theological Reflection (1990–2001): Part I." *Heythrop Journal* 46 (2005) 450–75.

———. "*Sensus Fidei*: Recent Theological Reflection (1990–2001): Part II." *Heythrop Journal* 47 (2006) 38–54.

Catechism of the Catholic Church. 2nd ed. Vatican City: Libreria Editrice Vaticana, 1997.

Catholics for Choice. *Amicus Curiae Brief Submitted to the Inter-American Court of Human Rights*. https://www.catholicsforchoice.org/topics/politics/documents/CatholicsforChoiceIVFamicusEnglishFINAL.pdf

Chesterton, G. K. *Orthodoxy*. Reprint, Chicago: Moody Classics, 2009.

Congar, Yves. *Tradition and Traditions: The Biblical, Historical, and Theological Evidence for Catholic Teaching on Tradition*. Translated by Michael Naseby and Thomas Rainborough. San Diego: Basilica, 1997.

Congregation for the Doctrine of the Faith. *Donum Veritatis.* http://www.vatican.va/roman_curia/congregations/cfaith/documents/rc_con_cfaith_doc_19900524_theologian-vocation_en.html.

———. *Letter to the Bishops of the Catholic Church on the Pastoral Care of Homosexual Persons.* http://www.vatican.va/roman_curia/congregations/cfaith/documents/rc_con_cfaith_doc_19861001_homosexual-persons_en.html

DignityUSA, "Declaration of Non-Reception of the Pastoral Letter on the Care of Homosexual Persons." http://www.dignityusa.org/nonreception (accessed May 22, 2014). This source is no longer posted on the DignityUSA website.

Dulles, Avery. "*Sensus Fidelium.*" *America Magazine: The National Catholic Review* 155, no. 12 (1986) 240–42.

Finucane, Daniel. *Sensus Fidelium: The Use of a Concept in the Post-Vatican II Era.* San Francisco: International Scholars, 1996.

Francis. "Address to Members of the International Theological Commission." http://w2.vatican.va/content/francesco/en/speeches/2013/december/documents/papa-francesco_20131206_commissione-teologica.html.

Gilby, Thomas. "Appendix 10: The Dialectic of Love in the *Summa.*" In *Summa Theologiae*, by St. Thomas Aquinas, edited by Thomas Gilby, 1:131–41. New York: McGraw-Hill, 1974.

Glaser, John W. "Authority, Connatural Knowledge, and the Spontaneous Judgment of the Faithful." *Theological Studies* 29 (1968) 742–51.

de Guibert, J. "A propos des textes de saint Thomas sur la foi qui discerne." *Recherches Science Religeuse* 6 (1919) 30–44.

Hammans, Herbert. *Die neueren katholischen Erklärungen der Dogmenentwicklung.* Beiträge zur neueren Geschichte der katholischen Theologie 7. Essen: Ludgerus, 1965.

Harent, S. "Note sur l'article precedent." *Recherches Science Religeuse* 6 (1916) 455–67.

Hattrup, Dieter. "Amt und Volk in der Kirche, Zum Sinn des *Sensus Fidei.*" *Theologie und Glaube* 85 (1995) 337–64.

International Theological Commission. *Sensus Fidei in the Life of the Church.* http://www.vatican.va/roman_curia/congregations/cfaith/cti_documents/rc_cti_20140610_sensus-fidei_en.html.

Joyce, G.H. "La foi qui discerne d'apres saint Thomas." *Recherches Science Religeuse* 6 (1916) 433–55.

John Paul II. "The Church Is a Prophetic Community." In *The Church, Mystery, Sacrament, Community*, 177–78. A Catechesis on the Creed 4. Boston: Pauline Books & Media, 1998.

———. *Familiaris Consortio.* http://www.vatican.va/holy_father/john_paul_ii/apost_exhortations/documents/hf_jp-ii_exh_19811122_familiaris-consortio_en.html.

———. *Novo Millennio Ineunte.* http://www.vatican.va/holy_father/john_paul_ii/apost_letters/documents/hf_jp-ii_apl_20010106_novo-millennio-ineunte_en.html.

Lamb, Christopher. "The Case for Mercy: Interview with Cardinal Walter Kasper." *The Tablet*, September 18, 2014. http://www.thetablet.co.uk/features/2/3401/the-case-for-mercy.

Lamb, Matthew. "Vatican II after Fifty Years: The Virtual Council versus the Real Council." *Fellowship of Catholic Scholars Quarterly* 35, nos. 3/4 (2012) 14–19.

Lawler, Michael. *What Is and What Ought to Be: The Dialectic of Experience, Theology and Church.* New York: Continuum, 2005.

Lewis, C. S. Introduction to *St. Athanasius on the Incarnation.* Translated and edited by a Religious of C.S.M.V. Crestwood, NY: St. Vladimir's Seminary Press, 1993.

Lynch, Robert. "What the People of God Said." *For His Friends: Thoughts and Reflections by Bishop Robert Lynch* (blog). February 7, 2014. http://bishopsblog.dosp.org/?p=6014.

Maguire, Daniel. "A Catholic Defense of Same Sex Marriage." The Religious Consultation on Population, Reproductive Health, and Ethics. http://www.religiousconsultation.org/Catholic_defense_of_same_sex_marriage.htm.

McBrien, Richard. "The Phoenix Case." *National Catholic Reporter*, July 6, 2010. http://ncronline.org/blogs/essays-theology/phoenix-case.

Metz, Johann Baptist, and Edward Schillebeeckx, eds. *The Teaching Authority of Believers.* Edinburgh: T. & T. Clark, 1985.

Newman, John Henry. *On Consulting the Faithful in Matters of Doctrine.* New York: Sheed & Ward, 1961.

O'Connor, Edward D. "Appendix 5: *Instinctus* and *Inspiratio*." In *Summa Theologiae*, by St. Thomas Aquinas, edited by Thomas Gilby, 24:131–41. New York: McGraw-Hill, 1974.

Pinckaers, Servais. "Morality and the Movement of the Holy Spirit: Aquinas's Doctrine of *Instinctus* (1991)." In *The Pinckaers Reader: Renewing Thomistic Moral Theology*, translated by Mary Thomas Noble et al., edited by John Berkman and Craig Steven Titus, 385–95. Washington, DC: Catholic University of America Press, 2012.

Pié-Ninot, Salvador. "Sensus Fidei." In *Dictionary of Fundamental Theology*, 992–94. Edited by René Latourelle. New York: Crossroad, 1995.

Pius IX. *Ineffabilis Deus.* http://www.papalencyclicals.net/Pius09/p9ineff.htm.

———. *Ubi Primum.* http://www.papalencyclicals.net/Pius09/p9ubipr2.htm.

Pius XII. *Deiparae Virginis Mariae.* http://w2.vatican.va/content/pius-xii/en/encyclicals/documents/hf_p-xii_enc_01051946_deiparae-virginis-mariae.html.

———. *Munificentissimus Dei.* http://w2.vatican.va/content/pius-xii/en/apost_constitutions/documents/hf_p-xii_apc_19501101_munificentissimus-deus.html.

Roman Catholic Womenpriests. "About RCWP." http://www.romancatholicwomenpriests.org/index.php.

Rush, Ormond. *The Eyes of Faith: The Sense of the Faithful and the Church's Reception of Revelation.* Washington, DC: Catholic University of America Press, 2009.

———. "Sensus Fidei: Faith 'Making Sense' of Revelation." *Theological Studies* 62 (2001) 231–61.

Salzman, Todd, and Michael Lawler. *Sexual Ethics: A Theological Introduction.* Washington, DC: Georgetown University Press, 2012.

Scheffczyk, Leo. "*Sensus Fidelium*—Witness on the Part of the Community." *Communio: International Catholic Review* 15 (1988) 182–98.

Second Vatican Council. *Ad Gentes* (English text). http://www.vatican.va/archive/hist_councils/ii_vatican_council/documents/vat-ii_decree_19651207_ad-gentes_en.html.

———. *Apostolicam Actuositatem* (English text). http://www.vatican.va/archive/hist_councils/ii_vatican_council/documents/vat-ii_decree_19651118_apostolicam-actuositatem_en.html.

———. *Dei Verbum* (English text). http://www.vatican.va/archive/hist_councils/ii_vatican_council/documents/vat-ii_const_19651118_dei-verbum_en.html.

———. *Dei Verbum* (Latin text). http://www.vatican.va/archive/hist_councils/ii_vatican_council/documents/vat-ii_const_19651118_dei-verbum_lt.html.

———. *Gaudium et Spes* (English text). http://www.vatican.va/archive/hist_councils/ii_vatican_council/documents/vat-ii_const_19651207_gaudium-et-spes_en.html.

———. *Lumen Gentium* (English text). http://www.vatican.va/archive/hist_councils/ii_vatican_council/documents/vat-ii_const_19641121_lumen-gentium_en.html.

———. *Lumen Gentium* (Latin text). http://www.vatican.va/archive/hist_councils/ii_vatican_council/documents/vat-ii_const_19641121_lumen-gentium_lt.html.

———. *Presbyterorum Ordinis* (English text). http://www.vatican.va/archive/hist_councils/ii_vatican_council/documents/vat-ii_decree_19651207_presbyterorum-ordinis_en.html.

Steinruck, Josef. "Was die Gläubigen in der Geschichte der Kirche zu vermelden hatten." In *Mitsprache im Glauben? Vom Glaubenssinn der Gläubigen*, edited by Günther Koch, 25–50. Wurzburg: Echter, 1993.

Thils, Gustave. *L'infaillibilité du people chrétien 'in credendo': Notes de théologie posttridentine*. Bibliotheca Ephemeridum Theologicarum Lovaniensium 21. Paris: Desclée de Brouwer, 1963.

Thompson, William M. "*Sensus Fidelium* and Infallibility." *American Ecclesiastical Review* 167, no. 7 (1973) 450–86.

Tillard, J. M. *Church of the Churches: The Ecclesiology of Communion*. Translated by R. C. De Peaux. Collegeville, MN: Liturgical, 1992.

———. "*Sensus Fidelium*." *One in Christ* 11 (1975) 2–29.

Wagner, Harald. "Glaubenssinn, Glaubenszustimmung und Glaubenskonsens." *Theologie und Glaube* 69 (1979) 263–71.

Walgrave, Jan. "Instinctus Spiritus Sancti: een proeve tot Thomas-interpretatie." *Ephemerides Theologicae Lovanienses* 45 (1969) 417–31.

11

Matthew Lamb on Retrieval in Catholic Theology

Robert J. Barry

INTRODUCTION

STUDENTS OF FR. MATTHEW Lamb, especially those arriving from a typical post-Vatican II Catholic religious studies department, would not automatically grasp what was going on around them in his classroom. Fr. Lamb's assignment of texts from the patristic and medieval eras would certainly have precedent in other courses, but his manner of engaging those texts could be novel and perplexing. This state of perplexity would gradually subside as students became accustomed to the activity of "Retrieval," as Fr. Lamb called it. Retrieval consists of a practice of constructive engagement with a living theological tradition which theologians understood themselves to be, not just heirs of, but also participants in continuing and expanding.

In the following chapter I will introduce and elaborate this notion of Retrieval by exploring three elements of this dynamic as practiced and taught by Fr. Lamb. For each of these elements I will discuss two elements of Retrieval that might positively contribute to academic theology today.

THE MONASTIC BACKGROUND

Theologians engaged in Retrieval take a sympathetic stand toward the insights and practices of their religious tradition. From this stance, the deepest resources for theological understanding may be found in the integrated life of communal study, contemplation and prayer such as that found in the monastic setting. Fr. Lamb used to recount to students his theological formation in the monastery library in Conyers, Georgia. In that library, then-Brother Lamb engaged in an unhurried study of the Fathers of the Church through the direct reading of the primary texts in the original languages. Self-paced reading was coupled with spiritual formation accomplished through the structured life of work, prayer, and study, measured out in proportions determined by years of practice and revision.

The tradition of monastic study, and the norms governing its proper exercise, is of course quite diverse in its many manifestations in different times, locations, and particular religious orders. Individual monasteries shift the weight of that balance of work, prayer, and study in accord with the charism of their founders, and in accord with the resources of the monastery and the abilities of the monks, both individually and collectively, as these have varied or developed over time. The perception that this balance was in need of realignment often arose in these diverse communities; this spurred various reform efforts within particular monastic houses or orders, and at times prompted the founding or re-founding of houses and orders. Sometimes such reforms might be moderate revisions of existing structures; sometimes such reforms or new foundations appear radical in terms of the existing structures, but are proposed by their founders as ways to remain faithful and true to Christ's teachings and example despite the obvious discontinuity from previous structures and practices. Thus, the mendicant orders of the Middle Ages did not embrace the stability of monastic life characteristic of the dominant Benedictine example, but rather exemplified the itinerant life of the disciples sent by Jesus in Mark 6; the Jesuits coupled the flexibility of the itinerant life with missionary zeal and military discipline to engage the intellectual needs of the church in the dawn of the modern era, while the new orders of sisters and lay brothers that emerged at the same time dedicated themselves to teaching and catechizing the children of the church.

The practice of Retrieval involves regarding one's religious tradition as a foundation and continuingly fruitful source for theological judgments, specifically out of the conviction that one is living in continuity with this tradition. Jean Leclercq's description of this dynamic as operative in the Middle Ages holds true for monasticism in general: "The part played by what can be called the living tradition in the continuity linking Western monasticism to the past of the whole Church must not be underestimated. It is often affirmed that monasticism maintained tradition by copying, reading, and explaining the works of the Fathers, and that is correct; but it did so also through living by what these books contained."[1] It is precisely in this exercise of realignment of communal life in terms of a living tradition that we see the practice of Retrieval at work. In each of these widely-varying instances of formation, reformation or re-founding of monastic life, the same faith produces specific practical forms of life; the shape of this life is governed by the virtue of prudence, a power of the intellect elevated by the love of God made possible through Christ's redemptive work, but guided by the resources of the very tradition in which one lives.

This continual process of formation, reformation, and re-founding responds to the continually developing external conditions of the world, and corrects for the biases that develop within individuals and orders due to the calcification of practices and the creeping vices that distort the practical judgments implemented in the various forms of monastic life. These reforms accomplish this, however, not by rejecting monastic traditions, but by relying upon those very traditions as foundational criteria for those reforms. In this process, Retrieval does not replicate the past, but rather produces a new mode of life that is related, but substantially distinct from both the tradition by which it is informed and the condition of the world in which it seeks to live in fidelity to that past: "All this is not to say that the monastic Middle Ages are not medieval or that they added nothing to patristic culture. To this assimilation of the church's past, the monks brought the psychological traits proper to their own time. But the foundations, sources, and the general atmosphere in which their culture grew were patristic. By prolonging patristic culture in a period different from that of the Fathers, they produced a new and original, yet traditional, culture deeply rooted in the culture of the first centuries of Christianity."[2] The guidance of monastic reform by the practice of Retrieval is not the exclusive domain of communities from the patristic and monastic eras.

1. Leclercq, *The Love of Learning*, 106.
2. Ibid., 107.

Even in the midst of the tumultuous change surrounding religious life in the era of the Second Vatican Council, Fr. Lamb's fellow Trappist brother, Thomas Merton, integrated this practice of Retrieval into his call for renewal of monastic life in the modern age. By engaging the deep tradition of monastic life and teaching, vowed religious are not merely informed about possible models that might be considered safe to follow, but rather are challenged by the voices from that tradition to examine the very basis for monastic practice: "Studying the original monastic sources, seen in their historical and cultural contexts, monks begin to ask themselves more disturbing questions than those which merely bear on meaningful observance. It is no longer just a matter of recovering a genuine understanding of monastic enclosure, silence, worship, fasting and trying to adapt these to a modern situation. The very concept of a vowed and cloistered life, of a life devoted to prayer apart from the world, of silence and asceticism, has to be examined."[3] It is precisely this exercise of Retrieval within a community embedded in a living tradition that fosters the monastic pursuit of freedom, not for the self, but for transcending the self, and enabling a conscious lived participation in a community beyond one's immediate vicinity.

While we may expect Retrieval to produce dramatic reforms and new monastic foundations, such a radical dynamic is not the necessary defining quality of the exercise of Retrieval. More frequently, monastic communities demonstrate the dynamics of Retrieval in their exercise of non-dramatic judgments regarding revisions to their communal life in accord with the founding rule of the order. Such ordinary functions of Retrieval are frequently easy to miss, as they can operate in an automatic and intuitive manner, in which the judgments one makes about the specific practical goods of the monastic life are considered as continuations and applications of the more general practical judgments expressed in the founding rule and constitutions, and in their previous application to the life of the community.

Monasticism's integration and living out of the wisdom of deeper tradition stands as a vivid example of Retrieval at work. Yet Retrieval is not limited to monastic life and practice alone. Two aspects of Retrieval that are integral to monastic life may serve to enrich theologians outside the monastery in this day and age, granted some necessary adaptations. First, the monastic practice of contemplative study of the sources in the

---

3. Conner, "Monk of Renewal," 179.

tradition, whether most ancient or most recent, serves as a fruitful manner of engagement. It is difficult for that fruit to ripen, however, within the typical framework of an academic semester or sabbatical. For example, while students grow profoundly through reading texts like St. Augustine's *City of God* for their courses, a semester-long course on Augustine that dedicates a month to the work can only assign carefully-chosen selections for students to read, and the professor might reasonably expect students to digest only a mere fraction of the wisdom of St. Augustine contained therein. A professor might encourage those students to continue reading these texts beyond the course, but must remain aware that the other academic obligations and the limits of time and energy that students face make such further independent reading unlikely.

This incompatibility between the fixed semester schedule of the academy and the practice of sustained contemplative study may be overcome, if only in a partial way, through the activity of a reading group of like-minded faculty and students. Such reading groups may operate according to a schedule, but that schedule can reach beyond the strictures of a specific semester, and can in fact proceed at a modest enough pace to encourage the deep reading and re-reading of the text to which the group commits itself. The product of such reading groups can be anything from informal discussion, either in person or online, to formal presentations, where one's questions and insights regarding the text can be tried and tested against the questions and insights of the other participants. This subsequent engagement of the participants may certainly go beyond the traditional monastic practice of contemplative reading, but being accountable to others can ensure that each participant engages in at least a minimal amount of contemplative reading, if only not to embarrass oneself in front of one's colleagues, students, teachers, and friends. One such reading group led by Fr. Romanus Cessario and Fr. Lamb met regularly at St. John's Seminary to discuss the articles in Thomas Aquinas's *Summa theologiae* on Law.[4] A core group of readers from different schools, frequently with interested guests, would read through an article or two of the *Prima Secundae* in preparation for our common time together. Like most reading groups, its participants were frequently pressed for time, so it only encouraged rather than insisted on extended contemplation of the reading ahead of time. Like many good reading groups, however, it included a reading of the relevant passages together, followed by combined contributions of the collective insights of the readers.

4. Fr. Lamb describes this reading group in Lamb, "*Contemplata Tradere*," 314.

A second element that makes Retrieval natural to the monastic life is the integration of theological study and spiritual development, especially through liturgy and prayer. Such integration may remain common to seminary settings in which theological education continues to take place. Outside of seminary however this dynamic is complicated by a number of factors, including the plurality of religious traditions among the students and faculty at centers of theological education and the constraints on schedules for both study and classroom meetings. To be part of the theological tradition upon which the exercise of Retrieval draws, however, is to be part of an ongoing activity aimed at knowing the subject matter of study more clearly and thoroughly, in both subjective and objective manners.

While liturgy and prayer may be available to students and teachers of theology at most academic centers, the mere availability of these spiritual resources does not automatically create the close-knit communal life that is itself a source for Retrieval. The challenge for Retrieval today lies in the integration of liturgy and prayer in the non-communal settings for theological study, as we have in academic departments sited in colleges and universities which are not themselves committed to the activity of Retrieval. This integration may arise, then, primarily through the initiative of like-minded students and faculty who come together to consciously create these conditions for a communal spiritual life where none was to be found before. Such an exercise need not take on the trappings of sectarianism or challenge existing institutions; it may involve something as simple as student-led evening prayer or regular attendance at a specified liturgy. It may find precedent in the existing integration of liturgy into even large-scale meetings of professional societies such as the Catholic Theological Society of America, and issue in a regular expectation that theological study and reflection should be accompanied by these activities of the collective liturgical life.

Fr. Matthew Lamb's formation as a Trappist monk provided profoundly rich resources for his integration of Retrieval as an essential element of his theological project. He conveyed the love of deep contemplative reading and the integration of the spiritual life with theological study to generations of his students. He has provided not only the inspiration, but also the practical models by which these dynamics of Retrieval that naturally operate within a monastic setting might take root in the practice of theologians in the contemporary departmental setting of theological formation.

APPROPRIATE ATTITUDES
FOR THE APPROPRIATION OF TRADITION

Fr. Matthew Lamb inculcated into his students the habits of mind necessary for gaining a knowledge of the tradition appropriate to the practice of Retrieval. Such appropriation of the tradition, however, needs to be systematic and sympathetic, two characteristics that are not universally evident in the manner in which theologians are formed and trained in the discipline in today's academy.

A hallmark of the modern academy, which serves as a common setting for theological education, is the habit of specialization. The scholarly world has noted the profound insights into a single aspect of some subject matter that is possible when scholars are given *carte blanche* to raise and answer questions on that aspect of the field and nothing else. In the best-case scenario, the achievements of the specialist scholars are integrated by other scholars with a more comprehensive wisdom about the subject, or are integrated by the program itself which sponsors these studies.

Theologians teaching and studying in the modern academy can be tempted to imitate such specialization, devoting virtually all efforts at one specific figure or question within the theological enterprise, again with the intended goal of deeper and more profound understandings about that particular figure, era or question. This attempt, however, runs the risk of ignoring the central fact that the subject matter of theology, properly speaking, is not figures, eras or intellectual questions, but rather the God whom these figures seek to understand, who is studied or worshiped in specific ways characteristic of particular eras, or who is the one about whom those questions are raised. Unlike other fields, where abstracting from other elements of a field can bring a researcher to a more intense understanding of the workings of a certain molecule or the influence of a particular economic factor on exchange rates, in theology such specialization might very well contract the scholar's understanding of God unless that research is connected to the fullness of the theological tradition dedicated to knowing God.

The study of theology adequate to the task of Retrieval, then, must be integrative rather than atomistic. The more comprehensive a theologian's engagement with the whole of the tradition, the more that theologian's grasp of God's being and activity is expanded and illuminated. While such an insight can generate a dictum that any good theologian should "read everything," even the most leisurely monastic life would not afford a single individual the time to do this impossible thing. Instead of attempting to or pretending to read everything, scholars should read, as a start, a set of central texts whose study would be systematically structured to lead the student to a comprehensive grasp of the outlines of the genetic development of theology's understanding of God. It is just such a conviction that lay behind the ordering of the program of study of theology at Ave Maria University under the leadership of Fr. Lamb.

A systematically-ordered engagement with the tradition would be multi-layered, so a familiarity with foundational texts could become the skeleton on which the further layers of flesh could hang. At a bare minimum, a possible program for theologians in training should ensure they know the major parts of the Scriptures, decrees from ecumenical councils, Augustine's *Confessions*, a selection from Thomas's *Summa Theologiae*, Newman's *On the Development of Doctrine* and the decrees of the Second Vatican Council. This or a comparable set of texts would provide the barest of outlines of the central insights of the tradition, and present them as the progressive attainment of greater understanding of God by theologians from across the whole of the tradition. Students who are immersed in a program for longer periods of time could then fill in the 800-year gaps between the authors and councils with other theologians, and deepen their understanding of the major theologians to whom they would be introduced. This deepening understanding of the fullness of the tradition should not be expected to be completed by the end of a student's theological training.

As any experienced teacher knows, the way to master a topic is to teach it, repeatedly, informed by the scholarship of specialists in the field. Such an exercise expands, deepens and enriches a scholar's knowledge, not just of that specific topic but of the field as a whole. Toward that end, scholars who wish to engage in the Retrieval of the theological tradition of the church in a systematic fashion would not shy away from teaching introductory or survey courses. They should conceive of preparing for and teaching that course as a conversation with the great theologians from the tradition; what might be the students' first encounter with such a topic will come to be the professor's second, tenth or twentieth time through a text. Even if such a text were to lay outside one's area of specialization, the teaching of it with the aid of trained specialists constitutes a form of continuing professional development in the discipline of theology, and enables that scholar to better engage in the activity of Retrieval.

Such a practice would likely transgress the (relatively) recently-imposed divisions within the theological discipline: a theologian trained as a biblical scholar might find herself plunging into a classroom discussion with students on *Fides et Ratio*, or a scholar publishing in Thomas Aquinas might find himself leading students through an investigation of Matthew's infancy narrative. Such engagement ought not to be thin; the advantage of specialization in specific fields in theology is the regular production of articles and books that communicate to other scholars, even outside the specialities, the fruits of focused research. If a scholar has a basic foundation in that specialty through his or her graduate training, that further research can then add to the understanding the scholar brings to even the introductory classroom.

One challenge to promoting this aspect of Retrieval in the current academy is that one cannot simply turn to a former golden age of theological instruction as a model for the systematic appropriation of the tradition that is both integrated and comprehensive. Certainly the monastic tradition of theological education appears integrated and comprehensive; whether such a formation was systematic, however, would depend on the wisdom of the particular instructor and the diligence of the specific students who had available to them the riches of the monastic library under what might, say at Brown University, be termed an "open curriculum,"[5] and only as long as they set the tone for the schooling.

The medieval example of theological education in the form of biblical lecture and commentary accompanied by Peter Lombard's *Sentences* bears the virtue of being more systematic, and in the curriculum of the medieval schools perhaps even integrated, but its engagement with the tradition was by representative rather than a comprehensive encounter with the great works of the tradition. This was not fundamentally altered when Thomas Aquinas's *Summa Theologiae* displaced the *Sentences* in some quarters in the early-Modern era, for shortly thereafter the study of the scriptures would devolve into the study of the texts and the sources of the bible, but merely as texts and sources, and the *Summa* itself would be summarized and condensed, forming handbooks that might be connected to the revealed sources on which their cogency depended, but which might equally be not-so-connected.

In our age, then, the systematic appropriation of the tradition that is both integrated and comprehensive is a project to be accomplished. Perhaps one might find examples of places in which this has chanced

---

5. See Brown University, "The Brown Curriculum."

to happen, and hold up those as models to imitate. Otherwise, those responsible for organizing and administering programs of theological study must consciously and intelligently develop the habits of mind by which its faculty and its students will come to know and critically engage that tradition. Fr. Matthew Lamb's training of his students has aimed to do just this, and has begun and continues to bear fruit in the field. Matthew Levering[6] stands as a notable example of a student of Fr. Lamb who has been formed by a systematic appropriation of the tradition that has been both integrated and comprehensive, and who now regularly writes and teaches theology that is both biblically and historically responsible.

Fr. Lamb has led his students to an engagement with the tradition fitted to the task of Retrieval that is not only systematic but sympathetic as well. Not every systematic approach to a tradition will bear this mark, and in fact Fr. Lamb's commitment to communicative praxis has been coupled with a critique of the development of the modern academy that has fostered approaches to academic subjects of study ranging from indifference (in a misguided attempt at objectivity) to hostile manipulation (out of, perhaps, a post-modern despair of objectivity). The workings of this dynamic are expressed, intentionally or not, by the specific term recently employed to describe the activity scholars conceive of themselves engaged in, namely, "Interrogation."

Scholars may intend nothing more by this term than the general scholarly activity of analyzing and raising questions about the subject of their investigations. Words, however, have power to reflect, or to delimit and shape, human behavior. "Interrogation" ordinarily describes the process in a criminal investigation whereby a person suspected of being guilty of a crime is placed under great duress, in the hope that the subject will be forced to admit the suspected violation of the law or norm that he is trying to cover and conceal. This process presumes the ill will of the subject under investigation, and likewise presumes the investigator conducting the interrogation is the faithful representative of the prevailing system of justice. It also presumes that a genuine crime has been committed, and that remedying this injustice is the primary objective of the investigator's actions.

The Interrogation is premised on a profound imbalance of power of the Interrogator over the subject who is under suspicion, laying that subject prone to the officially-sanctioned inquisitor who will threaten or

---

6. See chapter 3 for Matthew Levering's contribution to this volume, "Augustine on Creation: An Exercise in the Dialectical Retrieval of the Ancients."

employ actual violence in pursuit of his goal of justice. Frequently, the subject under duress will admit crimes he has not actually committed, especially if there are no defenders to testify to the truth of the matter alongside the helpless subject. The imbalance of power can be amplified when such an interrogation takes place in a revolutionary context, where the dynamic of *ressentiment* drives the interrogators, who formerly considered themselves to be oppressed by those in authority above them, who now find the positions reversed and see themselves no longer as judged by, but rather as the gleeful interrogators and judges of, their subjects.

This baleful dynamic of Interrogation reflects the approach that some have taken toward the tradition in the current state of academic theology. The tradition, and especially its primary representatives of Scripture, Augustine, and Thomas Aquinas, which formerly served as a starting point for Roman Catholic theology, have been made subject to interrogation by new inquisitors who exercise a newly experienced power and righteousness in direct proportion to how oppressed they previously experienced that tradition to be. As is true for many revolutionary systems, the first casualty in this interrogation is the truth; under the duress of forced interrogation, Augustine confesses that everything he wrote was because he actually hated women, Thomas Aquinas responds that Natural Law was actually just a clever device for pretending that merely conventional norms had some divine warrant, and the Bible reveals that it was merely a tool for oppressors all along.

Perhaps the most tragic dimension of conceiving of theology as an interrogation of the subject of tradition is the effect it has on theologians who re-conceive themselves as revolutionary interrogators, where the criterion for judgment is no longer the attainment of truth but rather the reversal of relations of power. When the academic discipline of theology falls subject to the power dynamics of the postmodern academy, then the discipline has simply fallen, rendering it nothing more than a vehicle for personal or group aggrandizement, distinguished from other departments only by the smug recognition by its practitioners that the subject matter of their study doesn't actually exist.

For the sake of truth and for the sake of the academic discipline, the systematic appropriation of the tradition conducted under the aegis of Retrieval must operate in a mode other than Interrogation. When a scholar envisions himself or herself as an integral part of an ongoing tradition, then the scholar approaches the voices of that tradition with a distinctive attitude that we might term "Conversational." Rather than envisioning the proper setting of theology as a darkened room with a subject cuffed to a chair under the glare of a piercing lamp, the kind of setting envisioned for theologians engaging in Retrieval is the conversation that takes place at the family table where generations of family and friends gather to celebrate a birthday or holiday. At such a table, you have many overlapping and interchanging conversations between people of different ages, from great-grandparents through babbling great-grandchildren. Each generation tells the stories that define them: those who fought in the war, those who lived in times of plenty, those who are uncertain about what the future holds, those who have fallen in love, those who have been abandoned. Each generation knows they are the children of the generation that has preceded them, and recognizes without resentment the debt they owe to their parents and grandparents, according them the prime seats and the first servings of the meal. The wisdom of the stories passed on from the prior generations is given primacy of place, even if their cogency or applicability is not immediately evident to everyone around the table. The younger generations perhaps have their own wisdom, not to displace but to add to the stories of who this family is, where it has been, where it is going, and how it is going to get there.

Thus Interrogation in no way is the appropriate mode for engaging the tradition of a church bound by the common love for and hope in a self-sacrificing God, who are called to be brothers and sisters to one another, bound up in one body as adopted members of the natural Son of the one true God. Retrieval must instead proceed by a mode closer to conversation among generations of a common family. In place of the contemporary dynamic of Interrogation of tradition under the guidance of a hyper-specialized focus on some portion of the theological enterprise, theologians today are responsible for engaging in an academic practice that may indeed have no precedent in order to ensure that the systematic appropriation of the tradition by faculty and students will be comprehensive and integrative. The mode in which this Retrieval is conducted must be generous and grounded in common love, less the love that scholars have for a common academic enterprise than the love family members have for their Father and for one another.

CRITICAL CONTINUANCE OF TRADITION

One might observe the dynamics and recommendations above and conclude that Retrieval may just be merely a more palatable word for an uncritical theological retrenchment or restorationism. An exercise of Retrieval that would take its inspiration in the work and thought of Fr. Lamb, however, could not be confused with any effort to restore or replicate a putative golden age in the discipline of theology. In one of the few synthetic accounts of the practice of Retrieval, John Webster says that its "immersion in the texts and habits of thought of earlier (especially pre-modern) theology opens up a wide view of the object of Christian theological reflection, setting before its contemporary practitioners descriptions of the faith unharassed by current anxieties, and enabling a certain liberty in relation to the present."[7] Fr. Lamb's practice of Retrieval is grounded in, and grows specifically out of, the communicative praxis outlined both in his book *Solidarity with Victims* and in his later reflections on the role of critical reason in the exercise of theology. As such, the form of Retrieval inspired by Fr. Lamb would only rightly consider itself "unharassed by current anxieties" triggered by modern critiques of religion and theological knowledge because it has thoroughly engaged those critiques, and either sufficiently addressed the problematic they raise or uncovered the critique itself as exhibiting a time-bound or culture-bound scotosis that can only be corrected by a more open-minded examination of the matter at hand.

There are two particular reasons why Retrieval fails if it simply tries to restore the practices of a prior pre-modern theological system. First, a genuine appreciation and understanding of the tradition will recognize the absence of a putative golden age of theology. One could argue that particular elements of theology were superior in prior times, but as noted above, the strengths of each age and style were coupled with limitations as well. The second reason is that an attempt to simply bypass the problems and challenges raised by the modern era, in particular its contrast between the authority of experience and the authority of dogma, will merely result in the unfortunate, and likely unconscious, importation of those modern concerns into one's "non-modern" theology itself.[8] Thus Protestant Fundamentalism's reaction to the threat of scientific rationality unwittingly incorporates that scientific view of "objective" reason in

---

7. Webster, "Theologies of Retrieval," 584–85.
8. Lamb, *Solidarity with Victims*, 101.

its casting of the truth of the scripture it holds dear, and Neoscholasticism's reaction to the modern philosophical concern for the universality and objectivity of truth claims leads it to press Thomas Aquinas's proofs for the existence of God and teachings on Natural Law into an apologetic role of producing subjective certainty that would be strange to Thomas himself. In the absence of a critical evaluation of the self in terms of the age in which one operates, one lays oneself prey to the general bias operative in the culture at large, even if, or perhaps especially if, one defines oneself over and against that dominant culture.

A scholar who becomes cognizant of modern modes of thought does not by that fact necessarily define himself or herself by that modernity. A theologian engaged in Retrieval must be trained in modern thought, both in order to recognize and account for the elements of modernity that might count as genuine advancements, and in order not to be limited by the strictures of the modern concerns: "We are all moderns and, if we are to take the self-correcting processes of learning within scholarship seriously, we have much to learn from the men and women of past ages. Communicative praxis is not restricted to the present generation. Every age and culture has its mistakes, biases and sins. Communicative praxis recognizes how cooperative consensus has to be universal if it is not going to self-destruct. One of the errors of modernity has been to misconstrue traditions and the past as no more than dominative and benighted authoritarian repression out of which modernity emerges."[9] Thus Fr. Lamb's seminars on works of St. Augustine would lead his unavoidably-modern students to engage those texts in light of what Jürgen Habermas took to be normative in modern thought: not its content of "intuitions, concepts, systems, rules, axioms or institutions, but rather [. . .] the effectively free exercise of intelligence and reason."[10]

Fr. Lamb's critical exercise of reason in communicative praxis was informed especially by the thought of Bernard Lonergan, but also engaged the critical thought of Jürgen Habermas, Johann Metz, Eric Voegelin, and others. His engagement with these figures was coupled with the critical insights that emerged through Retrieval, by which Fr. Lamb consciously sought to avoid and correct for modern distortions such as its bias against orthodoxy and authority. Lamb warns that "[t]heology will not be able to aid a genuine dialectic of enlightenment if

---

9. Lamb, *Eternity, Time, and the Life of Wisdom*, 147–48.
10. Ibid., 137.

it continues to internalize the caricatures of itself that the Enlightenment first portrayed."[11] Fr. Lamb's seminars were careful not to caricature the thought of any particular figure, for the dynamic questioning in which each of the figures was engaged in their own contexts was presumed to raise genuine questions and potentially generate intelligible insights, despite their distance in time or social context. This dialectical exercise of Fr. Lamb has been generous, but critical, recognizing the problems that could not just be brushed aside, and intent on responding to them in a fuller way than others had from the modern perspective.

Fr. Lamb's task in this effort of Retrieval has been to address a world that has been defined and deformed by the modern project. This effort relies on the wisdom of the Fathers and the Medievals, is inspired by the truth revealed in the Scriptures, and recognizes the strengths of contemporary diagnoses of the modern problem but does not limit itself to the remedies offered in this modern era. In his practice of Retrieval, Fr. Lamb tasks his students and his readers with transforming this world beyond its current maladies through the performance of raising ever further relevant questions rather than by an attempt to coerce the world to conform to an ideal falsely posited as universal. This exercise explicitly draws on Bernard Lonergan's development of Jürgen Habermas' critique of modern claims to objectivity:

> That to which Lonergan calls our attention is anything but the objectified "subject" or "consciousness" or "presence" described in the modern theories of the same. Habermas perceives the shortcomings of all such theories, whether they be totalitarian objectifications or all-inclusive totalizing critiques. His concern for "performative contradiction" is articulated in Lonergan's analysis of how our spontaneous sensitivity, intelligence, reason and evaluative activities are normed, not by extrinsic rules or axioms or principles, but by our spontaneous questioning that seeks to be attentive (sensitivity), intelligent (understanding), reasonable (truth) and responsible (value). In their disagreements, humans call attention to data overlooked, to alternate ways of understanding, to evidence or warrants not given, to values or goods not chosen. This self-correcting process of learning, as Lonergan indicates, is neither dominative nor dogmatically self-assertive.[12]

11. Ibid., 144.
12. Ibid., 139–40.

Thus this exercise of Retrieval does not reject the insights of the modern age, or of any other age; nor does it consider itself beholden to any particular era or system.

In its reaction against the limits of the modern project, one might then be tempted to label this activity of Retrieval as a "post-modern" enterprise. The hazard of this lies in overlooking the above critique and substituting one falsely universalized system with another. Retrieval, then, is best considered a critical and conscious continuation of a living theological tradition, neither seeking to identify with a distant past or subjecting itself to the criteria of the moment, whether that be modern or postmodern. For Fr. Lamb, the ultimate task of theology, and thus the end that sets the norms for its practice, is to take part in the transformation of the world from its subjection to sin to the glorification of God in all things. The criteria and resources for this transformation must aspire to something more than any modern or postmodern system offers, yet not dismiss the insights and achievements of these or any era out of hand. The reference point for judgment of what this transformed world might look like is not some novel arrangement or array of temporal goods, but the eternal good as we perceive and prepare for it in this world. The presumption is that our current state is sinful and fallen, but in the midst of being redeemed. This redemption includes a resolution of what a postmodern analysis might be content to let remain problematic and ambiguous. Theology then must be evangelical, not only in its source, but also in its aim, addressing a world in need of change with truths and realities that are designed for and capable of effecting that change.

CONCLUSION: THE FUTURE OF RETRIEVAL IN CATHOLIC THEOLOGICAL EDUCATION

The integration of the activity of Retrieval would rely on the opportunity for sustained reflection on the tradition, coupled with a tight integration between the academic and the spiritual dimensions of the theologian's pursuit of faith seeking understanding. This exercise of Retrieval would involve theologians in a task that encourages and requires them to step beyond the traditional boundaries of specialties in the field, and to engage that task with the sympathetic ear of a conversation partner rather than the harsh gaze of an interrogator. The result will not be to seek to restore the past nor to make peace with the present intellectual milieu, but rather will always seek to pursue the kingdom that transcends the particulars of this or any given moment.

Matthew Lamb's incorporation of Retrieval into his own teaching and writing is a fitting example of how Catholic theological education can fruitfully and critically turn to the deeper traditions of thought through Retrieval. Roman Catholic theology has evidenced a stubborn refusal of the domestication that has been attempted with other academic fields according to the model of academic mentorship and hyper-specialization in research. Granted, there are many schools in which such attempts at theological husbandry are regularly conducted, generating self-replicating lines of thought. The stubborn refusal of the discipline likely traces to the stubborn subject matter it is seeking to understand: the triune God who makes Himself known by an incarnate self-revelation. Students of theology regularly recognize that their object of study is not just the words about the subject; rather, they experience their study as an encounter with the very divine Subject of study itself. At that point, "study" according to the canon of modern academia ceases to be the dominant driving force, and instead students find themselves moved to what is truly appropriate to this field, the self-surrender of all one's other loves and interests to that Subject that one might otherwise merely study.

There will likely be two models by which the above elements that accompany Retrieval will become part of theological education. The first will be in a setting where the institution itself consciously seeks to nourish the faith which the academic exercise serves, and the instruction and extracurricular life of the academy are integrated. The graduate program in theology directed by Fr. Lamb at Ave Maria University is a prime example of this model. This program has provided Fr. Lamb with the opportunity to implement his vision for a rigorous and critical study of theology, where Retrieval can be conducted in a systematic, integrated and comprehensive manner. The well-formed graduates of this young program have achieved a remarkable placement record in teaching positions in just the few short years.

The other place that this Retrieval takes place is at academies where students of professors like Fr. Lamb engage in this task in a setting institutionally indifferent or even hostile to this task. At some schools there may be a critical mass of faculty engaged in Retrieval, and thus that school becomes a fresh source for passing on the habits of mind and the knowledge of the tradition essential for engaging in Retrieval. At other places, individual scholars may be the lone voices of a missionary standing in the midst of a hostile population, insisting quietly or vociferously against the injustice committed against the tradition to which he or she is committed. In such cases, students inspired to look beyond their own times and experiences can be inspired to engage in Retrieval as a rebellion against the tyranny of the modern deformities and a protection against the introduction of novel deformations of the world and their souls. It would be just such an exercise that would continue the legacy of Fr. Matthew Lamb.

BIBLIOGRAPHY

Brown University. "The Brown Curriculum." https://www.brown.edu/academics/college/degree/curriculum

Conner, Tarcisius. "Monk of Renewal." In *Thomas Merton, Monk: A Monastic Tribute*, edited by Br. Patrick Hart, 173–93. New York: Sheed and Ward, 1974.

Lamb, Matthew L. "*Contemplata Tradere*: Embodied Interiority in Cessario, Pinckaers, and Lonergan." In *Ressourcement Thomism: Sacred Doctrine, the Sacraments, and the Moral Life: Essays in Honor of Romanus Cessario, O.P.*, edited by Reinhard Hütter and Matthew Levering, 312–29. Washington DC: Catholic University of America, 2010.

———. *Eternity, Time and the Life of Wisdom*. Naples, FL: Sapientia, 2007.

———. *Solidarity with Victims: Toward a Theology of Social Transformation*. New York: Crossroad, 1982.

Leclercq, Jean. *The Love of Learning and the Desire for God: A Study of Monastic Culture*. New York: Fordham University Press, 1982.

Webster, John. "Theologies of Retrieval." In *The Oxford Handbook of Systematic Theology*, edited by John Webster et al., 583–99. New York: Oxford University Press, 2007.

Author Index

St. Albert the Great, 138–48
Alter, Robert, 64
St. Ambrose of Milan, 86, 105, 108
Aristotle, 16, 67, 86, 92n43, 105, 142
Ashton, John, 99
St. Athanasius, 184
Athenagoras of Athens, 67
St. Augustine, 2, 4–8, 16, 25–27, 29, 31,
    47, 49, 51, 52, 54–64, 68, 105–24,
    126–36, 157–62, 166, 168, 169,
    171, 178, 209, 212, 215, 218
  on creation, 49–64
  on divine illumination, 2, 126,
    127, 134
  on eternity and time, 105, 106,
    114, 117–24
  on ignorance and difficulty, 158
  on intellectual conversion, 25–27,
    128–30
  on philosophy, 107–15, 117, 119,
    120, 127, 129–32, 134–36
  on politics, 8, 160–62, 166,
    168n84, 169
  rationes seminales, 54, 58–62
  on Scripture, 54–64, 68
  on the Trinity, 47, 56
  on the two cities, 8, 162, 168n84,
    169

St. Benedict of Nursia, 136
Balthasar, Hans Urs von, 47
Barry, Robert, 2
Pope Benedict XVI/Joseph Ratzinger,
    69, 70, 71n16, 76n32, 77n35,
    78n38, 80, 91n41, 135, 136, 149,
    150, 152, 155, 156, 166–68, 171,
    175, 181n23, 184, 197
Benoit, Pierre, 72, 76–78
Blondel, Maurice, 14
Boersma, Hans, 97n63
Burkhard, John, 185n33, 196n79
Burnaby, John, 115n48

Cessario, Romanus, ix, 14, 209
Chesterton, G. K., 199
Childs, Brevard, 83n6, 87n22, 88,
    89n31, 91–94
Christiansen, Drew, 167nn83–84, 168
Cicero, Marcus Tullius, 107, 108, 127
Congar, Yves, 76, 78, 79, 92n43, 98
Coyle, Kevin, 114n44
Crowe, Frederick, 20n64
Curran, Charles, 176n5
St. Cyril of Jerusalem, 105

Daley, Brian, 95
Daniélou, Jean, 88n24
Dante Alighieri, 91n40
Dauphinais, Michael, xi, 1n1, 2, 3
De la Taille, Maurice, 38, 41n17
De Letter, P., 38n6
De Lubac, Henri, 15
Descartes, Renée, 26, 51
DiMattei, Steven, 88n24, 99n73
Diocletian, 162n61
Dionysius the Areopagite, 105n4, 140,
    141

AUTHOR INDEX

Djuth, Marianne, 110n28, 113n40, 114n44
Donceel, Joseph, 14, 15

Eliot, T. S., 104
Eusebius of Caesarea, 160–62, 165
Evans, Christopher P., xi

Farkasfalvy, Denis, 78n39
Fitzmyer, Joseph, 90
Flanagan, Joseph, ix
Fortin, Ernest L., ix, 7, 158n42, 159, 161, 162n61
Fowl, Stephen, 88, 93n47, 94n50
Pope Francis, 184, 197
Froehlich, Karl, 87

Gilkey, Langdon, 157n37
Grant, R. M., 90
St. Gregory the Great, 74
St. Gregory of Nyssa, 54
Grisez, Germain, 70, 71
Gutierrez, Gustavo, 157

Habermas, Jürgen, 50, 218, 219
Harrison, Brian, 70–72
Hattrup, Dieter, 181n23
Hawking, Stephen, 53, 54, 61–63
Hays, Richard, 82n1, 83n6, 97
Henriquez, Raul Silva, 70, 71
Henry, Paul, 115n48
Heraclitus, 87n23
Hobbes, Thomas, 163
Hopkins, Gerard Manley, 122
Husserl, Edmund, 17

St. John Damascene, 143
St. John Paul II, 155, 167n83, 184, 197
John of St. Thomas, 191
Jovian, 161, 162

Kant, Immanuel, 11, 15–18, 23, 32, 166n80
Kasper, Walter, 89n32, 177n12
Keating, Daniel, 95, 96
Knasas, John, 14
Krauss, Lawrence, 52, 53, 61–63

Lamb, Christopher, 178n12
Lamb, Matthew L., vii–x
Lawler, Michael, 176n6, 177n7
Lawler, Peter Augustine, 163n63
Lawrence, Frederick G., viii, ix, 166
Leclercq, Jean, 207
Pope Leo XIII, 28, 31, 43n27
Levering, Matthew, xvi, 1n1, 2, 3, 89n32, 93n47, 94–96, 98n69, 214
Levy, Ian, 98n70
Lewis, C. S., 73, 75, 184n31
Licinius I, 160
Locke, John, 163
Lombard, Peter, 145, 213
Lonergan, Bernard viii, xi, 7, 11–33, 37–39, 40nn13–15, 42, 44n28, 45, 47, 50, 77, 78, 166, 170, 218, 219
Louth, Andrew, 82n2, 88n24, 90n39, 98n69, 117n56, 119n64
Lynch, Robert, 176n4

Maguire, Daniel, 177n10
Mandouze, Andre, 115
Manent, Pierre, 168n84
Marechal, Joseph, 14–17
Marius, Gaius, 161n57
Martin, Francis, 88
Mary, Mother of God, 42n21, 184, 198
McBrien, Richard, 14, 176n5
McCamy, Ronald, 14
McCool, Gerald, 14
McEwan, Ian, 52n13
McGrath, Alister, 58n47, 61
Merton, Thomas, 208
Metz, J. B., 12, 13, 218
Mlodinow, Leonard, 53, 54n22, 61, 62
St. Monica, 104–24
  as ecclesial symbol, 107, 116
Moyise, Steve, 82n1, 84, 88n24
Muck, Otto, 14, 16
Murray, Paul, 138

Newman, John Henry, viii, 76, 178n12, 181n22, 183n26, 199, 212
Nietzsche, Friedrich, 51

O'Donnell, James, 106n7, 115
Olmsted, Thomas, 176n5

Orosius, Paulus, 162n61

St. Peter, 181
Philo Judaeus, 54
Pinckaers, Servais, 190n55, 191n60
Pope Pius IX, 183, 184
Pope Pius XII, 183, 184
Preus, James Samuel, 93
Rahner, Karl, 15, 78, 79
Rodgers, Eugene, 88
Rousseau, Jean-Jacque, 7n17, 163–65
Rousselot, Pierre, 14
Rynne, Xavier, vii

Sala, Giovanni, 15
Salzman, Todd, 176n6
Savanarola, Girolamo, 91n40
Scheffczyk, Leo, 182n23–24
Scheuer, Pierre, 14
Socrates, 105, 115n46, 127, 129, 130, 133
Spinoza, Benedict, 5n11, 26, 79, 80
Stanley, Christopher, 97
Stebbins, J. Michael, 42n20
Sternberg, Meir, 83n6

Synave, Paul, 72, 76–78
Taylor, Charles, 93
St. Teresa of Avila, 7n17
Theodore of Mopsuestia, 91n40
Theodosius, 161
St. Thomas Aquinas, ix, 1, 4n7, 5, 6, 15, 16, 25, 26, 29, 40nn11–13, 41, 42n20, 43n26, 44, 47, 49n2, 51, 66–70, 72–80, 83–100, 138, 145, 185–98, 200, 209, 212, 213, 215, 218
  on christology, 39–44, 47
  on Scripture, 50n2, 66–70, 72–80
Tyson, Neil DeGrasse, 53

Vertin, Michael, 16
Voegelin, Eric, 218
Vonier, Anscar, 42

Wagner, Harald, 185n33
Wagner, Ross, 83n6
Watson, Francis, 84n6, 92n46
Webster, John, 217
Wilhelmsen, Frederick, 14
Wilkins, Jeremy, 47

Subject Index

abortion, 176
academic specialization, 19, 211, 213, 221
Academy of Catholic Theology, 3
aggiornamento, vii, 4, 27, 31
America Magazine: The National Catholic Review, 2
ancients and moderns, 7, 51–52
angels, 55, 58, 59
Apollinarianism, 47n35
apostolic succession, 98, 170
Assumption, Dogma of the, 198
Augustinian view of history, 67
authenticity, 23, 32
Ave Maria University, viii, ix, 1–3, 8, 37, 46, 138, 212, 221
    Patrick F. Taylor Graduate Program in Theology at Ave Maria University, 8

baptism, 105, 115n48, 178n12, 179, 181n21, 196n79
beatific vision, 44
beauty, 24, 47, 117n59, 123
Boston College, ix, xv, 2, 3n5, 7
Brown University, 213

Cartesianism, 50
Cassiciacum, 106, 109, 110, 113, 114n44, 117, 123, 127, 131, 136
catechumenate, 104
Catholics for Choice, 177n11
Catholic Theological Society of America, 3, 210

Chalcedon, Ecumenical Council of, 46
charity, 4n7, 6, 38, 43–46, 140, 141, 143, 180n18, 182, 187n46, 192–197, 200
    as the form of faith, 44, 194, 195, 200
Church, viii, ix, 4, 46, 77–80, 85, 87–89, 96–100, 115, 132, 146, 149–57, 162, 169–71, 175–201
    and the Bible, 77–80, 85, 87–89, 96–100
    as Body of Christ, viii, 4, 46, 169
    hierarchy of, 200
    magisterial teaching, 170, 175–201
classicism, 12
cogito ergo sum, 26, 51
cohabitation, 176
Communion and Liberation, 198
conceptualism, 12
Congregation for the Doctrine of the Faith, 177n9
connatural knowledge, 193
consciousness, 20, 21, 25, 29, 31, 219
Constantinople, Third Council of, 40n14
contraception, 176
Couples for Christ, 198
creation, 39, 41n16, 52–64, 84, 90n39, 96, 114n45, 117, 122, 124, 127, 135, 140
Crisis Magazine, 3
culture, 4, 5, 17, 21–24, 28, 68, 135, 207, 217–18

SUBJECT INDEX

deposit of faith, 153, 167n82, 170, 176, 180n19, 181n21, 181n23, 182, 184, 196, 199, 200
development of doctrine, 4, 69, 170, 178n14, 199, 212
devil, 167n82, 190n53, 198
dialectic, 8, 22, 52, 120n67, 170
dialectic of enlightenment, 51, 218–19
DignityUSA, 177n9
divine pedagogy, 73–75, 120n69, 168, 169
divinization, 46
divorce and remarriage, 176–77, 196n79
dogmatism, 50

Enlightenment, 3, 6, 28, 166n80, 219
Epehsus, Council of, 46
esse, 16, 37–47
Eucharist, 105, 120n69, 139–47

faith, 3, 4, 6–9, 12, 27, 28, 30, 31, 44, 47, 51, 63, 69, 74, 75, 79, 80, 85, 88, 91, 93, 95n53, 96–100, 107, 109, 113, 115, 136, 139, 150, 153, 176–200, 207, 220, 221
  act of, 96, 185n33, 187–90, 198, 200
  assent of, 113, 115, 182, 183, 186, 188–90, 192, 198, 200
  explicit, 187, 189n51
  as initiated by God, 189, 190
  and the intellect, 189, 195
  and reason, 3, 8, 167, 171
  as transpolitical, 161n55
  unbelief, 188n48
Fathers of the Church, ix, 6, 49, 67, 98, 99n73, 168, 188n48, 199, 206, 207, 219
Focolare, 198
Frankfurt School, 13
friendship, x, 12, 117n56, 129, 130, 134, 135, 142
  with God, 25, 96, 100, 136, 194
  with Christ, 146, 147, 197
fundamentalism, 19, 217

gifts of the Holy Spirit, 44, 145, 185n34, 190–97, 200

globalization, 156n32, 167n84
glossa ordinaria, 98
grace, 27, 38, 42n21, 43–47, 84, 87, 89, 93, 121, 131, 140, 141, 144, 146, 154, 167n84, 169, 189, 190, 192n63, 196–98, 200
  divine indwelling, 43, 46
  sacramental, 140, 144
  state of, 196, 200
grammar, 26, 112, 132
great books, 7

haruspices, 158
heterosexism, 177
Hexaemeron, 55n30, 54
historical consciousness, 157, 162–68
historicism, 5–7, 155, 157, 163n63, 165, 166, 171
homo assumptus theory, 143
homosexual acts, 177
hope, 4n7, 6, 44, 93, 96, 105–107, 109, 113–16, 121–24, 134, 139, 187n46, 216
human dignity, 156n32
human rights, 156n32
hypostatic union, 38–47, 143n18, 146

image of God, 21
imagination, 67, 88n28, 187
Immaculate Conception, Dogma of, 183, 198
incarnation, 38–47, 93, 121n69, 143, 144, 154n18, 155, 169
insight, act of the mind, 20
instinctus of the Holy Spirit, 188–90, 191n60
intellectus fidei, 28
Inter-American Court of Human Rights, 177n11
International Theological Commission, 181n23
in vitro fertilization, 177

judgment, act of the mind, 5, 7, 8, 20, 21, 29–31, 50, 114n45, 118n59, 127, 186n38, 192, 193

La Civilta Catholica, ix
last judgment, 169

liberal arts, 107–14, 128, 130, 134
libido dominandi, 7
light of glory, 38, 43–45, 139

Marquette University, viii
marriage, 176n4, 177
mass media, 175, 182, 198
mendicant orders, 206
Middle Ages, 7, 206, 207
miracles, 86n14, 154n18, 188, 189nn51–52
mixed relation, 40n12
modernity, 6, 7, 49, 50, 156, 164–68, 171, 218
monasticism, 135, 206–13
mystagogy, 104–24

natural knowledge of God, 39
natural law, 152, 215, 218
natural science,
    DNA, 61n63
    evolution, 52, 61
    gravity, 52–54, 62
    physics, 49–54, 58, 59, 61, 62
    quantum gravity, 52–54, 62
    quantum physics, 53, 62
    scientific positivism, 50
negative theology, 140n6
Neo-Kantianism, 23
Neo-Scholasticism, 49n2
Nestorianism, 47
The New Yorker, vii
Nietzscheanism, 51
nominalism, 5–7, 26
nouvelle theologie, 49n2
NOVA, 53
numerology in the Bible, 158n40

obediential potency, 41, 43
ontological argument for the existence of God, 133
ordination of women to the priesthood, 177
Origenist view of history, 67

PBS, 53
philosophy
    Augustine and, 54, 127

and biblical interpretation, 80, 83, 91–96, 99, 100
cognition/cognitional theory, 15, 25, 26, 85, 126–28, 193n70
early modern, 7
empiricism, 26, 50
of history, viii
and literature, 129
metaphysical realism, 12, 26, 29, 30
metaphysics, viii, 6, 18, 19, 26, 82–100, 127, 167n83
philosophical education, 7, 130
political, 7, 8, 163, 166
role in theology, 4, 38, 132, 134
St. Monica and, 106–14
St. Paul on vain, 109
Stephen Hawking on, 53
universals in, 26
piety, 1, 140, 158, 160, 183
Platonism, 50, 110, 115, 122, 140
    Neo-Platonism, 47, 67, 94n51, 115, 117n59, 135
    Plotinean Ascent, 115–17, 121n69, 135
poetry, 86n16, 91n40, 122, 129, 131
politics
    reduction to technique, 7
    the transpolitical, 8, 161n55
Pontifical Academy of Theology, 155n28
Pontifical Biblical Commission, 90
Pontifical University Gregorianum, 12, 37
postmodernity, 28, 84–87, 89, 215, 220
praxis, 12, 13, 17, 20, 22, 24, 25, 32, 50, 157, 214, 217, 218
prayer, ix, 28, 32, 89, 196, 206, 208, 210
Protestant Reformation, 89n32, 139

regula fidei, 98
religious studies, 3n5, 23, 205
ressentiment, 215
ressourcement, 4, 27, 28, 31, 49n2
Roman Catholic Womenpriests, 177

Sack of Rome by Alaric, 160
Sacred Scripture,

SUBJECT INDEX 229

allegorical Sense of, 67, 68, 87, 88, 90, 145
anagogical Sense of, 67, 68, 87, 90
authorship of, 64, 67–78, 83, 85–87, 91–96, 98, 99
canon of, 69, 74, 78n38, 79, 92
historical-critical method, 5n11, 49n2, 63, 68, 79, 82, 84, 85, 90, 94n50, 95
inerrancy of, 69–72, 80
inspiration of, 66–80, 83, 86n14, 91, 96, 97n65
literal sense of, 67–72, 74, 85–93, 97n63, 99n73, 100
literary theory and, 76, 77, 86n15, 87n20, 88n24
postmodern interpretation of, 84–89
role of virtue in reading, 85, 89n33
St. John's Seminary, 209
senses of, 67, 83, 85–99, 91n40
salvation history, 69, 71n19, 74, 78, 79, 95
same-sex marriage, 177
schoolmen, Medieval, 6
Second Vatican Council, vii, 70, 149, 150, 153, 175, 176n6, 178, 181, 183, 195, 199, 208, 212
sectarianism, 210
sensus fidei, 176, 185
sensus fidelium, 175–201
sin, 42n21, 44n28, 143, 144, 158, 168n84, 190n53, 194n72, 220
mortal sin, 193n69

theodicy/problem of evil, 109, 111, 114n46
theological virtue, 4, 6, 27, 43, 109, 114, 176, 182, 186, 187, 194,
theologico-political problem, 8, 161
theology
academic, 25, 27, 31, 33, 205, 210–15
of beauty, 47
biblical, 66, 92

christology, 47, 143
dissent in, ix, 181n23, 196
education in, ix, 2–7, 211–21, 223
liberal protestant approach to, 3
eschatology, 25, 100, 117n56, 121, 165
fundamental, 19
and history, 29
importance of conversion for, 6, 12, 24–27
and joy, 138, 139
liberation, 166n80
and metaphysics, 19, 26, 42n21
method in, 11, 12, 18
and modernity, 7
political, 166n80
renewal of, 6, 9, 49n2, 66, 205–22
and the saints, 197n80
sapiential, 6–8, 37, 46
as science, 18, 28
and scriptural exegesis, 68, 72–80, 84, 90–100
soteriology, 44
as subalternated science, 31
theological *praxis*, 181n23
transposition in, 4, 5, 27, 29–32
Trinitarian, 45
Thomism
Ressourcement Thomism, 49n2
transcendental Thomism, 14, 15
transcendental idealism, 11, 15
transnationalism, 167n84
Trinity, Most Holy, 37, 38, 43, 45–48, 56, 184n31
mission of the Holy Spirit, 6, 43n26, 45n33, 46

United Nations, 167n84
University of Münster, 12
University of Notre Dame, 3n5

veneration of images, 42n21
voluntarism, 5n11, 7, 19

wine, 138, 145–47

www.ingramcontent.com/pod-product-compliance
Lightning Source LLC
Chambersburg PA
CBHW051055230426
43667CB00013B/2308